STAIRWAY TO HEAVEN

STAIRWAY TO HEAVEN

A Novice's Guide to Traditional Jewish Prayer

Zale Newman

FIRST EDITION

Copyright © 2015 by Zale Newman

All rights reserved.

No part of this book may be copied or transmitted by any means whatsoever without written permission of the author.

Published by STH Publishing
www.stairwaytoheaven.ca

Editor: Farla Klaiman
Book design and formatting: Yuda Braun, Anna Monnier-Shraer

Library and Archives Canada Cataloguing in Publication

Newman, Zale, 1955- author
Stairway to heaven : a novice's guide to traditional Jewish prayer /
Zale Newman.

Includes prayers in classical Hebrew, transliteration,
and a new English translation.

Issued in print and electronic formats.
ISBN 978-0-9939210-0-1 (bound).
ISBN 978-0-9939210-1-8 (paperback).
ISBN 978-0-9939210-4-9 (pdf)

1. Prayer--Judaism. I. Title.

BM669 N48 2015   296.4'5   C2015-903520-1
                  C2015-903521-X

Printed and bound in Canada/USA by Ingram Spark
Distributed by Lightning Source

AUTHOR'S DEDICATION

This book is dedicated to the memory of two giants of the past Jewish generation, both of whom had a profound influence on my life. Their teachings permeate every page of this work.

Their philosophy of life, how they conducted themselves, provided guidance, leadership, inspiration, and love, how they were guided by and in turn guided others with the Torah's teachings, their total dedication to G-d and to the Jewish People, both collectively and individually, serve as the "peak of the mountain" that I hope to ascend to at least a small elevation.

They were the closest of friends and soulmates, brought together through the depth of Torah and their total devotion to every member of our Nation. They played a crucial role in rebuilding our People after the destruction of the Holocaust and the upheaval of European Jewry. For one, the world was his workplace. For his dear friend, Montreal was the primary area of focus.

May their memories be blessed and may they serve to watch over us from Above.

Dedicated in memory and in deep appreciation of the Lubavitcher Rebbe,
*Rav Menachem Mendel Shneerson za"tzal, **the visionary leader and Rebbe of his generation**, and HaRav HaGaon Rav Pinchas Hirschprung za"tzal,*
the Chief Rabbi of Montreal, one of the generation's
pre-eminent Torah scholars and a tzaddik in every sense.

DEDICATION

In loving memory of

Saul and Margit Seidenfeld *a"h*

שמחה בן שלמה ע"ה   חיה מירל בת אברהם ע"ה

Daniel and Vera Rubinstein *a"h*

דניאל בן מרדכי ע"ה   מינדל בת חיים ע"ה

Annie Kohn *a"h*

בלימא רבקה אדל בת דניאל ע"ה

May their lives — which were dedicated to the values of G-d, Torah, and the Jewish People — and the myriad of good deeds performed by these exemplary individuals be a great merit to their family and to all of Am Yisrael.

Dedicated by Dr. Allan and Susie Seidenfeld

DEDICATION

Sarah bat Yisrael *a"h*

שרה בת ישראל ע"ה

Tovah bat Yisrael *a"h*

טובה בת ישראל ע"ה

Sarah bat Yisrael Bank and Tovah bat Yisrael Bank were sisters born in pre-Holocaust Europe in Ścinawa, Poland.

Their lives were cruelly snuffed out by the evil Nazi regime when Sarah was only thirteen years of age and Tovah was just an eleven-year-old child.

The precise date of their death and the location of their burial remain unknown. In spite of the pain of their loss, their memory remains a source of inspiration for their surviving family members.

May their memory be a blessing for their family and for all of Israel.

Dedicated in loving memory by Barry and Donna Bank

DEDICATION

Avraham Shlomo ben Menashe Levi HaKohein *a"h*
אברהם שלמה בן מנשה לוי הכהן ע"ה

Avrum Jeffrey Duke was born into the loving arms of his parents, Judy and Lorne Duke, on March 5, 1972.

As a toddler, Avrum was a very curious, happy, energetic, active, and athletic child. At the age of three, Avrum discovered skiing while visiting his Bubby and Zaida. As he grew older he explored many activities, including skating, playing hockey, camping, and swimming. He was a bright, handsome, and "spunky" kid. He loved playing with the first versions of computer games and liked to learn how things worked.

Although he was "a real boy" in every sense, Avrum was a good friend to his cousins and his classmates. He was well loved and was a very loving person. He was kind and sharing. He was very intelligent and knew how to play fairly, have fun, and sometimes even act silly, like any young boy his age.

On Yom Kippur 5742, when Avrum was only nine years old and in Grade 4 at Associated Hebrew School in Toronto, he was diagnosed with lymphoma. On the 20th day of Iyar, May 13, 1982, seven months after the cancer diagnosis, Avrum passed away.

Although Avrum's classmates would now be in their forties, one of them recently remarked to Avrum's mom that he often thought of Avrum. His memory still lies within the hearts of the many people who knew him.

Had Avrum grown up, he would have become a mentor who was strong, caring, and helpful. He was taken "back home" at such a young age but his memory remains a blessing to all those who knew him.

His epitaph reads as follows:

The tears in our eyes can be wiped away
But the tears in our hearts will always stay

Dedicated in loving memory of Avrum Shalom ben Menashe Levi HaKohein a"h
by his mother Yehudit Chaya (Judy) Duke a"h. *May their memories be blessed.*

TABLE OF CONTENTS

Preface	xiii
Transliteration Guide	xviii
Introduction	19
How to Use This Book	21
An Introduction to Prayer: Why, What, and Wherefore?	27
Ahavat Yisrael - Love Another Jew: The Key to Getting Our Prayers Answered	49
Tzedakah: The Gift of Giving	52
Major Themes of Prayer	56
Shema Yisrael: The "Jewish National Anthem"	59
Tallit and *Tefillin*	62
The Kaddish Prayer	64
The Mitzvah Groove: A Summary of the Multiple Morning Mitzvot	66
Shabbat: Day of Heaven	68
The Five Steps of the Daily Morning Prayers	72
The Daily Morning Prayers	73
The Shabbat Morning *Shemoneh Esrei*	107
The Weekday Morning *Shemoneh Esrei*	128
The Six Remembrances (and then some)	153

Minchah: The Weekday Afternoon Prayers	163
Maariv: The Weekday Evening Prayers	164
The Friday Night Prayers	171
Additional Prayers for Various Times and Events in Life	195
Prayers Throughout the Day	204
Bikur Cholim: Visiting the Sick	211
Prayer Stories	220
For Further Reading	240
Approbations	245
About the Author	252

PREFACE

The Talmud, in *Pirkei Avot* ("Ethics of our Forefathers"), teaches, "In a place where there are no men, try to be the man." The basic interpretation of this instruction is that when something needs to done and no one will stand up and take responsibility for fulfilling the task, then I am responsible for taking action and addressing the situation to the best of my abilities.

Back in the early 1980s, I noticed that there seemed to be very few "tools" for those who were raised without a strong Jewish background, yet wished to get closer to our Tradition. It was virtually an all-or-nothing situation. There were no traditional prayerbooks or High Holiday Machzors and few Passover Haggadahs designed specifically for the novice.

This effectively closed off the world of traditional Jewish prayer to those who did not read Hebrew and did not understand what the prayers were about or the concepts behind this central and ancient practice.

And so on a winter break in a condo in Manzanillo, Mexico, I began to write a siddur for the novice. After a couple of years, I put the project aside, leaving it for someone more knowledgeable and worthy of such a holy responsibility than I. But over the next two decades, while teaching and leading multiple beginners' services and prayer workshops, I still could not find an appropriate beginners' siddur that would serve as a tool to help bridge the gap between a student's first prayer and regular daily prayer.

So I attempted to be "the man" who would fill this apparent need and thus started to write again. Then, over a period of many years, at the weekly "Stairway to Heaven" prayer classes and workshops at Toronto's unique Village Shul, we "beta-tested" the work and asked the participants for ongoing feedback. This exercise ultimately led to what is contained in this book, more than thirty years after the start of this project.

One of the many lessons we learn from traditional Jewish prayer is that we should become accustomed to expressing our thanks. Therefore, we begin each day with the *Modeh Ani* prayer, which expresses our thanks to Hashem for giving us another day of life.

In that vein, first and foremost I express my thanks to Hashem for allowing me the privilege of working on this project, among the millions of miracles that Hashem has performed for me every moment of my life. He has blessed me in every way and has given me so much more than I could ever recognize. This project is but one of many, many aspects of my life wherein Hashem has provided me with an opportunity to live a life of meaning, purpose, and beauty.

Mah ashiv l'Hashem kol tagmulohi alai, wrote King David in Psalm 116. "How can I possibly repay Hashem for all that He has done for me?" In my case, perhaps one small way is for me to help some of "Hashem's children" achieve a deeper and closer relationship with our glorious Jewish tradition. This is but one attempt on my part to do just that. I pray that we will achieve some measure of success in this regard.

This book could not have been produced without the immeasurable contribution of its editor, Farla Klaiman, who worked for hundreds of hours to edit, re-edit, and edit yet again this work in multiple languages and formats. We met in NCSY Montreal in the 1970s, and how fortuitous it is that she came back into my life in Toronto a generation later to serve as the perfect editor of this work. Farla understood exactly what we were trying to accomplish. May she be blessed with *simchah* and *nachas* in her life. May we merit working together on future projects of a similar nature. And may she be blessed to inspire many people for many generations to come through her invaluable work as editor for the Azrieli Foundation Holocaust Survivors Memoirs Program.

The extremely challenging role of designing a book with many directions, options, changes, innovations, and nuances was expertly and artistically managed by the brilliant Israeli artist/designer Yuda Braun and his design team in Jerusalem. His good humor and insightful suggestions made what could have been an arduous process both interesting and enjoyable.

Rabbis Elazar Robinson and Yitzchok Hirschprung, two genuine, humble, and brilliant *talmidei chachomim* (wise Torah scholars), read through the manuscript and provided in-depth, thoughtful, and extremely beneficial comments and suggestions.

Every person, but perhaps a teacher most of all, is in turn the product of his teachers, in all of their various forms. To this end, I must first thank my parents, Cyril (Reb Yisrael) and Helen (Honey) *a"h*. They instilled within us a great love for Torah, tradition, our fellow Jews, the Land of Israel, and *tzedakah*, and a sense of truth and purpose. They undertook great sacrifice to provide us with a full-scale Jewish education, both formal and informal, in all of its forms. But the best education they provided was via the life they led and the example they portrayed in the way they lived each day. May my father (one of my two best friends) and my mother *a"h* be blessed with *nachas* and fulfillment and may they rest in Gan Eden. Their shining example lives on in my two sisters, Judith and Chaviva, who are both supremely dedicated, committed, activist Jews, living in Israel with their wonderful, highly dedicated families.

Over the years, I have been graced with wonderful teachers. From my earliest years, I was touched by the teachings of Mrs. Menzelefsky (kindergarten), Mr. Yitzchok Eisner (Grade 1), Rabbi Avraham Glukowsky *a"h* (Grade 2), and Reb Yisroel Yitzchok Cohen (Grades 3 and 4). I have remained close with them my entire life. In fact, I taught with Mr. Eisner on the March of the Living in the 1990s, learned how to run a beginners' *minyan* from Rabbi Glukowsky at youth conventions in my young adult years, and still receive guidance and teaching from Reb Yisroel Yitzhok Cohen at the Village Shul.

I received much of my outlook on life from the teachings of the Lubavitcher Rebbe *ob"m*, whom I identified at a young age as the visionary leader of the post-Holocaust generation. I continue to study his teachings on a regular basis.

Since my marriage, my main teacher has been Rav Reuven Silver *shlit"a*, who has taught our group Talmud and Halachah twice each week and has answered all of our halachic questions and moral dilemmas for over thirty years. I have also had the privilege of studying Talmud and Halachah on a regular basis with Reb Elazar Robinson *shlit"a*, my Rebbi and friend, for over thirty years.

While I have garnered an immense amount of knowledge from my primary Torah teachers, of paramount importance was their teaching by example as models of humility, to the extreme. This was the case with my holy and saintly father-in-law, Rav Pinchas Hirschprung *ob"m*, whose overwhelming and vast knowledge of Torah was only surpassed by his power of instant recall, Talmudic analysis, and unbridled generosity of spirit, body, time, and possessions. May his merit and that of his Rebbetzin *a"h* bring their offspring blessings of long life, good health, *hatzlachah*, and *nachas* in every way.

Rabbi Immanuel Schochet *a"h* and Rabbi Elisha Schochet introduced me to the wonders of Chassidic thought. Mr. Kurt Rothschild served as the ultimate model and mentor of selfless Jewish leadership and activism. Rabbi Sholom Schwartz taught me the meaning of tenacious dedication to a higher cause. Rabbi Mordechai Machlis taught me the higher levels of *chessed*. Rabbi Glenn Black taught me how to take the lessons taught by mentors and far exceed their accomplishments. Dr. Allan Seidenfeld has shared the morning study hour with me with the study of *hashkafah* and *Nesivos Sholom*.

I have been blessed with many other great Torah teachers, who remain unaware of whom they have touched and the depth of impact their lectures have had upon me and, in turn, my students. I have listened to hundreds of hours of lectures by Rabbis Berel Wein, Moshe Weinberger, Aryeh Lebowitz, Sholom Rosner, Efraim Wachsman, and Akiva Tatz, as well as by the illustrious Torah teachers Bryna Yocheved Levy, Shani Terrigin, and Shira Smiles, among many others. The common denominators shared by all these teachers are their immense knowledge, their ability to impart this knowledge to others, and their complete dedication to our People. But above all, the greatest common denominator is their sincere humility. It permeates their every word and action and draws me toward them with magnetic force. The word "I" has rarely been heard from their lips, while the word "we" is heard consistently.

The legendary Rabbi Shlomo Carlebach *a"h* taught me the power of song and of storytelling and a great deal about *ahavat Yisrael*, love for another Jew.

The awesome high school students from NCSY at hundreds of weekend *Shabbatonim* across North America and beyond, and those who diligently attended the ten-year Shabbat afternoon *Pirkei Avot* classes, often walking tens of miles in torrid heat or torrential rainstorms, taught me much about the purity of the Jewish soul and its desire to be deeply connected to our heritage.

The adult students at Aish Toronto and at the Village Shul's High Holiday alternative services and the weekly "Issues at 11," "Soul Spa," "Meaningful Date Night," and "Stairway to Heaven" classes have compelled me to seek to understand many of the deeper aspects of Judaism and to try to share this knowledge with them in an understandable, approachable, meaningful, and relevant way. I thank Rabbi Ahron Hoch, the Board, and all of the attendees at the Village Shul for allowing me the opportunity to learn, teach, share, dance, laugh, cry, celebrate, pray, and grow with them in that unique center for personal growth.

I have learned an immense amount from my children Chayim Ezriel, Batsheva, and Dovid Tzvi ("DZ"). I believe that I learned much more from them than I ever taught them. And I am filled with wonder when watching our grandchildren Yaakov Shlomo, Pinchas Yadin, Keira Biba, and Yehuda. May they all be blessed with many years of learning and teaching and connecting themselves and others to the One Above. They are the greatest of the many gifts that Hashem has bestowed upon me. Except for one….

The Talmud teaches that *acharon acharon chaviv*, the last is the most beloved. Indeed. My dear wife, soulmate, partner, mirror, life coach, audience, and in-house therapist has shared everything with me for the past thirty-six years. She has been my greatest teacher and my other best friend.

May Hashem bless all of those mentioned above with long life, good health, true Jewish *nachas*, accomplishment, and joy, and may they live and be well to witness the Ultimate Redemption. I pray for all of you.

Zale Newman
Kislev 5775,
December 2014

TRANSLITERATION GUIDE

Consonants:

בּ	b	ל	l
ב	v	מ ם	m
ג	g	נ ן	n
ד	d	ס	s
ה	h	פּ	p
ו	v	פ ף	f
ז	z	צ ץ	ts*
ח	ch	ק	k
ט	t	ר	r
י	y	שׁ	sh
כּ	k	שׂ	s
כ	ch	ת	t

*exceptions: mitzvah, mitzvot, rebbetzin, tzedakah, tzedek, tzitzit, Yitzchak

Vowels:

ָ ַ ֲ   a, as in "ma"

ֶ ֱ   e, as in "met"

ֵ   ei, as in "rein"

וּ   u, as in "rule"

ִ   i as in "cozy" (exceptions: Breisheet, reisheet)

ֹ   o, as in "row"

ְ   consonant' (e.g., v'___) unless pronounced as part of previous syllable (e.g., lif-nei, not li-f'nei)

י   ai, as in "aisle, Mordechai"

INTRODUCTION

Often when we perceive something as incorrect or puzzling, we view it as lacking something. "This is old-fashioned, this is unfair; it must be wrong," we might say. If what we perceive is problematic, we assume that it is lacking and therefore should be disregarded or even discarded.

But this is not the correct way to perceive Jewish tradition. If we do not understand or if something appears to be wrong, what we ought to do is question *ourselves*, *our* perceptions, not simply the validity of what we perceive.

Why do we perceive this practice as being outdated? Why do we perceive something in Jewish tradition as being wrong or G-d as being unfair? Do we lack knowledge or understanding of this particular practice or tradition? Have we searched for various explanations and studied the underlying meaning and significance? Have we looked at the total picture, the ultimate goal, or are we just viewing one "frame of the film," as it were. Have we discussed the issue with scholars and spiritual leaders whose vast storehouse of knowledge may hold the answers we seek? While our first instinct may be to doubt the validity of that which we perceive, we ought to stop and reconsider our perception. Perhaps our perception is invalid because we are lacking in some way.

If we are honest and perceive ourselves as lacking knowledge and deep understanding, then we can take comfort in the knowledge that people far wiser than we are, with far greater understanding, have asked similar questions and have received satisfactory answers. They have achieved understanding. They have perceived the truth. The answers are available. It is incumbent on us to question our perceptions and to search for meaning and truth. The truth may lie "just around the corner" or may only be discovered at the end of a long journey of probing and questioning. But in the end, truth will be found, as others have found it. What we need are knowledgeable and credible guides on this journey.

So it is with the Jewish concept of prayer. It may look archaic; it may appear to be outdated, irrelevant, and incomprehensible. But when we search for the true essence, we find the keys to one of the two most awesome Jewish experiences available to us (the other being deep Torah study). Prayer is a Jewish tradition, which has survived and thrived for 4,000 years, for 2,000 generations of Jewish parents and children. It is a tradition practiced in the shuls of Australia and the prisons of Siberia, a daily practice in the Yeshivas of America and the bus stations of Israel.

The Lubavitcher Rebbe, in his commentary on *Pirkei Avot* ("Ethics of our Forefathers" — the section of the Talmud dealing with the moral and ethical foundations of the Jewish People), provides the following explanation of the instruction that we are to "build a fence around the Torah." Most commentators explain the mishnah as providing a direction to the rabbinic leaders to enact laws that will safeguard the practice of Jewish tradition. Thus, if they perceive that the Jewish people are lax in a particular area of observance, the leaders must establish laws to ensure that the Jewish tradition survives intact.

However, the Lubavitcher Rebbe points out that an instruction in the Talmud must be for all Jews, not just for the few in leadership roles. He explains the mishnah in the context of our moral obligation to bring authentic Jewish tradition to our fellow Jews. He explains that not everyone is ready for the full measure of Jewish observance at a particular moment. Observance of a particular practice may be too strange, too intimidating, or too difficult at this time. So, says the mishnah, if some cannot enter the arena of total observance, we are instructed to "build fences" for them so that our fellow Jews can climb the fences and observe the practice of Jewish tradition from them. Soon the observers may want to try it themselves, to taste our tradition, and over time may even come to accept the practice of that particular aspect of Judaism on a regular basis.

So it is with prayer. A traditional Hebrew prayer book can be very intimidating. Even if we can read the Hebrew words, do we know what they mean and the point of the whole exercise? And what about a myriad of other questions that we need answered? This brief work is but one small picket fence on which the novice can stand to observe the great Jewish tradition of daily prayer.

Climb up. Take a taste of tradition. Enjoy the adventure. Pray that it never ends.

AMEIN.

HOW TO USE THIS BOOK

Objective

The objective of this book is to introduce the reader to the key concepts and practice of Jewish prayer. The concept seems difficult and foreign to many of us. We don't understand it and we don't know how to have a relationship with G-d. The purpose of this book is to act as the first step on the "Stairway to Heaven" that is Jewish prayer.

The ancient Temple in Jerusalem had fifteen steps, which led from the public area to the area where the Temple rituals were performed. One of the lessons of this is that there are many steps in the process of achieving a close relationship with G-d. As with all relationships, there are times when we feel closer and times when we feel some distance.

It is important to know that G-d does not turn away from us. The distance is caused when we turn away from G-d. Daily prayer ensures a level of closeness every day. And while there will, of course, be times when we feel a greater closeness, a daily discussion with G-d ensures there is rarely, if ever, a great distance between ourselves and G-d.

This book is designed to help you begin to bridge that distance, to guide you on the initial steps of the path that Jews have used for 4,000 years to achieve a high level of closeness to G-d.

Basic Stage — The 180-Day Program

The first step of a journey is always the most difficult. The first step in this case is to begin with the daily morning prayer. Try to do this every day for ninety days. (There is a slightly different prayer for Shabbat (Saturday) morning.) Then try adding the afternoon prayer for the next sixty days (i.e., days 91-150). For the subsequent thirty days (i.e., days 151 to 180), try to add the evening prayer as well.

If you have completed these steps, you have really made great progress as you begin to climb the "Stairway to Heaven." If you have found this too difficult a task to complete — relax! Take it a little slower. Start again. The key is to do it daily. It must become a part of your daily life. If you can't say all of the Basic Stage prayers, say at least a part of them until you are able to complete all of them.

Advanced Stage — The Next 180 Days

Now you are ready for the Advanced Stage. For the next 180 days (i.e., days 181 to 360), say the Advanced Stage prayers, which are identified with an orange sidebar, as well as the Basic Stage prayers.

After the first 180 days you will have completed a half-year of prayer. If you missed some days, don't worry. Move on! If you missed a lot of the prayers, don't be concerned. Keep going! If you found it difficult and, at times, really, really difficult — Mazel Tov! You are a true Jew fighting the battle to attain spirituality. Did you think that your body would give in to your soul so easily? Not for someone who has such a holy soul. Keep climbing!

And if you fall, don't worry. Rebbe Nachman of Breslov, the early nineteenth-century rabbi whose main path to G-d was through prayer and daily meditation, said that he used to fall a thousand times a day. That is the human condition. Just get up again and keep climbing. Make sure your spiritual energy is driving you forward and don't give in to a state of spiritual inertia. Ask Hashem to help you. You don't ever have to climb alone.

Last Stage — The Rest of Your Life

Now you can move on to the Last Stage. That is beyond the scope of this book. You have completed the steps outlined in this volume. You are ready to move on to an accessible traditional prayerbook like the one we have used for the past 2,500 years. Join the club.

You are the next link in the chain of the Jewish People.

Try the Artscroll translated linear version of the siddur, the Metsudah linear translation, or the Nusach Ari volume in English. You can use these and other similar user-friendly siddurim (traditional prayer books) forever.

See if you can find a traditional shul that is warm, friendly, spiritual, and accessible. Talk to the Rabbi and Rebbetzin. See if they can act as spiritual guides for you — not only with prayer but with all of the other mitzvot, too.

What's in a Name? How We Refer to G-d

We have tried to use the name "Hashem" when referring to G-d, rather than using the English word "G-d" or one of the commonly used English terms, such as "Lord" or "Almighty." These terms each have some connotation but, in Hebrew, each "name" that is used for G-d represents a specific manifestation of G-d in the world. For example, the Hebrew word *Adonoy,* which is commonly translated as "Master," refers to G-d as the One who sets and controls the rules of nature. In the traditional prayers, there are many ways of referring to G-d, depending on the theme of that particular prayer.

We Jews are careful when and how we refer to G-d. As such, we are careful when we use any of the Hebrew terms that the Torah uses to refer to G-d. Instead of specifically saying the names, it has become an accepted tradition around the world to substitute the word *Hashem,* meaning "The Name," when we are not praying in the original Hebrew language.

Therefore, most often we use the word *Hashem* when referring to G-d. At times, when a verse or prayer refers to G-d by a number of different names (e.g., the prayer *Ein Keloheinu*), we have chosen to use various terms that attempt to express the meaning of the names that were used in that particular Hebrew verse.

In the Hebrew text of the siddur, we refer to G-d as *Adonoy* even though this name is not pronounced in the way that it is spelled in Hebrew. We have chosen to use the classic *yud yud* symbol (יי). But we pronounce the name as Adonoy as it appears in the transliteration below the blessing or the verse.

Icons — Signs of the Time

As you go through this book and try the suggested path of prayer for the novice, you will notice certain icons. Specifically they are as follows:

> **Kavanah:** *This indicates what you may wish to focus on before and during the upcoming prayer. The word* kavanah *means "to direct" or "to aim." It is what your thoughts can be focused on during that particular prayer, as that is the key theme of that prayer. Ideally,* all *mitzvot should be performed with* kavanah, *meaning the intent to fulfill that mitzvah as well as the intent to fulfill Hashem's instructions.*

Dance: This indicates that this is an ideal time to join in a traditional Jewish dance to express the feeling of joy with our entire body.

Do: This indicates that there is something specific to do at that point, aside from something to think and say.

Remember: This indicates that there is something specific to say or do at that point.

Say: This indicates that there is a particular phrase or verse that should be said at that place in the prayers.

Sing : This indicates that this prayer is usually recited in song. If you aren't familiar with one of the traditional tunes, use any tune you enjoy or compose one of your own!

Sit: This indicates that after a section of prayer which was said standing, one can be seated and continue the prayers from this point.

Smile: This indicates that the theme suggests that we ought to be happy when reading that particular prayer. Although all of prayer is best said while in a state of happiness and appreciation, this prayer has a theme that should ignite happiness and joy when said.

Stand: This indicates that if possible, it is preferable to stand while saying this particular prayer. It usually means that we are talking *to* Hashem rather than *about* Hashem, or it is a section that refers to a clear, public revelation of Hashem at some time during history.

Think: This indicates that there is a point that requires some serious thought before proceeding further.

The Translation

In the introduction to his monumental translation of the Torah (called *The Living Torah*, Moznaim Publishing), Aryeh Kaplan quoted Maimonides, who states in *his* magnum opus, the *Mishneh Torah* (also called the *Yad*), that one who dares to translate the Torah in a literal way is deserving of the death penalty for disseminating heretical literature. The reason is that, while the Torah is meant to be taken seriously, it is not meant to be translated or deciphered literally. The Torah is comprised of the Written Law and the Oral Law. The Oral Law was given to us on Mount Sinai and provides the true translation and explanation of the Written Law of the Torah. Without it, the Torah can be, and has been, misinterpreted.

The same holds true for the prayers. When the prayer says, "G-d is our rock," that in no way implies that we believe for even one moment in a god of stone. It means that G-d is there for us to lean on, to depend on, to give us strength. And so, in this work, we have attempted to reflect the intent and the meaning of the words rather than the literal translation of the words.

While this can be the subject of some controversy and some criticism, we felt strongly that, as long as we relied on a major traditional Jewish commentary (e.g., Rashi, Radak, Ba'al Shem Tov) for the source of that particular translation, we were indeed enhancing the prayers rather than detracting from the original intent. This view has been confirmed to us by a number of leading authentic Orthodox authorities.

We have attempted to use the explanation that we feel would be most meaningful to the readers of this book. As such, we also incorporated the methodology of Aryeh Kaplan in his translation of the Torah, in which he utilizes various commentaries on the same verse rather than relying on the explanation of one particular commentator for the whole verse.

Because of this, you will find that other accepted translations of the siddur vary somewhat from this translation. Please do not be alarmed and do not lose faith in the efficacy of either work. We are simply relying on different classical commentators. In any case, you will find the translations are fairly close to one another in almost all cases.

The Disclaimer

This book is *not* meant to replace the traditional siddur. It is meant to be a handle, enabling the newcomer to traditional Jewish prayer to grasp the traditional siddur. It represents only the first two steps on a ladder that contains an infinite number of steps.

It is in no way meant to usurp the traditional siddur. I strongly believe that it is improper to develop new versions of the siddur (e.g., feminist, poetic, humanistic, etc.) with the intent of replacing the tradition. Parts of the siddur come directly from the Torah, a G-dly document. Other parts were written with G-dly inspiration by our Patriarchs, our Prophets, our greatest people, including Adam, Abraham, Moses, and King David. The siddur was organized by the "Men of the Great Assembly," the leaders of the Jewish people, who included the prophets Daniel and Mordechai, some 2,500 years ago. New words cannot replace their words. The words of the traditional siddur are the keys to the heavens. New keys cannot be fashioned to replace the traditional ones.

Thus we are clear that this book is only a stepping stone, using excerpts from the traditional siddur. No new prayers have been added. No deviation from the original intent has been put forth. This book is simply a temporary measure designed to help guide the novice to the regular use of a traditional siddur.

AN INTRODUCTION TO PRAYER: WHY, WHAT, AND WHEREFORE?

What is the Jewish concept of prayer? What does prayer mean? Why are we supposed to pray so often? What do we gain by praying? What is the goal of prayer? Why is there a prescribed order of prayer rather than a free-form dialogue? Who wrote our prayers? Why do we pray in Hebrew and why does Jewish law dictate that men and women should pray separately?

These and many other bothersome issues are the current focus of young and old Jews alike, who find today's synagogue service formal and aloof and today's synagogue a cold, foreign mausoleum, rather than a place where our Jewish soul can "come home" to rejuvenate. So let's examine some of them.

Who Invented Prayer?

Prayer as a part of daily life was "invented" by Avraham Avinu, Abraham, the first of the three founding fathers of our people.

Avraham's concept was revolutionary in his day, perhaps even more so than it is today. Only twenty generations after the creation of the world and only ten generations after the destruction of the world during the time of Noach and the Great Flood, G-d's power was evident to all.

The world's inhabitants felt that mortal man, subject to emotional hurt, loneliness, physical pain, and ultimately death itself, could never hold a direct dialogue with the All-Powerful G-d who created a world of towering mountains, vast oceans, and great verdant forests. He created millions of species of animals and, of course, all kinds of people. Furthermore, G-d alone held the power to destroy it all in one brief nanosecond.

How could mere mortal man converse with the Ultimate Ruler? Could we imagine ourselves sharing our innermost feelings, problems, and desires daily with, let us say, the President of the United States, who is of course just a fellow human being, subject to the same emotional and physical frailties to which we are all subject. How much more so would it be inconceivable to talk, at will, about any subject at all, with the Creator of all existence? So they thought. Avraham established what was to become the basis of our Jewish legacy. He dared to be different, dared to go against the tide of popular wisdom.

Among his many innovations and revolutionary concepts, Avraham invented people-to-G-d "direct distance calling." He let the people of his day and of every subsequent generation know that this person-to-G-d dialogue was not only possible, was not only acceptable to G-d, but was in fact desirable to G-d. After all, G-d is the Father of all people. And what father or mother does not want to hear their children's innermost feelings, desires, dreams, and problems? What bubbe or zaide doesn't feel warmth and compassion when their grandchildren sit upon their knee and share their saddest and happiest moments or their deepest feelings?

So too, taught Avraham, does our Father in Heaven, the Father of our parents and grandparents, the Father of all people, desire to hear our deepest thoughts and feelings. Not for His benefit, but for ours. Avraham therefore began the practice, now established in Jewish law, of daily morning prayer. Thus we would begin each day in the right frame of mind, with the right perspective and the right sense of purpose and mission.

This practice was further extended by Avraham's son, Yitzchak (Isaac), who established the afternoon prayers, and again by Yaakov (Jacob), Avraham's grandson, who established the evening prayer. The purpose of each of these three prayers will be discussed shortly.

What Does The Term *Davening* Mean?

These innovations from Avraham, Yitzchak, and Yaakov, our forefathers (*avos* in Ashkenazic Hebrew, *avot* in Sephardic Hebrew, or *avuhon* in Aramaic, the language of the Talmud), tell us the origin of the colloquial term for praying known as *davening*. The term likely comes from the Aramaic *di-avuhon*, meaning "that which emanated from our three founding forefathers."

Additionally, every Jewish child traditionally learns how to pray (*daven*) from his or her father or mother when he or she is very young. Although our tradition teaches that children instinctively know that they can talk to G-d but later become inhibited about doing so, the formal prayers must be taught to each child. Typically, the first prayer is taught by a child's parents and the chain of Jewish tradition is thereby passed down from generation to generation. We can thus see the parallel between *davening*, meaning "emanating from our parents," and *davening*, meaning "emanating from our founding fathers." As we become the next link in the chain of the Jewish people, we take on the mission of passing on the heritage of *davening* to our children.

Others opine that the etymological root of the word *daven* is the word "divine," and the term means to speak to the Divine One.

Why Does G-d Want Us To *Daven*?

Does G-d need our prayers, just as a parent requires that his children share their feelings with him? No, G-d does not require that we *daven*, for He needs nothing from us. He existed prior to the creation of the world over 5,770 years ago and will continue to exist beyond the time when the world, as we know it, might cease to exist, replaced by a new form of worldly existence. He does not need our prayers for His existence or for His benefit.

Furthermore, G-d already knows our deepest thoughts and feelings. The fact is, however, that the Jewish concept of prayer is a gift that allows us to achieve a greater level of spirituality, a greater measure of self-improvement, and a closer relationship with G-d. This is what He desires, that we constantly seek to raise ourselves, to reach ever closer to Him, to seek greater spirituality, to grow as human beings, to become as G-d-like as we can. To bridge the apparent gap between Human and G-d, between the Creator and the created.

But What Is *Davening*?

At its most basic level, the objective of *davening* is to put our lives, meaning our thoughts, words, and actions, into proper perspective. *Davening* can eventually lead to the elevation of one's soul out of one's body and result in a total spiritual experience. At its highest level, *davening* can be the ultimate spiritual experience, leading the soul through each of the spiritual worlds to the highest levels of spiritual experience, emanating from the inner recesses of the heavens.

But between the various levels (that is, from the most basic to the most lofty), there are immeasurable stages and steps. Let us examine but a few of these.

Level I. Putting Our Lives into Perspective – *L'hitpalel*

(N.B.: The Hebrew language is based on the structure of root words. A word can come from more than one root, and when that is the case, those multiple meanings are conceptually related to each other. The root of the Hebrew word *l'hitpalel* is *pll*, which can be pronounced as *pallel* or *pallal*, depending on the vowel markers used. *Pallel* means to evaluate, which is discussed below, while *pallal* means to work towards achieving potential, which will be elaborated upon later.)

At its most basic level, *davening* is a tool of evaluation (*pallel*), which can serve to put our lives into perspective. This can be more easily understood by examining each of the times established for *davening*.

Morning Prayers

Shacharit, the body of morning prayers, is ideally said at the beginning of each day before we begin any of our regular daily actions, such as eating breakfast or doing work. It focuses on an appreciation of G-d's gift of life itself — our ability to walk, talk, breathe, discern right from wrong — the very abilities that we normally take for granted.

In the Chassidic Bobov Shul in Toronto, a young father, Reb Yitzchak, discovered that he had a life-threatening illness. After successful surgery, he accepted the practice of making an annual *seudat hoda'ah*, a feast of gratitude, to celebrate his recovery from a potentially fatal illness. At one of these feasts, he asked the participants, "When was the last time you remembered that you had a finger?" We all stopped and thought for a moment. "When it hurt," he answered.

A point well made. The simple movement of a finger, the blink of an eyelid, the routine motions of breathing, walking, speaking, laughing, or reaching for a handshake are all activities that we generally take for granted. In fact, we normally only realize their significance, the enormity of each gift when we, G-d forbid, lose the ability to perform these routine activities.

Yet, G-d gives us these gifts, every day, for a purpose. We are alive! But why? For what purpose? How will we be of benefit to our people, to humanity, to our families, and to those whom we touch in our daily lives? What mitzvot will we do today? How will we grow and develop? How will we use the gift of life that we've been given? What will our true accomplishments be if we are given yet another day of life and what will be the "measuring stick" by which we gauge these accomplishments?

This is the key objective of Shacharit: to focus our mind, our thoughts, and our actions for that day. This is our morning "psych-up," a spiritual "shot in the arm," so that we leave for work, school, vacation, or wherever, with the proper sense of mission and purpose; indeed, with the proper sense of appreciation for the gift of life itself. We will then lead meaningful lives. We will make a difference — at least some small difference. And a lot of small differences make a huge, dramatic difference.

When we carry a great sense of appreciation and of mission, when we recognize all of the awesome gifts that we have been given, this will manifest itself in the three quintessential characteristics or basic qualities that define the Jewish People. These are the qualities of compassion, modesty, and the desire to be constantly on the lookout to perform acts of kindness. When we understand that we are given a gift of life for another day, when we understand that every movement, talent, and ability is a G-d-given gift, then this awareness will eventually come to permeate every thought, word, and action, resulting in a life that is focused and channeled to achieve goodness in the world.

The manifestation of appreciation will be a deep-rooted sense of compassion or *rachmonus*. When we appreciate the gifts that we have been given, we realize how fortunate we are and have compassion for those who are lacking. We will be willing to share our gifts with others. G-d's kindness and compassion towards us will manifest itself in our kindness and compassion toward others.

In fact, this is the key objective of so many aspects of Judaism. Each Shabbat, Jewish Holiday, fast day, and blessing that we recite allows us to focus, sometimes just briefly and sometimes at greater length, on our individual gifts and the gift of life itself, so that we, in turn, will recognize how fortunate we are and conduct our lives in a purposeful fashion, in accordance with G-d's purpose in creation, as outlined in the Torah, G-d's "instructions for living."

Afternoon Prayers

But what happens to this sense of purpose, this sense of mission, this sense of goodness, this desire to make a difference, to take action, to be ever more compassionate, that we felt in those early morning hours? Often it can dissipate as we sit in a busy downtown office, with a cup of coffee in one hand, the phone receiver in the other, two lines on hold, a report due by tomorrow, a desk full of files, a computer flashing numbers, and clients waiting in the lobby.

So what does Judaism instruct us to do? Shut the door, put the phone on "do not disturb," and put our life back into perspective with Minchah, the afternoon prayer. Minchah is brief, but enough to serve as the "breeze" that cools us off in the heat of a pressure-filled day. That is why the afternoon prayer is called "Minchah," from the Hebrew word *menuchah* — to rest, to calm down, to relax our mind and our spirit.

If you have been at a summer home on the water or by an ocean just before sunset, at *minchah* time, you will see how nature "calms down" and "relaxes" before it begins the second half of the day. Since Judaism teaches that everything in nature is put here for our benefit and to teach us lessons for living, we too can see that it is best for human nature to take time out in the day — not just to "clear the cobwebs" and get a caffeine jolt in regards to our work day, but to calm ourselves down, clear the spiritual cobwebs, and get a "spiritual latte" to keep us focused for the second half of the day. Or, as Judaism teaches, before the next day begins, since the new day begins at nightfall (e.g., Shabbat begins on Friday night).

Evening Prayers

Finally, at the end of our work day comes Ma'ariv, the evening prayers. This is when we review our day. We look back at the objectives we set for ourselves during Shacharit, the morning prayers, with an eye toward self-improvement. It is the recap, the evaluation and, at the same time, the setting of objectives and commitments for the next waking day's challenge, should we be fortunate enough to be granted another day of life. Ma'ariv also allows us to direct our subconscious to higher thoughts while we sleep.

Thus we can see how *davening* at this most basic level allows us to tune in thrice daily to a higher purpose in living and keep our lives in perspective. This also explains why we are required to *daven* so often. In fact, ideally we should recite one hundred blessings, which are little prayers, every day!

While driving on the highway, with my father at the wheel of the car, I noticed that although we were driving on a straight highway towards our destination, with no apparent curves on that particular stretch of road, my father constantly moved the wheel slightly back and forth. I asked him why he was adjusting the steering wheel if we were driving in an apparently straight line. Why did he not simply hold the wheel in one stationary position?

He replied that small bumps on the road, little stones and other impediments, knocked the tires slightly off-track and he was constantly required to make minor corrections and adjustments in order to stay on a steady course. The same is true with our spirit, our focus, our sense of purpose. Events during the day take our minds off our real purpose in life and *davening* is that "adjustment of the wheel" that steers us back on track. It is the friendly tap on the shoulder that says, "Remember to focus" on what really matters.

It is worthwhile to note that the most common expression to describe *davening* in classic Jewish writings is *l'hitpalel*, which means to "evaluate one's self." G-d, as we say so often in the Rosh Hashanah and Yom Kippur *davening*, knows our thoughts, desires, and motivations. The purpose of relating them to G-d is so that we get an honest view of ourselves — all with an eye to constant self-improvement.

Heightening our awareness of G-d can play a central role in our lives or it may play a very secondary role. Rabbi J.B. Soloveitchik notes that there are two types of awareness. There is an acute awareness of someone or something, and there is a latent awareness of that same individual, object, rule, or concept.

This can best be illustrated with Rabbi Soloveitchik's example of a mother and her child. While she is playing, feeding, or talking to her child, the mother is acutely aware of the presence of her child. When she is away from her child, say, on vacation, she is still aware of her child but this awareness is more in the "back of her mind" than in the forefront. This Rabbi Soloveitchik calls "latent awareness."

For many of us, our awareness of G-d is very latent, as we go about the hectic routine of life in the twenty-first century. Prayer time gives us a few moments of acute awareness as we talk directly with our Creator, our Heavenly Parent.

Level II. Improving Ourselves – *L'hitpalel/Avodah*

(N.B.: Here, we are discussing *l'hitpalel* as *pallal*, working to achieve our ultimate potential. In the Talmud, this aspect is expressed by referring to prayer as *avodah*, which literally means "to work," but in this case means to work on ourselves.)

Perhaps the most often discussed aspect of *davening* is its use as a means for self-evaluation and thus a means for self-improvement. Rabbi Aryeh Kaplan described this as "taking a G-d's eye view of oneself," meaning that as we stand in discussion with G-d, if we are sincere and totally honest, we also see ourselves as we really are, the way G-d perceives us. We see our potential and our abilities, and we see the areas that require work and improvement.

As such, it is proper during *davening* to stand before G-d in humility and modesty. We should talk to G-d about those areas that require improvement and ask G-d for help in overcoming the barriers to self-improvement. If we are sincere in our requests for help, G-d will assist us in the way that is best for each of us.

In fact, just identifying the areas that need self-improvement and subsequently asking G-d for assistance helps us become aware of these areas and keep these areas for improvement in mind. We become more conscious of ourselves and therefore more cautious of life's pitfalls and better focused on life's objectives.

This root word can be seen in the other classical Hebrew word for prayer, namely *avodah*, work. We have discussed the term *l'hitpalel*, from the root word *pallel*, to evaluate, but, as the great eighteenth-century rabbi, holy man, and spiritual leader known as the Ba'al Shem Tov teaches, there is yet another expression used for prayer, meaning "to work" on something as one would work a raw piece of leather into a finely-crafted, soft, delicate piece of useful material, or "work" a field, turning it from one that is fallow into one that is productive.

First we *pallel*, evaluate ourselves, and then we utilize *avodah* to *pallal* ourselves, work on ourselves to improve those areas in which we require improvement and self-control. It is a good idea to take one attribute that we perceive as requiring improvement, such as better control over anger, jealousy, *lashon hara* (saying things that one should not), miserliness, being judgmental, or lack of sensitivity, and by talking to G-d through *davening* and serious contemplation, make a concerted effort to work on this attribute.

At the wedding of a close friend, Reb Noach Weinberg *a"h*, the founder of Aish HaTorah, delivered a *dvar Torah* (insight from the Torah). He explained that in Jewish tradition, marriage is forever. That is, marriage binds two souls together for eternity. They are bound in this world and in the next world as well (assuming, of course, that the couple does not, G-d forbid, divorce).

But how does our soul become bound forever to that of our partner? By what methodology do these two souls become one? We accomplish this binding by simply saying seven words. In one short phrase, our life is changed drastically, forever. The phrase translates as, "You are betrothed to me according to the laws of Moshe and Israel." The point Reb Noach was making was that this ceremony illustrates that in one moment, with seven short words, one's life can change drastically. And just as this happens at the beginning of a marriage, so too can it happen countless times throughout our lives.

Through the words of *davening*, and the accompanying moments of contemplation, we can make these changes. Some will be small changes like being more appreciative of our spouse and children, and some will be larger, more dramatic changes such as taking on the lifelong observance of an additional mitzvah. If we are to climb the ladder that our forefather Yaakov envisaged in his famous dream, leading towards the heavens and the heights of spirituality, then we must ascend one step at a time.

The process of self-improvement is one that never ends. There are an infinite number of small steps that we can take. Sometimes we fall down the ladder and have to climb up again. Each human quality can be refined and improved. Each mitzvah can be done in greater quantity (i.e., more often) and with better quality (i.e., more feeling, more sensitivity). Perhaps this is the intention of the Ba'al Shem Tov when he teaches that if we are the same after *davening* as before *davening*, if we have not experienced at least a small change in awareness or self-improvement during *davening*, then indeed we have not truly *davened*.

If we have not achieved at least a minor mental or emotional adjustment, then our *davening* was for naught. It was simply lip service and not *Avodat Halev*, a service of the heart, a realization of the mind taken to heart.

Level III. Channeling the Power of One's Brain – *Kavanah*

We know that our brain is the central system that controls all of our bodily functions, actions, and words. The brain serves as the "command post" for all thoughts and activities.

Furthermore, we know from Jewish tradition that the source of our soul resides in the brain. (That is the reason that one of the *tefillin* is placed upon the head). The very essence of both our soul and our body resides in the brain. If the challenge of life itself is to utilize our thoughts, words, and actions for the pursuit of good, as defined by the Torah, G-d's guidebook to humanity, then success in this challenge must lie with the ability to channel the power of our brain. This will allow us to achieve the measure of discipline and focus required to use our thoughts, words, and actions to fulfill the mitzvot, which are the true measure of our life's accomplishments.

But is it possible to achieve control over our brain power? Aren't our emotions stronger than our intellect? If we *feel* something, is this not stronger than if we *know* something?

The answer is that we *must* achieve this measure of control if we are to lead productive, successful lives. Our intellect must constantly override our emotions if we are to live successfully among other people. And knowing the truth is always stronger than just a momentary emotion.

We all know this, but we haven't necessarily focused on it and how to become better at it. We know that at times we get so angry with our children that we'd like to yell at them. However, our brain tells us that this isn't necessarily the right thing to do.

At times we'd like to yell at our boss or our client and tell him what we really think of him, yet our brain steps in before we find ourselves unemployed. Upon deeper analysis, we see that the difference between a positive action (i.e., a "good thing") and one that is not positive is often in our brain. One can give charity with a sense of joy, thankfulness, and empathy or one can write out a cheque to a charity begrudgingly and filled with negative feelings. The only difference is in the mental approach. Proper channelling of our brainpower can discipline our thoughts, block out negative thoughts, and create positive ones in their place.

Whether the "bottle is half full or half empty" depends on our ability to channel our thoughts.

Does this mean we are not free to "feel," to let our emotions flow freely? Of course not. Authentic Judaism stresses the need for deep-rooted feelings.

Tisha B'Av, the day when we focus on Jewish tragedies, including the destruction of the Temple in Jerusalem and the last 1,900 years of physical torment and spiritual exile, is the appropriate time for deep, soul-felt tears, while Purim, when the Jews even in the midst of a difficult exile reaffirmed their acceptance of the Torah and thus were saved from their Persian enemies, is the time for wild expressions of real joy. Simchat Torah, when we complete the annual reading of the Torah and begin reading anew, is the time to celebrate with joyous dance and song, while the day we commemorate the victims of the Holocaust is a time for tears and somber reflection.

We see that authentic Judaism wants us to experience and utilize our emotions in an intense, deep-rooted manner.

It is a great mitzvah to dance at and dress up for weddings, just as it is a great mitzvah to mourn in torn clothes, sitting on a stool unshaven, in a room for a full week following the burial of one of our seven closest relatives (i.e., mother, father, sister, brother, son, daughter, spouse).

The Torah wants us to feel these emotions with the full force of our being. Yet all of the emotions must be experienced with control and discipline. The fast of Tisha B'Av and the mitzvah of sitting shiva do not mean that one is to experience suicidal depression, and the Simchat Torah celebration or a wedding feast is not to be experienced in a drunken stupor. Our intellect, our brain must always be in control over our emotions and our initial "gut reactions."

Perhaps the best illustration of this is via an examination of love. There are many beautiful, exalted, holy forms of love. One of the highest levels that G-d instructs us to achieve is the spiritual level called love of G-d, sometimes represented by love within the family. G-d wants every family to be filled with love between husband and wife, parents and children. The embodiment of all mitzvot is the all-encompassing mitzvah of *ahavat Yisrael*, that is, love of another Jew. Nevertheless, there are many times when love is forbidden. There are situations where love can be ruinous to a Jew, to his or her family, or even to the entire Jewish People.

We are all familiar with the all-too-common occurrence of Jews allowing themselves to "fall in love" with non-Jews. By not exercising control over our emotions, we can, G-d forbid, end our family's chain in the Jewish People going back more than 3,300 years. The very event that generations of Jews fought and died to prevent could, G-d forbid, occur if we lack the discipline that allows our mind to overrule our emotions.

Allowing oneself to love an already married man or woman is another example where lack of control can lead to consequences so serious that one deserves the most severe penalty, according to the Torah.

So it can be easily understood that we *must* be able to exercise discipline over our brainpower in order to lead a productive, moral life.

If that is the case, how does one achieve this measure of discipline? How do we "train our brain"? In authentic Judaism, there are only two ways this can be done with guaranteed results.

One way is through intense, focused prayer, and the other is through the concentrated, intense study of Torah. It is through channelling our brainpower that we add intent, desire, and meaning to a mere physical act. It is this intent that changes an act from just a plain, perhaps inadvertent action, to an act of holiness.

As the eleventh-century Sage, Rabbi Moshe Ibn Ezra, teaches, "Things that come from the heart enter the heart," meaning that anything done with pure and proper intent will in turn touch the heart of another.

If, for example, charity is given by simply writing out a cheque, with no empathy, it is still a positive action, but one done on a very low level. But if, on the other hand, we contemplate and try to feel the plight of those receiving the charity — the pain, anguish, and suffering that led them to so debasing a situation that they must beg for charity from another — then the giving of charity becomes a truly pure and holy act. The gift will be accompanied by warmth and a smile of compassion. It means much more in the heavens and much more on earth as well.

There are many other examples. If one expresses love towards another and does not really mean it, we view it as being false and manipulative. If, on the other hand, it is said with full honest intent, it is an expression beyond words, which touches someone's spirit, far beyond intellectual comprehension. It can make us swallow hard, shed a tear, or turn away from the searing light of truth emblazoned in the words, "I love you."

Intent is added by the use of *kavanah*, that is, focus, concentration, aiming at the proper objective like a spiritual laser beam. It is interesting to note that heartfelt intent, the deep-rooted feeling of doing what is right, of fulfilling our mission in this world, is not necessarily to be achieved only by concentrating on the positive intent, but also can be achieved by blocking out extraneous thoughts and emotions. This will allow our soul, our *neshamah*, to flow and fill our brain with deep-rooted feelings of truth and proper intent.

This helps us understand why we *daven* so often. Achieving the ability to channel our brainpower takes constant practice. Every measure of control can be surpassed by a greater measure until we achieve total control of our brainpower during the waking and sleeping hours. Our soul can overtake and permeate every thought, word, and action, overcoming negative and frivolous thoughts and instinctive, harmful emotions. Of course, achieving control over our brainpower is really hard work. It is the hardest work we could ever possibly do.

And this is another reason that *davening* is called *avodah* in the Talmud, for *avodah* means "work," from the root word *eved*, "servant," to subjugate and subordinate our emotions to our intellect, to make our emotions serve our intellect.

This is one of the key reasons that the two primary actions that Judaism instructs us to perform at the beginning of each day, and as often as we can during the day, are *davening* and Torah study. Our brain will change and will become more disciplined, more controlled, and more focused on our true nature and on fulfilling our mission or purpose in this lifetime.

Level IV. Seeking a Deep Spiritual Experience – *D'veikut*

(N.B.: The Torah instructs us *l'davka bo*, that is, to attach ourselves to Hashem. One means of achieving *d'veikut*, attachment, is through davening. We see a similar concept in the Hebrew word *t'fillah*, the most commonly used term to describe prayer. It comes from the root words *toffel*, to be attached, and *niftal*, to be twisted together (like strands of a rope).)

The highest objective of *davening* that we will examine is one that has no limits and no bounds. The potential is no less than the most awesome experience that we are capable of having in this lifetime.

While the greatest spiritual experiences have not been attainable for the last 1,700 years due to a decline in our spiritual purity and sensitivity, nevertheless, great spiritual experiences are still attainable.

We spend most of our lives pursuing physical or material experiences, or at best, a combination of physical and spiritual experiences.

We work hard to earn a living, which, in turn, will provide what we perceive to be the necessities of life as well as some well-deserved luxuries. To this end we obtain an education, which enables us to enter a profession, which will provide an income that can be used to purchase a home, furniture, cars, jewelry, clothes, and vacations, and enable us to pay for our children's education so that they in turn can do the same thing.

In doing this we achieve a sense of gratification in acquiring success and growth. However, if we examine our day more carefully, much of each twenty-four-hour segment of life is spent sleeping, eating, and working, which are for the most part physical experiences. These satisfy our body's needs. But what about our soul's needs? When does our soul achieve growth? When do we express our spirit, our true essence? We get so caught up in this complicated world we live in that our soul, our spirit, our true essence gets covered up. Jewish mysticism refers to this as having a *klipah*, a "peel" or "husk" on the soul.

The soul can be best thought of as a flame that resides in our brain. In Proverbs 20:27, we read, "The soul of a person is the candle of G-d." This is one reason that, in a shiva home, on the anniversary of a close relative's death (*yahrtzeit*), and prior to leaving for the shul on the eve of Yom Kippur, we light a candle. This is to remind us that although a person may no longer be alive in the physical sense, her soul continues to live on in the "eternal world." The light of the soul still shines.

But what happens to the flame within each one of us? Unless we constantly work to fan the flame into a brightly burning torchlight, it can become covered up, concealed, and diminished, until what remains is no more than the tiny flicker of a lonely spark.

Conceptually, what happens is similar to the nature of an onion, where peel upon peel, layer upon layer covers up the core of the onion. Similarly, our soul can become encased in layer upon layer of these "peels," which diminish the brightness of our spiritual flame.

When do we have an opportunity to peel away layer after layer and uncover our soul? When does that small ember of spirituality that burns inside us get its chance to be fanned into a bright burning flame?

Davening is one of these opportunities. For a few minutes each day, we can peel some of the layers off and let the true essence of our soul burst forth and express itself.

Davening should be a time for spiritual rejuvenation, a time to get in touch with our soul and to have our soul get in touch with its Source, G-d. The Jewish soul is inextricably connected to G-d, since its central core is an actual piece of G-d Himself. (Just as a flame can be taken from a roaring fire without in any way diminishing the fire). When we do this, we can feel true awe or fear of G-d. When else can we feel attachment to and love for G-d? When else can we feel undeniable truth, which will permeate our lives in totality?

Aryeh Kaplan, among many others, has written on the power of *davening* as a deep meditative experience. *Davening*, over time and with constant work, can be one of the deepest human experiences. As we said, the ultimate potential is no longer available, that being to enter the innermost heavenly chamber, the source of G-d's presence. In the past, there have been great, holy angel-like people, who have experienced and written of their souls leaving their bodies behind as they ascended through higher spiritual worlds to enter Gan Eden, the upper recesses of Heaven. For them the experience was totally spiritual.

But even if we are unable to achieve the highest and most powerful levels of spirituality, we can still achieve deeper and higher levels than we have ever experienced before. These experiences can become deeper and higher as we learn to release our soul from the bonds of everyday life and let it expand and shine.

In this sense, *davening* is the "call of the soul." At times it may be lonely, a still small whisper, and at other times a dramatic shout, yet no matter what the intensity, its value to our lives is immeasurable.

If we understand *davening* as a deep-rooted, intense spiritual experience, we can understand why large synagogues have become cold and unpopular. In fact there is a strong trend today to *davening* in a *shtibel* ("little home" in Yiddish), which is a small intimate place designed exclusively for study and prayer, a place where our soul can soar.

It is simply hard, if not impossible, to have an intense, uninhibited spiritual experience when surrounded by hundreds of people in a large room, often with a choir and an operatic cantor.

In this context, we can also understand the Jewish law of having a *mechitzah* or separation between men and women. This *mechitzah* is in no way meant to be discriminatory. It is designed for women as much as it is for men, if not more so.

It is simply impossible to be spiritually uninhibited, to let our soul loose, to allow our spirit to flow forth and express itself in pure, intense prayer in the company of members of the opposite sex.

Human nature is such that we are all more comfortable expressing ourselves honestly, emotionally and spiritually, when we are free of the feeling that we are being scrutinized or observed by members of the opposite sex. Discussions with women confirm that those who understand the depth of *davening* much prefer a *mechitzah* that allows no scrutiny by men at all and vice versa.

The Talmud relates that when the Temple in Jerusalem was first built to serve as the spiritual center of the world, all Jews (and many non-Jews) went there to achieve closeness to G-d and clarity in life. There were huge crowds there. In order to keep those in attendance focused on their personal holiness and the holiness of the place itself, the Rabbinic leaders saw that it was necessary to separate the men and the women.

At first they put the women at the front of the Temple and the men behind them. There was still too much distraction and mixing of the sexes — hardly a deep spiritual experience. So they attempted to put the men in front and the women behind them, thinking that the women would be more adept at keeping their spiritual focus. This too proved to be fruitless.

So the Rabbis instructed that a balcony be constructed so that the men would pray downstairs and the women upstairs with nothing to distract them from being focused on the Temple service.

The need to remain focused during *davening* also explains why many men cover their heads with a *tallis*. While there is a mystical source for this as well (i.e., having two head coverings, the *kippah* and the *tallis* or the *kippah* and a hat, represents the two spiritual lights or auras, an inner light and an encompassing light that surrounds every Jew), it is simply a practical way of providing privacy during *davening*. If we cut off our peripheral vision, we can concentrate totally undisturbed on our *davening*.

If this is the case, that some form of privacy helps us achieve real, intense *davening*, then why do we not *daven* alone, at home?

Why Do We *Daven* as a Group?

We can use the analogy of a dark room and a single candle to explain this. If we walk in holding a single flame, we have alleviated total darkness in the room. However, the room is far from being bright. If ten or one hundred or one thousand people came in holding candles, the light would become much more intense, much brighter, and the room would begin to shine. The same holds true with spiritual energy. If we pray alone, then the spiritual flame that constitutes our soul begins to shine. However, if this flame is joined by ten, one hundred, or one thousand flames, the atmosphere begins to radiate light.

Of course, if we *daven* in the presence of a Tzaddik, one who is so spiritually alive that he is like a torch rather than just a candle, then he has the power to intensify the spiritual power in the whole room. Put simply, if many are *davening* at the same time, the spiritual energy in that location is multiplied exponentially and this will affect those who are attuned to spirituality.

When we *daven* together, we strengthen each other through our own spirituality and others in turn give spiritual strength to us.

The late Rabbi Ziggy Wolkenstein of Toronto taught me that Rebbe Nachman of Breslov, a grandson of the Ba'al Shem Tov and nineteenth-century spiritual leader (whose movement stresses *davening* and meditation), explains this spiritual impact as a mathematical exponent similar to a chemical compound.

Say person A & B are *davening* together. There is prayer A, prayer B, prayer AB, and prayer BA. Now if person C joins them, there are prayers A, B, C, AB, AC, BA, BC, CA, CB, and ABC. Thus two people together form four prayers. Three people together form ten prayers and so on. The multiple gets huge when one considers a whole shul of people praying.

Furthermore that is why we encourage *every single person* to pray. We don't want to miss even one person. For that person's individual prayers can form enormous multiple prayers when joined with other people's prayers.

From a simple, practical perspective, we also understand that it is easier to get caught up or swept away in the environment in which we find ourselves. For example, if we attend a concert and the emotions of the audience compel its members to give the performer a standing ovation, then we tend to get swept up in the excitement of the moment as well and we rise in applause.

If we find it hard to *daven* because there are other things on our minds, it is easier to push these aside and concentrate on prayer if we are surrounded by an environment permeated with intense spirituality.

This is the reason that many people leave their regular shuls during Rosh Hashanah and Yom Kippur, the High Holidays, and go to Israel or go back to their yeshiva or join the rabbi who is their spiritual mentor. They want to achieve a high level of spirituality and this is facilitated more easily in a more vibrant spiritual environment. We know that in some environments, spirituality is so latent that it can only be found in the deepest reservoirs of a person. In others, the environment is filled with the acute, palpable presence of G-dliness and spirituality.

One of the leading scholars of pre-war Poland, Reb Tevel of Dukla, wrote that he found it virtually impossible to achieve a proper level of *kavanah*, intense concentration, if he did not *daven* with a *minyan* (quorum) of at least ten Jewish men. He simply was unable to climb to the same heights of spirituality when davening privately. And if he, a holy man, one of the spiritual greats of his generation, was unable to achieve his spiritual objective without a *minyan*, then we who are many rungs on the spiritual ladder below him can learn an obvious lesson.

Nevertheless, if we are unable to find a shul that follows the guidelines set forth in Jewish law or that provides a stimulating and uplifting spiritual environment, then we should *daven* as best we can individually, in the privacy of our home or in a spiritually motivating place, like in a park or on a mountain, as was the custom of many great mystical rabbis of yesteryear.

We should note, however, that many great rabbis throughout the ages have stressed the importance of attempting to *daven* in a *minyan* (a group of not less than ten Jewish men who are praying together).

Why are almost all prayers in the plural form ("We") rather than the singular form ("I")? We Jews are interconnected. Just as we share similar physical genetics, we share spiritual genetics. Our souls are part of all Jewish souls. We are all flames from the same fire. We are likened to parts of one body. Some Jews are the head. These are the leaders, the teachers, the thinkers. Some are the heart of the Jewish People. These are the healers, the consolers, those who inspire. Some are the hands. These are the doers.

No matter what part of the Jewish body one functions as, he or she is an integral part of the body, performing a function that no else can perform. If one part of the body is in pain, it affects all of the body. It would be absurd, if you hurt your foot, to say, "Well, it is only my foot. Why should my head or any other part of me care?"

So it is with the Jewish People. Your pain hurts me. Your joy makes me happy. Your concerns are mine. Your life is inextricably connected to mine. Your mistakes affect me. Your goodness affects me; your needs are my needs. That is why we must pray in the plural. We pray for all of us, for we are all part of one body and one soul. This too will help us concentrate and focus on our prayers and is another reason we *daven* in a *minyan*, with others present. Perhaps I and my family members are healthy. How can I concentrate on the prayer of healing? It doesn't affect me at this time. But when I look around the shul, I begin to think of others and what they might need in their lives. Who needs healing in their family? What about those in the hospitals and the nursing homes and the old age homes? You see that *davening* with others expands our vision beyond what we see in our own lives. We learn to look outwards, to care and work for others.

It drives us to fulfill a whole category of mitzvot called *bein Adam l'chavero*, that is, the mitzvot between one person and another.

When you pray, stop, look around, and think of others. Shuls are meant to be a community within a community where we learn to think of others besides ourselves.

Perhaps this is one reason why a synagogue is referred to as a "shul," which means "school" in German. In Hebrew, a shul is often referred to as a *beit midrash* or "house of study." It is where we learn Torah. It is where we learn what to do, what we are here in this world to accomplish. It is where we learn to care for others. It is where we learn about life.

Why Is A *Minyan* Defined As A Quorum Of Ten Jewish Men?

Why is a *minyan* defined as a group of ten men (at least six of whom are *davening* with the *minyan*) while a woman is not included in this count?

While this work does not provide an in-depth analysis of the role of Jewish women, and particularly their role as spiritual leaders, it is worthwhile to note the primary spiritual role of women and why their participation in public *davening* takes on a secondary role.

Every part of a body has its specific function. The brain thinks, the heart pumps blood, the nerves feel, the eyes see. Each part has its own purpose. When all parts work in harmony, we see a healthy functioning person. The same is true for all of nature, indeed for all things that G-d or people create. In the case of a tree, the roots, bark, trunk, branches, leaves, and fruit all serve a separate yet vital function in the life of the tree. In a clock, every working part must be exact and must work in harmony with the other parts to tell time accurately. The same is true in a family, in a community, in a nation. Look at a school, a business, or a country. It is the way of the world.

In the Jewish nation, G-d delineated separate functions for specific parts of the people. As one illustration of this principle, it should be noted that each of the twelve tribes had its own specialty and its home in the Land of Israel from where it could best serve the world.

For example, the Tribe of Levi served as the peacemakers and the spiritual leaders, and therefore was spread around the country to live in forty-eight designated cities. The Tribe of Zevulun was to affect the other nations of the world, and so their specialty was shipping and their home was on the Mediterranean coast. G-d further delineated the tasks of the Jewish nation by splitting the Tribe of Levi into Kohanim (from the lineage of Aaron) and Levi'im (the rest of the Tribe of Levi, other than Aaron and his lineage).

The elders (*zikeinim*) had their specialty, as did the tribal leaders (*nesi'im*), the judges (*shoftim*), the Kings (from the lineage of King David), and all other members of the Jewish People.

So it is with men and women. Each gender branch of the Jewish people has its specialty. Obviously, we are born with physical and emotional differences. This is to indicate to us that we have different specialties, different tasks to accomplish. Who is superior? Neither — or both. Each fulfills a function that is vital to the mission of the Jewish People and to the continuance of the nation. As a general rule (and virtually all rules have exceptions), the Torah ascribes most functions in the community (i.e., the outside world) to the male segment of the Jewish nation while ascribing most functions in the home and in the family (i.e., the inner world) to the women. The Talmud (in the volume entitled *Yevamos*) states that all blessings that come to the home and the family, come through the woman of the family.

But since *davening* in a *minyan* in a shul is a community function that takes place in the "outside world," it is ascribed to men.

A popular misconception, likely taken from our Christian neighbors, is that the shul is the center of Jewish life. This is far from the truth. While the shul is indeed a place to achieve spiritual growth through prayer and Torah study, in fact the true center of the Jewish People is actually the Jewish home. It is here that the basics of our people, namely our beliefs and values, are transmitted from one generation to the next. The eternal, everlasting nature and mission of the Jewish People is dependent upon successfully transmitting the spirit of the Jewish home.

Furthermore, the three "pillar mitzvot" of the 613 given to us in the Torah — Shabbat, keeping kosher, and family purity — are performed primarily in the home. Just as biologically women have been given the supremely spiritual gift of carrying and delivering human life, which is the activity that most closely emulates G-d's creation of the world, so the women of Israel have been entrusted with many supremely spiritual gifts, including these three "pillar mitzvot" and the overriding responsibility of the transmission of Judaism to future generations.

There is a place in the World to Come for all good people and a special place for all Jews who fulfill their mission in this world — whether they be men or women. And just as all good parents love each of their children, no matter what the child's gender might be, G-d loves all of *His* children, whether they be male or female.

But Do My Prayers Really Matter?

Yes, they most certainly do. Does this mean that every single prayer matters? Does every one make a difference, have some impact, bring about a cause-and-effect response from the heavens? Are my words really and truly significant?

The Ba'al Shem Tov (the founder of the Chassidic stream of Judaism some 250 years ago) taught that *every prayer* is answered. And the answer is *not* "No!" So if that is the case, why don't we see that every request receives an affirmative response?

That is because Hashem, in His infinite wisdom and understanding of our future, sometimes "banks" our prayers. When someone turns to Hashem and beseeches Him for an act of kindness or compassion, it elicits a positive response. Sometimes this response is immediate and sometimes the request is answered in the future. Sometimes it is held in reserve for a person's child or grandchild or family member. And sometimes the positive response is utilized on behalf of the Jewish People. But *no prayer is wasted*.

The Jerusalem Talmud explains that the *Amidah*, which is the central part of each prayer service, originally comprised eighteen blessings (on a regular weekday) because at the end of the second book of the Torah (i.e., *Parshat Pikudei*), when the Torah explains how the Jews built the first travelling temple, it says that the Jews did as Hashem commanded eighteen times.

Why is it from this particular part of the Torah that we learn how many blessings to say? Chassidic thought teaches that this section of the Torah explains in meticulous detail the work of every single member of the Jewish People in the construction of the travelling temple. Every aspect of the construction and of the artwork mattered. Every contribution was significant. No contribution was deemed to be too small. If anyone had failed to fulfill his or her task, the temple would have been incomplete.

So it is with prayer. Every single prayer matters. Each one is significant. Each one elicits a response from Above. None is too small. So take your prayers seriously. Don't ever dilute the potential impact of your prayer. And don't get despondent if it seems all of your prayers are for naught. They *are* being answered. And those responses are being allocated by Hashem for use at the right time in your life and the life of your family that is the Jewish People.

AHAVAT YISRAEL – LOVE ANOTHER JEW: THE KEY TO GETTING OUR PRAYERS ANSWERED

One of the key objectives of Jewish prayer is to connect us more closely to G-d. Another is to connect us more closely to our fellow Jews. A brief examination of this theme will show that these two objectives are really one and the same.

The mitzvah to love G-d and the mitzvah to love another Jew are inextricably linked. The early Chassidic master, the Maggid of Mezritch, said that his Rebbi, the Ba'al Shem Tov, would frequently repeat that we Jews are referred to as the "children of G-d," and when we truly love the father, we must also love his children.

Furthermore, to look at this from a deeper perspective, the Jewish soul (which is what differentiates a Jew from a gentile; both have a soul but each one has its own distinct makeup) is made up of five parts. Each part gives the life force or energy to a different aspect of our lives. The central part of a Jewish soul, known in mystical terms as the *yechidah*, is an actual part of G-d above. So when we show love towards another Jew, we are showing love to the part of G-d that is contained in every Jew.

This also explains why we Jews are connected. On a simple level, we share a common history and heritage. In truth, what we shared in common took place a long time ago. Think of a Yemenite Jew who only recently left the town where his ancestors had resided for a thousand years and a modern Manhattanite working on Wall Street. For the last thousand years, they have shared little in the way of history, language, customs, dress, and the like. What they do share is the common legacy of the Torah and early Jewish history.

But on a deeper level, we are connected because we are all part of one soul.

Consider this: The inner part of our soul is like a flame from the same fire. Proverbs states, "The soul of a person is the candle of G-d." Therefore we are literally connected, not only figuratively. We are part of the one soul of Adam, the first Jewish soul of Avraham, and the all-encompassing soul of Moses, who ascended Mount Sinai to receive the Torah directly from G-d. Thus the Talmud states that the Jews stood at Mount Sinai as "one person with one heart."

This is an unbreakable connection that makes us share a common destiny. Just as G-d is one, we the Jewish People are one. We are one with each other and one with G-d. That is why, when the Torah instructs us to love another Jew, it says to "love your neighbor (meaning your fellow Jew) as you do yourself." How can such an instruction be fulfilled? If we understand that we are really parts of one common entity, then when we love another Jew who contains within him or her part of our one common soul, we in fact love a part of ourselves.

This has a very practical application in Halachah (Jewish law), in the principle of *arvut*, which means both "joined together" and "responsibility for another." It is this principle that, under specific conditions, allows one Jew to perform a mitzvah on behalf of another. For example, one Jew can blow the shofar for another. One Jew can make a blessing for another.

Davening helps us focus on this. When we do focus, *ahavat Yisrael* becomes part of our psyche and that becomes manifested in a feeling of love and genuine acts of caring about and caring for our fellow Jews.

Consider this: Are you touched more deeply when you read about a tragedy that befell a Jewish person than you are by a tragedy that befalls a total stranger, even if the Jewish person lives in Argentina or Israel while the stranger lives right in your neighborhood? Ahhh. It is your Jewish soul that grieves.

And aren't you a least a little happier, a little more filled with pride when a Jewish person wins the Nobel Prize or an award of some sort? Even if you don't know the person and never heard of him or her before? That's your Jewish soul at work, too.

After such a diverse and varied history, with all our political, religious, socio-economic, and geographic differences, we still feel connected. And that is because we *are* connected. As discussed earlier, that is why we *daven* in the plural form, to remember the other parts of our people, of our soul.

That is why *davening* in a *minyan* and in a shul is the favored form of prayer. It helps us to feel the connection that exists between Jews. Think how G-d feels. His children are at peace with one another. They care about one another. They pray for one another. They help one another. It makes G-d feel, just as it would make any parent feel, the *nachas*, the sense of joy and inner peace that comes from knowing that the children feel a deep connection with each other and take care of each other.

From a practical perspective, this is why the great sixteenth-century kabbalist, Rav Yitzchak Luria (known as the "Arizal"), instructs us to open *davening* each day by reaffirming our acceptance of the mitzvah of *ahavat Yisrael*, love of another Jew. We make this acceptance real by beginning each day with a small donation to *tzedakah*, charity. We don't just speak of acceptance. We don't just feel it. We do it. We make it real. We make a difference every day.

(Note: We don't deal with money on Shabbat and the major Jewish holidays. Instead, we give *tzedakah* before Shabbat and the holidays to make up for the day(s) we will miss. Women have the custom of giving *tzedakah* just before they light the Shabbat candles. Many keep a special silver, ceramic, or other artistic *tzedakah* box next to the candlesticks to remind them to perform this mitzvah.)

It is in the merit of our daily acceptance of *ahavat Yisrael* and its practical application through the donation to *tzedakah* that our prayers are answered. This is what opens up the heavenly gates of kindness and compassion. When we feel and, more importantly, when we act in a way that shows kindness and compassion to others, we in turn are shown kindness and compassion in far greater measure by our common Father. This is why charity is referred to as "the wings of prayer." This concept will be further elaborated in the next section.

The Talmud relates the story of the great rabbi, Hillel. A prospective convert to Judaism once approached Hillel with an unusual request — to be taught all of Torah while "standing on one foot." After being turned away by other great scholars due to the apparent ridiculous nature of the request, his request was met by Hillel, who responded that all of the Torah is based on the mitzvah to love another Jew and that all the rest of the Torah was merely commentary. Now go and learn how to love another person, Hillel instructed.

Indeed, that is the purpose of the whole Torah. That is the key to creating a world of sensitivity, compassion, and kindness. That, as Rabbi Akiva said, is the great underlying principle of the entire Torah.

TZEDAKAH: THE GIFT OF GIVING

As has been mentioned, *tzedakah*, commonly translated as "charity," is referred to as "the wings of prayer." In many of our prayers, we ask Hashem to provide us with everything we need, and then some. We ask Hashem to go beyond what we really need and what we really deserve and grant us gifts in many forms, day after day, for many years. We are essentially asking Hashem to be extremely benevolent towards us.

But *tzedakah* doesn't really mean "charity." The term "charity" (from a Latin word meaning "dear") implies benevolence, in that we are giving to someone from the goodness of our hearts. The term *tzedakah* has the word *tzedek* at its root. *Tzedek* means to do what is right and what is just.

Hashem provides us with much more than we need. And we, in turn, are to partner with Hashem and take from the excess that He has given us and share it with others. In this way, we learn to be givers, just like Hashem, the ultimate Giver.

So when we ask for everything we want, the right thing to do is to tell Hashem that our true intentions are to use some portion of what we are given to give to others. And just as those people will receive from us, they are to "pay it forward" and share a portion with others. We will thus create a family, and then a community, a society, and ultimately a whole world of givers. The whole world will then learn to emulate this G-dly quality of giving.

The more we plan to give, the more we will be given. This puts us squarely in partnership with Hashem. How so, you might ask? As an example, in the case of a doctor, Hashem grants the doctor the wisdom and power to heal and the doctor uses it to heal someone who is ill. In the case of a farmer, Hashem provides him with rain, earth, sunshine, nutrients, and seeds. The farmer in turn works the field and gives a portion of the harvest to the poor. (It is interesting to note that, in times of old, when the Temple stood in Jerusalem and many Jews were farmers in Israel, ten gifts were given from the produce of the land. These gifts totalled about twenty per cent of the total bounty of that year).

So we see that the whole idea of *tzedakah* is to fulfill our part of the partnership with Hashem. Hashem gives us wheat and we make cake. Then we share the cake with those who are needy and we have completed the partnership of giving.

If our intent is to use what Hashem gives us for a higher purpose, including providing for those in need, then our prayers soar to high spiritual levels, as if they had wings. We become true partners with Hashem. And this justifies us asking Hashem for even more heavenly gifts.

But here's a novel and extremely practical concept for us to put into action immediately. *Tzedakah* is not only fulfilled by giving money and material possessions. *Tzedakah* is also fulfilled by giving of our time, our efforts, our homes, and our words.

In financial terms, the minimal obligation, as instructed by the Torah, is to give ten per cent of our after-tax income to Jewish charities and needy people. But we should also give a minimum of ten per cent of our waking hours for worthy causes and needy people. This charity time can be used in a myriad of ways. We can volunteer to work in an organization, to lead others, and to build lives, buildings, and worlds. We can use our charity time to comfort others, to celebrate with someone else, and to uplift or assist one who requires these emotional forms of assistance. We can use our homes to welcome guests, to uplift people, to assist single people in meeting their *bashert* (destined partner), to welcome new people to the community, to invite single or lonely people for a holiday or Shabbat meal, and to host a Torah class, perhaps in honor of a birthday or a *yahrtzeit*.

Maimonides teaches the phenomenal concept of *tzedakah* using words. A few thoughtful, sincere, heartfelt, and well-placed words can make someone feel comforted, build self-esteem, inspire, express thanks, and uplift. The *Zohar* (the main book of Kabbalah, Jewish mystical thought) teaches that just as we are ultimately responsible to answer to the One Above for what we said and should *not* have said, we are responsible to answer for what we should have said and did not say.

Words are the great tool of mankind. Used well, they can save lives, drive people to higher heights, build self-esteem, inspire others, build relationships, and create loving relationships between people.

And we can inspire others to follow our lead in all of these forms of *tzedakah*. The Torah relates the story of Yitro, the father-in-law of Moshe Rabbeinu (Moses our Teacher), who gave Moshe a sage piece of advice. When Yitro saw long lines of Jews waiting to seek advice and judgement in various disputes from Moshe, he advised Moshe to share the responsibility with many Jewish leaders. He recommended that Moshe set up a system of one judge/mentor/teacher for every thousand people, one for every hundred, one for every fifty, and one for every ten.

What is the practical lesson that we can learn from this story? The Lubavitcher Rebbe explained that every one of us is compelled to take responsibility for assisting others in our lifetime. Some can have a major impact and assist one thousand people. Others can affect one hundred and some fifty. But *everyone* can affect at least ten people in a lifetime. That's only one every five years of our adult life. So if we find someone who needs assistance in any way, or we find a worthy cause that requires our assistance, why not encourage a friend or relative to join us?

In doing so, we will have leveraged our caring into far greater results for the ultimate, needy recipients. It occurs to me that all revolutions were started by one person. That holds true for a revolution in acts of kindness, in education, in benevolence, in healing, in outreach, and in all other forms of *tzedakah*. One person who in turn inspires others can provide "wings" for many people to soar higher and higher and provide many needy people with many forms of *tzedakah*.

One more point. We gain more for ourselves and benefit more by giving *tzedakah* to others, than they do by receiving our *tzedakah*. Maimonides teaches that if a person wants to give a hundred dollars to *tzedakah*, it would be better to give one dollar one hundred times than it would be to give one hundred dollars at one time. Why, you might ask?

Because if we compel ourselves to do the act of giving a hundred times, we will change our basic nature and turn from being takers (the way all children are born) into givers. We will become habituated to giving. And can you imagine a society where everyone had that approach? Where everyone wanted to be a giver? Could you imagine if everyone on the planet were like that?

Well then, let us start with our own personal development. Let's turn ourselves into habitual givers. Let us make our family and our circle of friends into "giving circles." Here are some practical ways to accomplish this goal:

• Give *tzedakah* daily. Put money into a charity box each time you daven. Give *tzedakah* before Shabbat and Jewish holidays for the *davening* you intend to do on those days.

• Women should give *tzedakah* before lighting the candles at the start of each Shabbat or major Jewish holiday.

• Keep a charity box in your office. Put one in the room of each of your children. Give them a coin to put in it each day.

• Compliment your spouse and children at least once every single day.

• Become accustomed to giving people compliments and saying "thank you" all the time, even for the smallest of favors and tasks done on your behalf.

MAJOR THEMES OF PRAYER

The point of prayer is to connect, to live a more aware, thoughtful, appreciative, conscious, deep, and focused life. We accomplish this by taking a few moments first to *think* and then to *say* various prayers, which include parts of the Torah, Psalms, and a private, personal discussion with Hashem, our Parent Above.

When the last prophets of our Nation, who wrote the last books in the Jewish Bible, and their peers compiled the siddur, their intention was to give us an everlasting tool to help us grow by focusing on particular concepts, which we could use for self-development. To this end, the major themes of Jewish prayer are as follows:

Self-Awareness

Who am I? Who put us here and why were we put here? What impact can each of us have upon the world around us, as a partner with G-d? And alternatively, who are we not? What are we good at and what are the areas that we need to focus on for our individual personal growth in order to achieve our human potential?

These questions and the prayers that relate to them are found mostly in the beginning prayers of each day.

Self-Improvement

What follows from the previous prayer exercise is the essence of Jewish prayer. By knowing who we are and analyzing how we are doing relative to our human potential each day, we can constantly improve ourselves, our relationships, and the world in which we find ourselves.

Awareness of G-d

If we are to understand anything about our purpose in Creation, we must achieve some measure of relationship with Hashem. The first step to building this relationship is to become aware of Hashem and His impact in our lives. As we get more comfortable in our understanding of Hashem, we begin to achieve a relationship with our Parent Above. And the more conscious we are of Hashem in our lives, the more we live a G-d-centered life rather than a self-centered, hedonistic one, and the more we fulfill our purpose on this Earth, which is also the ultimate form of pleasure and self-fulfillment.

Awareness of Gifts

Awareness of Hashem leads to our becoming more aware of all that we have and all that we have been given, all the gifts in our lives. In a society that is focused on what we are lacking at any particular time (I know, I spent years as a marketing manager for one of the world's largest food, fashion, and toy companies; it was all about letting you know what you *don't* have but supposedly ought to), the focus of prayer begins with what we *do* have. This leads to a much more reassured, calm, and appreciative life.

Gratitude

Once we achieve the realization of all of the gifts that Hashem has granted us in our lives, we are obligated by sheer human decency to express our gratitude. And if we become accustomed to doing this, we will express gratitude in all areas of our lives. This will make our relationships richer and will make all of life a more balanced, happier, deeper, and richer experience.

Redemption (Personal, National, and Global)

With all of life's challenges — from the small, almost insignificant ones to the huge, life-altering ones, from the national challenges that we have faced throughout history and certainly face today to the broader global challenges — we have to stay positive. We must remain optimistic that just as Hashem has redeemed us personally and nationally from so many challenges in the past, He will indeed continue to assist us and redeem us from all personal, national, and global challenges.

Although we have a number of Jewish holidays focused on this theme (e.g., Yom Kippur, Chanukah, Purim, Pesach), we are to remind ourselves of this multiple times each day.

Requests

Once we know who we are and what we need, as well as a little about Hashem as the all-powerful Master of the World who is also our Parent

Above, we know "the address" to go to in order to ask for our personal needs and the needs of the people we know, our People as a whole, and the world at large. We can ask Hashem for anything and trust that He knows what is best for us and when the ideal delivery moments are for all that we need and all that we seek.

SHEMA YISRAEL: THE "JEWISH NATIONAL ANTHEM"

The verses of the Torah that we call *Shema Yisrael* or "The *Shema*" appear everywhere in our lives. They form the words that are on the parchment of the mezuzah that is to be placed on the doorpost of each door in our homes and offices (except the washrooms and similar rooms that are utilized for personal hygiene). We are surrounded by the words of the *Shema*. The *Shema* has the power to protect us.

The same words are written on one of the four parchments of the *tefillin* that is placed on the arm and the same words are once again written on the parchment of the *tefillin* that is placed on the head. We are tied to the words of the *Shema*.

The words of the *Shema* are taught to little children as soon as they can speak. These are the last words someone says before leaving the world. The words of the *Shema* are to be said every morning and every night of our entire lives. They form part of the morning and the evening prayers.

The words of the *Shema* are recited before we go to sleep at night. They are recited by the entire shul at the end of Yom Kippur services. They are constantly on our lips and in our hearts. They are the most important words in the Torah. So what is it about these words that make them the Jewish anthem?

The *Shema* reminds us about the very essence of life, of why we are here and what we are to do. The *Shema* is the mission, the goal, the point of life. It gives us strength. It gives us focus. It gives us encouragement. It gives us inspiration. The *Shema* is the essence of our faith, the reaffirmation of our acceptance of G-d. We are G-dly people. We work for G-d. We are G-d's People. We want to live in a world with G-d. We want to live in G-d's world.

Let us briefly examine the key words and ideas in the *Shema* from two different yet complementary perspectives. The first is the perspective discussed by Aryeh Kaplan in his phenomenal work *Jewish Meditation*.

The first phrase is the key phrase. "*Shema Yisrael, Adonoy Eloheinu, Adonoy Echad* "— translated as, "Listen Israel, Adonoy our G-d, Adonoy is one." What does that mean?

The *Shema* means to listen carefully, to internalize the message. Aryeh Kaplan, in *Jewish Meditation*, points out that when one examines the sounds of the letters of the word *Shema* on an oscilloscope, which deciphers and projects sounds waves, the very sounds of the letters of the word give us an understanding of the word itself.

The "shhhh" sound is chaotic. It is white noise. It is a mixture of all wavelengths. The next sound "mmmm-aaaaaah" is one perfect wavy line. It is a comforting, clear, simple sound. It is order. That is the point. Get out of the confusion of life and get ordered; find simple clarity.

In Jewish mysticism, the letter *shin*, which makes the sound "shhh," represents fire (the Hebrew word for fire is *aishhh*), while the letter *mem*, which makes the sound "mmm," represents water (the Hebrew word for water is *mayimmm*). When we say the *Shema*, we "cool down" from the "heat" of the confusion of our daily lives into a relaxed mental state of "cool" calm and clarity.

OK, so I'm calm and focused. But what am I focused on?

Yisrael (or Israel in English) was the name given to our forefather Yaakov (Jacob) after the famous story in the Torah when he fought with the angel of Eisav (Esau) and emerged victorious. It represents the Jewish People in the struggle to achieve mastery over the physical, over nature, over our nature, over foreign concepts and anti-G-d thoughts. So thus far the *Shema* says, "Cool down from your chaotic life and remember this as you struggle with the challenges of life . . ."

What are we to remember?

That *Adonoy* (i.e., Hashem), G-d, who is so awesome, powerful, and impossible to totally comprehend, is *Eloheinu*, our G-d. Infinite, but ours. And "*Adonoy* is one." The one and only G-d. The one life force who keeps recreating our world every microsecond. The only One who runs the world. The One who is everywhere. Hashem is one *with* us as we go through life. And Hashem is one *within* us, as we Jews have a "spark of G-d" within our souls. Hashem is the One who unites us, as we all carry a spark from the same source. And the same one G-d no matter how we experience G-dliness. Sometimes we will experience G-dliness with joy, sometimes with tears, sometimes by experiencing the beauty, complexity, and magnitude of nature.

The second perspective comes from the teachings of the great Rebbe Nachman of Breslov. Rebbe Nachman explained that the name *Adonoy* refers to Hashem when we perceive Hashem's kindness and compassion. *Eloheinu* refers to Hashem when we perceive Hashem's judgment and strength.

Rebbe Nachman of Breslov points out that the lesson of the *Shema* is that both *Adonoy* and *Eloheinu* are one. They are both *Adonoy*, meaning that, no matter how we might perceive G-d's effect upon us, the effect always comes from a place of G-d's kindness and compassion. Everything Hashem does has its source in Hashem's kindness.

How can these two manifestations of Hashem's power and influence be construed as coming from the same source and motivation?

At times parents must show love to their child by being strict or exercising their best judgment. This can result in the child being refused a request (e.g., no more jellybeans today) or going through a painful experience (e.g., going to the doctor). The same is true with our Parent Above. Hashem shows His love for us in many ways. But *all* of Hashem's ways are based on love, kindness, and compassion. We may not perceive this at times. We may not get what we want. We may not understand. We may go through very painful experiences.

But the absolute truth, which we must repeat to ourselves over and over again, is that everything that Hashem does is for the best and is based upon kindness and compassion. This is the meaning of *Shema Yisrael*, taught Rebbe Nachman.

And so the first phrase alone contains the concepts of the Oneness of Hashem, our acceptance of Hashem, and our understanding that Hashem is a loving, kind G-d. The rest of the *Shema* deals with our love of Hashem, our self-sacrifice for Hashem, and the study and spreading of Torah to our children and to the world.

These messages must permeate our thoughts, our emotions and, most of all, our actions. We need to remind ourselves constantly, as we live in a world where G-dliness is hidden rather than revealed. We can never allow the truth to be hidden deep within us. It should be the driving force of our lives.

TALLIT AND TEFILLIN

Just as every part of our body has its particular function and each function is critical to the overall workings of the body, so too the Jewish people are like a body. One person may serve as the "brain" of the nation, while another serves as its "heart," and yet another serves as its "hand."

As was mentioned before, the Jewish People were made up of various tribes. Each tribe had its own specific role within the nation. The same is true in a family, a corporation, an army, and other similar structures. We each have our particular role to fulfill in order to achieve overall success for the group.

Thus within the Jewish People, men and women have differing roles. This has been discussed, to some extent, in another section of this book. However, it is appropriate to repeat the teaching in discussing two particular mitzvot — the *tallit* and the *tefillin*.

Women are free from the obligation of performing these daily mitzvot, while they have great importance for men. Women are free from these mitzvot as they are "time-bound"; that is, they must be performed only during the day, and women are generally free from performing most (but not all) time-bound mitzvot. Women have their own special and unique mitzvot to fulfill.

However, for Jewish men, these two mitzvot are deemed to be among the most important ones that they can fulfill. The *tallit* is a special prayer shawl, which is worn during the morning prayers every day of the year. (Note that many of us grew up using a scarf-like facsimile of a *tallit*, which does not fit within the prescribed size of a proper *tallit*. A proper *tallit* is more the size of a large bath towel.)

While far more study is required to understand the depth of meaning of this mitzvah, simply put, every day a Jewish man wraps himself in the mitzvot. *Tallit* represents the idea that we should be surrounded by mitzvot in every aspect of our lives. Some Jewish men even wear a *tallit katan*, a small *tallit* under their shirts, so that they literally are encompassed by a holy article of clothing the entire day.

The *tefillin* are even more complex and the mitzvah requires study and investigation. The *tefillin* are considered the second holiest of articles, exceeded in holiness only by a Torah scroll.

Tefillin are worn only on regular weekdays (i.e., Sunday to Friday, when no major Jewish holiday occurs). Each leather box of the *tefillin* contains four paragraphs from the Torah, written by a trained scribe using a specially fashioned quill, ink, and parchment, similar to that used for the writing of a Torah scroll.

These boxes are placed upon the bicep muscle of a man's weaker arm, horizontally across from the heart, and then wrapped seven times upon the arm and then upon the hand. The other box is placed in the center of his forehead, between the two brain hemispheres, where his hairline was during his youth. A special knot is placed at the back of the head, at the base of the brain. In this way, the *tefillin* represent a man's binding of his brain, heart, and arm to the service of meaning and purpose, as articulated by Hashem in the Torah.

Thus a man should strive each day to have holy thoughts, feelings, and actions. He is literally bound to and bound up with the Torah every day. And while *tefillin* can be worn any time during the day, they are best donned while the morning prayers are being recited, as that is the time when one is usually in a state of unencumbered holiness.

See page 75 for instructions on how to put on *tefillin*.

THE KADDISH PRAYER

The Kaddish prayer is one of the best known of all Jewish prayers, as it is the prayer recited by a Jewish mourner following the burial of a close relative. There are, however, six versions of the Kaddish prayer, which are recited at different times. The first half of all of the versions is the same. The second half changes depending on the occasion when one recites the prayer.

Various forms of the Kaddish prayer are recited at the following times:

The "Half Kaddish" signals the end of a particular section of the prayers (or according to some early opinions, the beginning of a distinct section of the prayers). It contains the essential theme of the Kaddish prayer (see below).

The "Full Kaddish" is recited after every complete prayer service. In addition to the basic Kaddish prayer, it is a prayer that asks Hashem to accept and answer the prayers that the congregation has just recited.

The "Rabbis' Kaddish" is recited after the public study of the works of the ancient Rabbis. Aside from the basic theme of the Kaddish prayer, it is a prayer that asks Hashem to provide Divine assistance for the teachers and students of Torah and Jewish wisdom.

The "Siyum Kaddish" is recited at the public celebration following the completion of a significant work of Torah study (e.g., a complete volume of Talmud).

The "Graveside Kaddish" is recited by the immediate family members at the graveside following the burial of their deceased relative.

The "Mourner's Kaddish" is recited daily at a public *minyan* by the members of the immediate family for either eleven months or thirty days (depending if the deceased is a parent or one of the other seven closest relatives) following the burial and on the *yahrtzeit* (i.e., the anniversary of the death on the Jewish calendar) each year.

The main theme of all of the Kaddish prayers is to remind us of the "Big Picture." It is a prayer for the time of Mashiach, when the world will achieve its ultimate objective. At that time, all of humanity will recognize Hashem and have a relationship with our Parent Above. It will be a time of peace, higher purpose, and deep relationship with Hashem for all of humanity.

The inference of the Mourner's Kaddish is that, with the death of a good person, the world has lost someone who has helped bring the world closer to the time of Mashiach. The mourners proclaim that they will step up and increase their efforts to bring the Era of Mashiach by recognizing their higher purpose in life and increasing their observance of mitzvot and acts of kindness.

In this regard, the mourners (or the representative of the mourners) make a public declaration and affirmation of the goal of humanity and thus lead those in attendance to make a public affirmation of the higher goals and purpose of humanity. Thus the mourners have performed the great mitzvah of making a public *kiddush Hashem* (bringing people closer to Hashem). The goal is not for the mourner to recite the Kaddish prayer but rather to lead the congregation (as would a *chazzan*) in responding to the requests made in this prayer. The Talmud teaches that this is a tremendous merit for the deceased.

See pages 124 to 125 for the Mourner's Kaddish.

THE MITZVAH GROOVE: A SUMMARY OF THE MULTIPLE MORNING MITZVOT

The Talmud, in the section referred to as *Pirkei Avot* (Ethics of Our Forefathers), teaches that one mitzvah or positive action pulls along the next one. This is the source of the English expression, "One good thing leads to another." We all know this to be true in life. When one gets in a "groove," this tends to lead to more similar types of activities.

If we get into an exercise "groove," we tend to exercise more often, be more conscious of what we eat, read more articles about fitness, and discuss the matter with our friends. The same is true about a "bad groove." If we lose our self-control over eating healthy foods, before long we are binging on chocolate, milkshakes, pastries, fatty meats, nasty carbs, potato chips, and all sorts of "junk food."

With a mitzvah groove, not only is our headspace focused on doing mitzvot, and not only are good feelings generated as a result of doing so many worthwhile activities, but Hashem rewards those who do mitzvot with the opportunity to do more mitzvot. As the Talmud teaches, the reward for one mitzvah is the opportunity to do another mitzvah.

We should ask Hashem each day for the opportunity to do something worthwhile, to make a difference that day. By starting our day along the path prescribed by Jewish tradition, we get into the "mitzvah groove" every single day of our life.

Consider the following list of mitzvot that we are to do each morning:

- Washing our hands (i.e., spiritual cleansing; see page 73).

- Reaffirming our acceptance of the mitzvah to love another Jew (see pages 49 and 52).

- Praying.

- Reaffirming our belief and trust in the One and Only G-d (see page 101).

- Giving charity (see pages 52).

- Remembering the Exodus from Egypt (see page 103 or 153).

- Reciting the Shema (see page 100).

- Studying Torah (for at least a short while) (see page 81 and 82).

- Reconnecting with our love of Hashem.

- Reconnecting with our fear (i.e., awe) of Hashem.

- Reminding ourselves not to follow our inclination to do wrong things.

- Specifically for men, wrapping ourselves in the *tallit*, and wearing the *tefillin* for the arm, and the *tefillin* for the head (i.e., each one is an independent mitzvah).

Now you can see why we Jews start our day with so many mitzvot. It not only means we have accomplished so much in the first half hour of the day, it sets us in a "mitzvah groove" for the entire day. The challenge is to keep it going throughout the day. And then we set the pace again the next day, for we never want to leave the "mitzvah groove." That's what we are put here on Earth to do. That's how we fulfill our potential and achieve a complete and satisfying life.

No mitzvah should ever be taken lightly. We cannot measure the complete effect of a mitzvah that we have done, nor can we measure the loss of a mitzvah opportunity that we did not grab. The Ba'al Shem Tov said that sometimes a soul in a body, a person, is placed here on Earth for seventy or eighty years in order to do one person one favor on one particular day. And all the rest is commentary.

Think about it. Maybe that one mitzvah opportunity is the fulfillment of the whole purpose of our creation. Wow! Now does that give that one mitzvah significance or what? And maybe that one mitzvah will lead to another, which will lead to another and another and another and, well . . . . You get it. So start your morning in the "Mitzvah Groove" and it will lead to good things every day, every week, every month, and every year, throughout all of your life.

SHABBAT: DAY OF HEAVEN

To preface our brief discussion of Shabbat, let us examine succinctly the three basic relationships in life. They are:

- The relationship between a person and G-d,
- The relationship between a person and other people,
- The relationship between a person and one's self.

Take yourself as an example. There is your relationship with G-d. Do you think about G-d? Does G-d affect your decision-making? Do you wonder about G-d? Question G-d, talk to G-d? Do you feel that G-d has an effect on your life?

How about your relationship with other people? Whom do you feel close to? What do you do for other people? What do other people do for you? What qualities do you admire most in others? Who inspires you? Who uplifts your spirits?

What about your relationship with yourself? "What does that mean?" you are no doubt asking yourself. Well, what are the things you do for yourself? In most cases, people spend most of their lives in pursuit of personal gratification. It seems that this relationship is the driving force in most people's lives. But let us examine this more carefully.

If you are defined by your true essence, which comes from your soul, your G-d-given life force, you can ask yourself a set of different questions. When do you listen to your soul? You obviously listen to your body. You give it food, rest, medical care, pleasure, warmth, and the like. But what about your soul?

Do you give it nourishment, care, and attention? Do you listen to the subtle calls of your soul? Are you tuned into your true essence? Do you ever make time to hear your own soul?

It all sounds pretty complicated, doesn't it? Fortunately, there are instructions in the Torah for enhancing each of these relationships and for keeping the correct balance among all three relationships. These instructions are called *mitzvot*. The word *mitzvah* has two etymological root words. One is the word *tziva*, which means "to direct" or "to command." From here we get the expression "the commandments."

But there is a far deeper explanation for mitzvot, which stems from the root word *tzavta*, meaning "to join." That is because the purpose of all mitzvot is to join two entities in a closeness that exceeds the closeness they had before the mitzvah was performed.

For example, the mitzvah of *tzedakah* (charitable acts) connects the giver and the receiver. Before the gift or act of charity, the two parties may not even have known each other. But once a gift is given, the two parties are closer. They are connected. And the more often one gives to the other, the more connected the two people feel. This builds the relationship between one person and another.

The mitzvah of eating kosher food is one that primarily affects only the one eating the food. The food that we eat affects our physical nature. It gives us vitamins and other nutrients. It gives us fuel for energy, fuel for life. The wrong food can cause damage to the arteries and the heart. The same holds true for kosher food. The right food provides spiritual energy. It nourishes the soul and joins the body and the soul together to perform mitzvot, which achieves the purpose of creation.

On the other hand, the wrong food can block the spiritual arteries and damage the heart. It can cause a breach between, or a distancing of, the body and the soul. It can inhibit the body from joining the soul in doing mitzvot. It can prevent us from fulfilling our purpose in creation. This is the key mitzvah to help define and build the relationship between a person and one's inner self.

Of course, prayer is an example of a mitzvah that helps us to build a relationship between G-d and us.

What about the balance among these three sets of relationships? Let us look at a three-legged stool as an example. We know that if one leg is cut off, the stool will fall. If one leg is far too short, the stool will fall. If one leg is slightly shorter than the other two, the stool will be off-balance and will teeter.

The same is true in life. These three relationships must be in balance. True, some people excel in one of these three relationships more than the others, making our stool example less than perfect. But still, the principle holds true. The three relationships must be in balance.

Shabbat is the day when we get our lives back into balance. And it is the one day each week when we make time to enhance each of the three relationships. In the heavens, we are told that everything is in proper balance. Truth and peace live in balance. G-d and the souls of good people have an ever-growing relationship. Similarly, Shabbat is the "day of heaven." We take time to do some things and not do others so that we can put our lives back into equilibrium. That is why the Talmud says, "More than the Jews kept the Shabbat, Shabbat kept the Jews."

On Shabbat we pray longer, and in a more relaxed way, than on any other day of the week. We even say prayers at the Shabbat dinner and lunch table. We listen to the Torah reading, make time to study Torah, and hear the Rabbi's talk in shul. We sing songs of appreciation for all that G-d has given us. We think about G-d and all the goodness in our lives. All this serves to enhance our relationship with G-d.

A real Shabbat is a soul time. We remind ourselves that we are Jewish. We listen to the call of our soul, which tells us that we long to achieve closeness with G-d and with other Jews. We remind ourselves that we are G-d's partners in Creation. We remember that we have a G-dly mission to accomplish.

On Shabbat, we rest, we relax, we sleep a little longer. We walk slowly. No need to rush. We take it easy. We relax our minds. We read beautiful thoughts and ideas from Torah books. We eat special food. We rejuvenate our bodies. We rejuvenate our minds. Most of all, we rejuvenate our souls. We get the strength to go forward into a new week of challenges and accomplishments. All this serves to enhance our relationship with ourselves. On Shabbat we are good to ourselves. To all of our selves — to our body, our mind, and our soul.

And on Shabbat we build the relationship between ourselves and other people, especially our own family. Acts of kindness begin at home. Husbands and wives achieve greater closeness on Shabbat. Shabbat is a day of love. Husbands bring flowers and sing King Solomon's Song (*Eishet Chayil*) to their wives. Wives make special food for their families. Spouses forgive each other for words better left unsaid and for things that should have been done but weren't.

Parents talk sweetly to children — give them special Parents' Blessings every Friday night, take them to shul, tell them Shabbat stories, sing with them, laugh with them, and forgive them for the things that go wrong during our nervous week.

Before Shabbat, we call our parents to wish them a Good Shabbos. We invite guests for dinner. We greet newcomers to the shul. We wish each other "Shabbat Shalom" or "Good Shabbos." We forgive each other. We go to Kiddush — share a "l'chayim," share a thought, share a laugh with each other. We build friendships. Shabbat helps us to enhance relationships between us and other people — especially our family members. Since ideally we don't work, shop, or travel on Shabbat, we have time for all of the three relationships. We can put our lives back into equilibrium in all ways. We look at our lives and correct ourselves if we are out of balance or if we are headed in the wrong direction.

That is why Yom Kippur is referred to in the Torah as *Shabbat Shabbaton*, the Shabbat of Shabbats. It is the one day when we evaluate and correct our lives, and resolve to achieve balance and equilibrium in all relationships for the coming year. It may not be the most pampering of days but it is the most life-defining day. Just like the weekly Shabbat.

And that is also why the time of Mashiach is referred to as *yom shekulo Shabbat*, a time when every day is like Shabbat. Don't worry. It doesn't mean to imply that you will never be able to work or travel again. It means that the peace, serenity, and fulfillment of Shabbat will be present every day. Because, dear friends, Shabbat truly is a "day in Heaven" right here on Earth.

If you have never experienced a *real* spiritual Shabbat or haven't experienced one lately, call your local Orthodox Rebbetzin and ask her to arrange for you to be a guest at a special home one Shabbat. If you don't have a local contact, try the Internet at Chabad.org or Aish.com. They will be happy to use their international contacts to arrange a home for a Shabbat or Jewish Holiday experience.

THE FIVE STEPS OF THE DAILY MORNING PRAYERS

The Jewish prayer book is called a "siddur." You might recognize the word as being similar to the Pesach "Seder," the fifteen steps that are the order of business at the Pesach Seders, which take place on the first night of Passover in Israel and the first two nights of Passover outside of the Land of Israel.

The prophets who wrote and organized the siddur some 2,500 years ago set out a particular order to the prayers to help us achieve various levels of inspiration and insight. The five steps of the daily morning prayers are as follows:

Step 1. Moments of Awareness ("Who am I?")

Prayers that remind me of who I am, what I have, and what I am here to do today.

Step 2. Contemplating Hashem's Impact on the World ("Who is G-d?")

Readings and prayers that remind me of who G-d is and what He does in the world.

Step 3. Reaffirming the Oneness of Hashem and Our Connection with Him ("Connecting G-d and me together")

Using the *Shema Yisrael* set of prayers to reaffirm our connection to G-d.

Step 4. My Personal Dialogue with Hashem

Having a personal talk with G-d where I make requests and give thanks.

Step 5. Taking the Lessons, Awareness, and Inspiration of the Prayers into My Daily Life

Prayers that give me inspiration and direction as I head into the challenges of my life again today.

Now, friends, let the *davening* begin!

THE DAILY MORNING PRAYERS

Steps 1, 2, and 3 of the morning prayers are the same whether it's Shabbat morning or a weekday morning. However, you will come to a fork in the road, so to speak, when you get to Step 4, your personal dialogue with G-d in the *Shemoneh Esrei*, a prayer that differs on Shabbat and holy days from the regular weekday. Just begin with *Modeh Ani* below, and you'll come to the signs directing you to the appropriate *Shemoneh Esrei* and after-prayers of Step 5.

Modeh Ani

Some say the *Modeh Ani* prayer, to thank Hashem for another day of life, right when they wake up, even while lying in bed.

See page 78 for the text of prayer should you wish to say it prior to the formal morning prayer service.

Netilat Yadayim
Ritual washing of our hands to remove spiritual blocks

In Jewish tradition, sleep is considered to be a taste of death. We always counter a symbol of death with water, which is a symbol of life.

To do this ritual: When you get out of bed, take a large cup of water and pour it over your entire right hand from your fingertips to your wrist and then over your left hand, from your fingertips to your wrist. Repeat this two more times. (Thus you have poured right/ left, right/ left, right/ left.) Now dry your hands.

The blessing for this mitzvah is said as part of the morning prayers (see page 79).

Tallit
Surrounding yourself with spirituality (a mitzvah for men)

Unfold your *tallit* and, before you wrap it around your head and shoulders, say the blessing. This is done every day of the year and on the evening of Yom Kippur, commonly referred to as *Kol Nidrei* night. The *tallit* should large enough to cover most of your body.

See page 62 for a deeper understanding of this mitzvah.

Kavanah: *Today I should be surrounded with goodness and opportunities to perform mitzvot. Let me not be lead astray by negative desires and emotions.*

You, Adonoy our G-d, Source of all blessings, Master of the World, made us holy by giving us the mitzvot and commanding us to wrap ourselves in a *tallit*.

Baruch atah Adonoy Elo-heinu Melech ha-olam asher ki-d'shanu b'mits-votav v'tsi-vanu l'hit-a-teif b'tsi-tsit.

בָּרוּךְ אַתָּה יי אֱלֹהֵינוּ מֶלֶךְ הָעוֹלָם אֲשֶׁר קִדְּשָׁנוּ בְּמִצְוֹתָיו וְצִוָּנוּ לְהִתְעַטֵּף בְּצִיצִית.

Wrap your *tallit* around your head and shoulders, covering your face as well, and then drape it over your shoulders, the way you will wear it during davening.

NOTE: On Shabbat skip this next section and go directly to page 78 to begin the Shabbat Morning Prayers, as *tefillin* are not worn on Shabbat.

Tefillin
Channelling your thoughts and actions
(a major mitzvah for men)

(See page 62 for a deeper understanding of this very important mitzvah).

Tefillin are worn by Jewish men on every regular weekday, that is, Sunday to Friday, when no special biblical Jewish holiday occurs. They can be put on at any time during the day. However, it is ideal to wear them during morning prayers, when our minds are free and clear and our thoughts are pure.

Please note that there are many different traditions as to how to put on the *tefillin* and even how to make some parts of the *tefillin*, such as the knots at the back of the head *tefillin*.

We have used the classic *nusach sefard* version used primarily by Jews from Chassidic backgrounds in countries such as Poland, Russia, Hungary, and Czechoslovakia. There are slightly different versions for Jews with the traditions of Chabad, Germany, Lithuania, and the Sephardic countries of North Africa and the Middle East. It is best to follow the tradition of your family or your rabbi.

Place on Your Arm:

You have two black leather boxes with straps in your *tefillin* bag. One is for the arm, the other for the head. Take out the arm one first — that's the one comprising one smooth box, rather than four compartments. Remove the *tefillin* from the plastic case. The arm *tefillin* goes on the weaker arm — the left arm for right-handed people, the right arm for lefties. Roll up your sleeve so that the *tefillin* is in direct

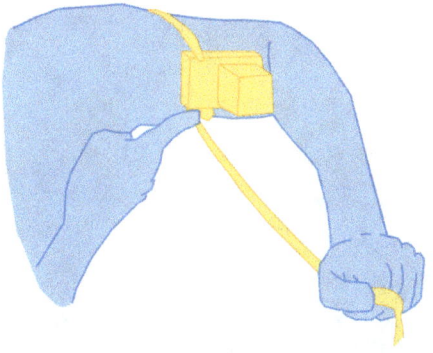

contact with your skin. Put your arm through the loop formed by the knotted strap. Place the black box on your biceps, just below the halfway point between the shoulder and the elbow, right across from your heart.

> **Kavanah:** *All of my actions, represented by the arm, and all of my desires, represented by the heart, should be for goodness.*

You, Adonoy our G-d, Source of all blessings, Master of the World, made us holy by giving us the mitzvot and commanding us to put on *tefillin*.

Baruch atah Adonoy Elo-heinu Melech ha-olam asher ki-d'shanu b'mits-votav v'tsi-vanu l'ha-ni-ach t'fi-lin.

בָּרוּךְ אַתָּה יי אֱלֹהֵינוּ מֶלֶךְ הָעוֹלָם אֲשֶׁר קִדְּשָׁנוּ בְּמִצְוֹתָיו וְצִוָּנוּ לְהָנִיחַ תְּפִלִּין.

Bind the Arm *Tefillin*:

Tighten the strap around your arm, mindful that the knot stays in direct contact with the box. Continue to wrap: two more times over the strap-socket of the black box and around the biceps, then seven times around your arm, and once around your palm. Leave the remainder of the strap loose.

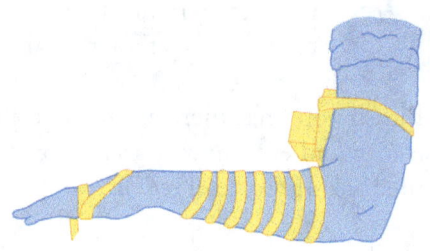

Place the Head *Tefillin*:

Next, take out the head *tefillin*. Remove the *tefillin* from the plastic case. The box goes on your head, just above your forehead. Center it in the middle of your head directly above the point that's right between your eyes. The knot at the back should rest on the base of your skull.

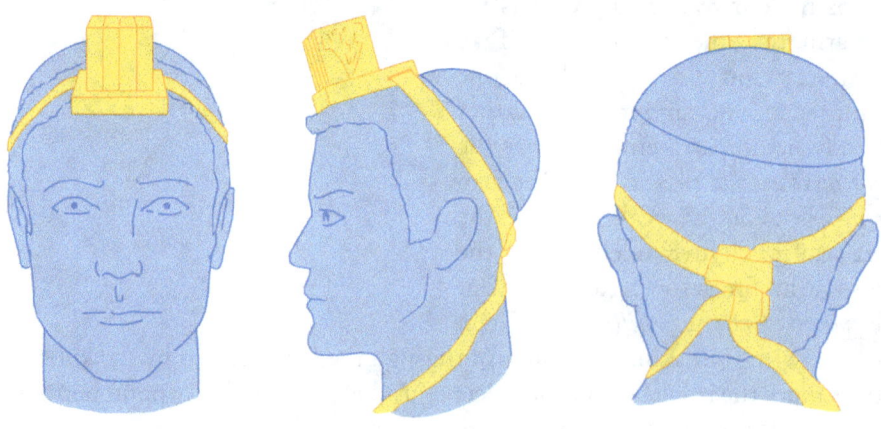

> **Kavanah:** *My thoughts and the power of my soul should only be utilized for goodness.*

Tighten the head *tefillin* and recite:
You, Adonoy our G-d, Source of all blessings, Master of the World, made us holy by giving us the mitzvot and commanding us regarding the mitzvah of *tefillin*.

May Hashem be acknowledged as the Source of blessing always.

Baruch atah Adonoy Elo-heinu Melech ha-olam asher ki-d'shanu b'mits-votav v'tsi-vanu al mits-vat t'fi-lin.
Baruch sheim k'vod mal-chu-to l'olam va-ed.

בָּרוּךְ אַתָּה יי אֱלֹהֵינוּ מֶלֶךְ הָעוֹלָם אֲשֶׁר קִדְּשָׁנוּ בְּמִצְוֹתָיו וְצִוָּנוּ עַל מִצְוַת תְּפִלִּין.
בָּרוּךְ שֵׁם כְּבוֹד מַלְכוּתוֹ לְעוֹלָם וָעֶד.

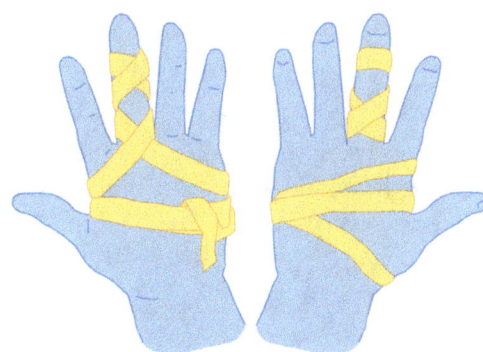

Tie on Hand:
Now back to your hand. Wrap the remainder of the strap three times around your middle finger, like this: once around the base, then once just above the first joint, then one more time around the base. You've got some strap left over, so wrap it around your palm and tuck in the tail end.

Wrap the *tefillin* around your left hand (right hand for a lefty) and say the following:

(Hashem says:) I will betroth you to Me forever and I will betroth you to Me with righteousness, justice, kindness, and mercy. And I will betroth you to Me with trust and you will know Hashem.

V'ei-ras-tich li l'olam
v'ei-ras-tich li b'tsedek
u-v'mish-pat u-v'chesed
u-v'ra-cha-mim.
V'ei-ras-tich li be-emu-nah v'ya-da-at et Adonoy.

וְאֵרַשְׂתִּיךְ לִי לְעוֹלָם
וְאֵרַשְׂתִּיךְ לִי בְּצֶדֶק
וּבְמִשְׁפָּט וּבְחֶסֶד וּבְרַחֲמִים.
וְאֵרַשְׂתִּיךְ לִי בֶּאֱמוּנָה
וְיָדַעַתְּ אֶת יי.

If you do not have time to recite all or part of the Morning Prayers, then, at the minimum, while wearing *tefillin*, say the *Shema*, found on pages 100 to 104.

 The main thing to remember when praying (and perhaps in all of life as well) is to *think* before you *speak*. Read the *kavanah* before saying each prayer and then take a moment to contemplate and integrate the idea of that particular prayer.

The Five Steps of the Morning Prayers:

As we explained earlier (see page 72), the morning prayers consist of a five-step program for awareness, self-growth, and building our relationship with Hashem. Let's take the first step . . .

Step 1: Morning Moments of Awareness (Who am I?)

The key concept behind Step 1 is to become aware so that we make the right decisions. By knowing who we are, what we have, and why we are here, we are bound to make the right decisions today and every day.

Modeh Ani: Thanking Hashem for another day of life.

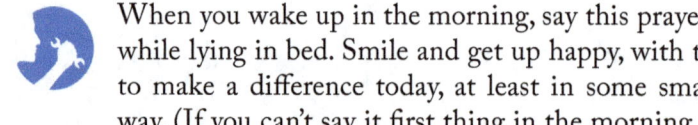 When you wake up in the morning, say this prayer right away, even while lying in bed. Smile and get up happy, with the determination to make a difference today, at least in some small but significant way. (If you can't say it first thing in the morning, then say it at the beginning of the morning prayers).

> **Kavanah:** *I am about to thank Hashem for giving me another day of life to fill with meaning and purpose.*

Thank you, Hashem, Master of the World, for giving me the gift of life today by returning my soul to me. Great is Your faith in *me*.

Modeh ani l'fa-necha, Melech chai v'ka-yam, shehe-che-zarta bi nish-mati b'chem-la; rabah emuna-techa.

מוֹדֶה אֲנִי לְפָנֶיךָ, מֶלֶךְ חַי וְקַיָּם, שֶׁהֶחֱזַרְתָּ בִּי נִשְׁמָתִי בְּחֶמְלָה – רַבָּה אֱמוּנָתֶךָ.

Reisheet Chochmah: Recognizing Hashem

> **Kavanah:** *I will try to "see" Hashem as I go on with my day. Hashem is the ultimate cause of everything that happens to me. He only does what is best for me. It's all good.*

The beginning of all wisdom is to see Hashem and to be in awe of Him. Performing the mitzvot gives one great understanding. May we, and our descendents, understand that Hashem is the Source of all blessings.

Rei-sheet choch-mah yir-at Adonoy sei-chel tov l'chol o-sei-hem, t'hila-to o-medet la-ad. Baruch sheim k'vod mal-chu-to l'olam va-ed.

רֵאשִׁית חָכְמָה יִרְאַת יי שֵׂכֶל טוֹב לְכָל עֹשֵׂיהֶם, תְּהִלָּתוֹ עֹמֶדֶת לָעַד. בָּרוּךְ שֵׁם כְּבוֹד מַלְכוּתוֹ לְעוֹלָם וָעֶד.

Al Netilat Yadayim: Blessing for the Daily Special Handwashing
(see page 73 for instructions on how to do this ritual)

 This is the blessing for the daily ritual handwashing. It can be said right after washing your hands first thing after you wake up or you can say it here as part of the structured morning prayers.

> **Kavanah:** *All things blocking my spirituality should be removed.*

You, Adonoy our G-d, Source of all blessings, Master of the World, made us holy by giving us the mitzvot and commanded us regarding the ritual of washing of our hands in this special way.

Baruch atah Adonoy Elo-heinu Melech ha-olam asher ki-d'shanu b'mits-votav v'tsi-vanu al n'tilat ya-da-yim.

בָּרוּךְ אַתָּה יי אֱלֹהֵינוּ מֶלֶךְ הָעוֹלָם אֲשֶׁר קִדְּשָׁנוּ בְּמִצְוֹתָיו וְצִוָּנוּ עַל נְטִילַת יָדָיִם.

Asher Yatsar: Blessing for Our Bodies

> **Kavanah:** *I thank you, Hashem, that all of the complicated functions of my body work. Without Hashem's life force, I could not survive for even one moment.*

You, Adonoy our G-d, Source of all blessings, Master of the World, created people with wisdom and made our bodies so complex with many cavities and many openings. It is obvious to You that if even one of them were to rupture or become blocked, it would be impossible to survive and stand before You. You, Adonoy, Source of all blessings, Master of the World, heal our bodies and make wondrous creations.

Baruch atah Adonoy Elo-heinu Melech ha-olam asher ya-tsar et ha-adam b'choch-mah, uva-ra vo n'ka-vim n'ka-vim, cha-lu-lim cha-lu-lim. Ga-lu-i v'ya-du-a lif-nei chisei ch'vo-decha, she-im yi-pa-tei-ach echad mei-hem, o yi-sa-tem echad mei-hem, i ef-shar l'hit-ka-yeim v'la-amod l'fa-necha. Baruch atah Adonoy ro-fei chol ba-sar u-maf-li la-asot.

בָּרוּךְ אַתָּה יי אֱלֹהֵינוּ מֶלֶךְ הָעוֹלָם אֲשֶׁר יָצַר אֶת הָאָדָם בְּחָכְמָה, וּבָרָא בוֹ נְקָבִים נְקָבִים, חֲלוּלִים חֲלוּלִים. גָּלוּי וְיָדוּעַ לִפְנֵי כִסֵּא כְבוֹדֶךָ, שֶׁאִם יִפָּתֵחַ אֶחָד מֵהֶם, אוֹ יִסָּתֵם אֶחָד מֵהֶם, אִי אֶפְשָׁר לְהִתְקַיֵּם וְלַעֲמוֹד לְפָנֶיךָ. בָּרוּךְ אַתָּה יי רוֹפֵא כָל בָּשָׂר וּמַפְלִיא לַעֲשׂוֹת.

Blessings For The Torah: Hashem's Instructions to Humanity

First Torah Blessing: For Giving Us the Torah

> **Kavanah:** *I thank you, Hashem, for giving us the Torah, which contains all of the instructions and directions for us to have a meaningful and purposeful life. It is life's most precious gift. May we always be blessed to discover the beauty and sweetness in its words and instructions.*

You, Adonoy our G-d, Source of all blessings, Master of the World, made us holy by giving us the mitzvot, and commanded us to study the Torah. May You make its words sweet for us and for all of the Jewish People. May we and our children and all Jewish children become close to You and study Torah in order to know and understand it. You, Adonoy our G-d, Source of all blessings, Master of the World, teach Torah to His nation Israel.

Baruch atah Adonoy Elo-heinu Melech ha-olam asher ki-d'shanu b'mits-votav v'tsi-vanu la-asok b'di-vrei Torah. V'ha-arev na Adonoy Elo-heinu et di-vrei Tora-t'cha b'finu u-v'fi am-cha beit Yisrael. V'ni-h'yeh anach-nu v'tse-etsa-einu v'tse-etsa-ei am-cha beit Yisrael. Ku-lanu yod-ei sh'mecha v'lom-dei Tora-techa lish-mah. Baruch atah Adonoy ha-m'la-meid Torah l'amo Yisrael.

בָּרוּךְ אַתָּה יי אֱלֹהֵינוּ מֶלֶךְ הָעוֹלָם אֲשֶׁר קִדְּשָׁנוּ בְּמִצְוֹתָיו וְצִוָּנוּ לַעֲסוֹק בְּדִבְרֵי תוֹרָה. וְהַעֲרֶב נָא יי אֱלֹהֵינוּ אֶת דִּבְרֵי תוֹרָתְךָ בְּפִינוּ וּבְפִי עַמְּךָ בֵּית יִשְׂרָאֵל. וְנִהְיֶה אֲנַחְנוּ וְצֶאֱצָאֵינוּ וְצֶאֱצָאֵי עַמְּךָ בֵּית יִשְׂרָאֵל. כֻּלָּנוּ יוֹדְעֵי שְׁמֶךָ וְלוֹמְדֵי תוֹרָתֶךָ לִשְׁמָהּ. בָּרוּךְ אַתָּה יי הַמְלַמֵּד תּוֹרָה לְעַמּוֹ יִשְׂרָאֵל.

Second Torah Blessing: For Choosing the Jewish People

Kavanah: *It is a privilege to be part of the Jewish People — the Chosen People, the Light to the Nations, the conduit of Torah to the people of the world.*

You, Adonoy our G-d, Source of all blessings, Master of the World, chose us from all other nations and gave us His Torah. You, Adonoy, are the Giver of the Torah.

Baruch atah Adonoy Elo-heinu Melech ha-olam asher ba-char banu mi-kol ha-amim v'na-tan lanu et Tora-to. Baruch atah Adonoy no-tein ha-Torah.

בָּרוּךְ אַתָּה יי אֱלֹהֵינוּ מֶלֶךְ הָעוֹלָם אֲשֶׁר בָּחַר בָּנוּ מִכָּל הָעַמִּים וְנָתַן לָנוּ אֶת תּוֹרָתוֹ. בָּרוּךְ אַתָּה יי נוֹתֵן הַתּוֹרָה.

A Few Moments of Daily Torah Study

From the Torah (*Bamidbar* (Numbers), chapter 6, verses 25-27)
May Adonoy bless you and watch over you.
May Adonoy enlighten you and show you favor.
May Adonoy turn towards you and grant you peace and fulfillment.

Y'va-re-ch'cha Adonoy v'yish-m'recha.
Ya-eir Adonoy pa-nav ei-lecha vichu-neka.
Yisa Adonoy pa-nav ei-lecha v'ya-seim l'cha shalom.

יְבָרֶכְךָ יי וְיִשְׁמְרֶךָ.
יָאֵר יי פָּנָיו אֵלֶיךָ וִיחֻנֶּךָּ.
יִשָּׂא יי פָּנָיו אֵלֶיךָ וְיָשֵׂם לְךָ שָׁלוֹם.

(NOTE: If you have difficulty reading Hebrew, it is preferable to read this section in English rather than in transliteration, and so no transliteration has been provided.)

(From the Jerusalem Talmud (part of the Oral Torah tradition))
These are the halachic obligations for which there is no set measure:
Leaving a corner of the field for the poor to harvest, the annual first fruit offering that was brought to Jerusalem in the Temple times, how much time one spent in the Temple during the thrice yearly pilgrimages, acts of kindness and Torah study.

These are the obligations for which a person benefits in this world but the ultimate reward is reserved for the World to Come:

Honoring one's father and mother, acts of kindness, attending at the place of Torah study in the morning and evening, providing hospitality to guests, visiting the sick, providing for a bride, escorting the deceased, praying intensely, bringing peace between one person and another and between husband and wife and know that Torah study is equivalent to all of these.

אֵלּוּ דְבָרִים שֶׁאֵין לָהֶם שִׁיעוּר:
הַפֵּאָה וְהַבִּכּוּרִים וְהָרֵאָיוֹן וּגְמִילוּת חֲסָדִים וְתַלְמוּד תּוֹרָה.
אֵלּוּ דְבָרִים שֶׁאָדָם אוֹכֵל פֵּרוֹתֵיהֶם בָּעוֹלָם הַזֶּה וְהַקֶּרֶן קַיֶּמֶת לוֹ לָעוֹלָם הַבָּא.

וְאֵלוּ הֵן: כִּבּוּד אָב וָאֵם, וּגְמִילוּת חֲסָדִים, וְהַשְׁכָּמַת בֵּית הַמִּדְרָשׁ שַׁחֲרִית וְעַרְבִית, וְהַכְנָסַת אוֹרְחִים, וּבִקּוּר חוֹלִים, וְהַכְנָסַת כַּלָּה, וּלְוָיַת הַמֵּת, וְעִיּוּן תְּפִלָּה, וַהֲבָאַת שָׁלוֹם בֵּין אָדָם לַחֲבֵרוֹ וּבֵין אִישׁ לְאִשְׁתּוֹ – וְתַלְמוּד תּוֹרָה כְּנֶגֶד כֻּלָּם.

Elohai N'shamah: Blessing for the Soul

> **Kavanah:** *Thank you, Hashem, for giving me my soul for another day.*
> *It is the source of my goodness.*
> *My unique Jewish soul makes me part of the Jewish People,*
> *which has been chosen from all other people for a special G-dly mission.*

My G-d, the soul you have given me is pure. You created it, formed it, and blew it into me and You safeguard it within me. Eventually You will take it from me and return it to me in the World to Come. As long as my soul is within me, I thank You, Adonoy, my G-d, the G-d of my parents, and the Master of all Creation. You, Adonoy our G-d, Source of all blessings, return souls to non-living bodies.

Elo-hai, n'sha-mah shena-tata bi t'ho-rah hi. Atah v'ra-tah, atah y'tsar-tah, atah n'fach-tah bi, v'atah m'shamrah b'kirbi, v'atah a-tid lit-lah mi-meni, u-l'ha-cha-zirah bi le-atid la-vo. Kol z'man sheha-n'sha-mah b'kir-bi, modeh ani l'fa-necha Adonoy Elo-hai vei-lohei avo-tai, Ri-bon kol ha-ma-asim, Adon kol ha-n'sha-mot. Baruch atah Adonoy ha-ma-cha-zir n'sha-mot lif-ga-rim mei-tim.

אֱלֹהַי, נְשָׁמָה שֶׁנָּתַתָּ בִּי טְהוֹרָה הִיא. אַתָּה בְרָאתָהּ, אַתָּה יְצַרְתָּהּ, אַתָּה נְפַחְתָּהּ בִּי, וְאַתָּה מְשַׁמְּרָהּ בְּקִרְבִּי, וְאַתָּה עָתִיד לִטְּלָהּ מִמֶּנִּי, וּלְהַחֲזִירָהּ בִּי לֶעָתִיד לָבֹא. כָּל זְמַן שֶׁהַנְּשָׁמָה בְקִרְבִּי, מוֹדֶה אֲנִי לְפָנֶיךָ יְיָ אֱלֹהַי וֵאלֹהֵי אֲבוֹתַי, רִבּוֹן כָּל הַמַּעֲשִׂים, אֲדוֹן כָּל הַנְּשָׁמוֹת. בָּרוּךְ אַתָּה יְיָ הַמַּחֲזִיר נְשָׁמוֹת לִפְגָרִים מֵתִים.

Blessings of Differentiation

Life can be confusing. Yet we have the responsibility to make choices. The key is the ability to differentiate — between good and evil, right and wrong, when to speak and to remain silent. Often the world appears very confused and unable to differentiate and therefore make the right choices. Each morning we remind ourselves of who we are and what our individual and national roles are.

Natan Lasechvi: Blessing for Intellect

> *Kavanah: Hashem has given me the power of intellect. I can use it wisely to discern the difference between right and wrong.*

You, Adonoy our G-d, Source of all blessings, Master of the World, gave me the understanding to discern between day and night.

Baruch atah Adonoy Elo-heinu Melech ha-olam asher natan la-sech-vi vi-nah l'hav-chin bein yom u-vein lai-lah.

בָּרוּךְ אַתָּה יי אֱלֹהֵינוּ מֶלֶךְ הָעוֹלָם אֲשֶׁר נָתַן לַשֶּׂכְוִי בִינָה לְהַבְחִין בֵּין יוֹם וּבֵין לָיְלָה.

Lo Asani Goy: Blessing for Being Jewish

> *Kavanah: I am privileged to be part of the Jewish People. I am a link in the chain of the Chosen People going back almost 4,000 years to Abraham and Sarah, the first Jews.*

You, Adonoy our G-d, Source of all blessings, Master of the World, have not made me a Gentile (with the responsibility of fulfilling only the seven Noahide mitzvot), but instead have given me the responsibility to fulfill all of the mitzvot that a Jew is required to fulfill.

Baruch atah Adonoy Elo-heinu Melech ha-olam shelo a-sa-ni goy.

בָּרוּךְ אַתָּה יי אֱלֹהֵינוּ מֶלֶךְ הָעוֹלָם שֶׁלֹּא עָשַׂנִי גּוֹי.

Lo Asani Aved: Blessing of Freedom

> **Kavanah:** *I am free, in body (i.e., from slavery and bondage) and in thinking (i.e., from the world's ideologies that go counter to my Jewish beliefs).*

You, Adonoy our G-d, Source of all blessings, Master of the World, have not made me a servant (with the limited responsibility of fulfilling the mitzvot that a converted servant in a Jewish home must fulfill). Instead You have given me the responsibility of fulfilling all of the mitzvot that a Jew is required to fulfill.

Baruch atah Adonoy Elo-heinu Melech ha-olam shelo a-sa-ni a-ved.

בָּרוּךְ אַתָּה יי אֱלֹהֵינוּ מֶלֶךְ הָעוֹלָם שֶׁלֹא עָשַׂנִי עָבֶד.

Lo Asani Ishah: The Gender Blessing for Men

> **Kavanah:** *I have been given the responsibilities of a Jewish man. I will try my best to fulfill them today.*

You, Adonoy our G-d, Source of all blessings, Master of the World, have not made me a Jewish woman (with women's awesome overriding responsibility of ensuring the future of the Jewish people and their unique mitzvot). Instead You have given me the responsibility of fulfilling an additional quantity of mitzvot each day.

Baruch atah Adonoy Elo-heinu Melech ha-olam shelo a-sa-ni ishah.

בָּרוּךְ אַתָּה יי אֱלֹהֵינוּ מֶלֶךְ הָעוֹלָם שֶׁלֹא עָשַׂנִי אִשָּׁה.

She'asani Kirtsono: The Gender Blessing for Women

> **Kavanah:** *I have been given the responsibilities of a Jewish woman. I will try my best to fulfill them today.*

You, Adonoy our G-d, Source of all blessings, Master of the World, have made me to fulfill His Purpose in creating the world (which is, above all, to ensure that the Jewish People serve as G-d's messengers and teachers in this world).

Baruch atah Adonoy Elo-heinu Melech ha-olam she-a-sa-ni kir-tso-no.

בָּרוּךְ אַתָּה יי אֱלֹהֵינוּ מֶלֶךְ הָעוֹלָם שֶׁעֲשַׂנִי כִּרְצוֹנוֹ.

Blessings for My Gifts and Capabilities

Now we focus on the gifts that Hashem has given us today. We should be grateful for these and resolve to use them for good.

Pokei'ach Ivrim: Blessing for Sight and Insight

> **Kavanah:** *I have been given the great gifts of physical sight and of insight, to "see" truth and not be blinded by those things that cause spiritual blindness.*

You, Adonoy our G-d, Source of all blessings, Master of the World, give sight to the blind.

Baruch atah Adonoy Elo-heinu Melech ha-olam po-kei-ach iv-rim.

בָּרוּךְ אַתָּה יי אֱלֹהֵינוּ מֶלֶךְ הָעוֹלָם פּוֹקֵחַ עִוְרִים.

Malbish Arumim: Blessing for Clothing

> **Kavanah:** *I have been given the gift of clothing to protect and decorate my body, and I have been given the mitzvot to clothe and decorate my soul.*

You, Adonoy our G-d, Source of all blessings, Master of the World, provide clothes for the naked.

Baruch atah Adonoy Elo-heinu Melech ha-olam mal-bish a-ru-mim.

בָּרוּךְ אַתָּה יי אֱלֹהֵינוּ מֶלֶךְ הָעוֹלָם מַלְבִּישׁ עֲרֻמִּים.

Matir Asurim: Blessing for Movement

> **Kavanah:** *I am blessed with the gift of physical movement. I have been given the ability to break away from those desires, thoughts, and habits that would hold me back from achieving greater spiritual potential.*

You, Adonoy our G-d, Source of all blessings, Master of the World, free those who are held back.

Baruch atah Adonoy Elo-heinu Melech ha-olam ma-tir a-su-rim.

בָּרוּךְ אַתָּה יי אֱלֹהֵינוּ מֶלֶךְ הָעוֹלָם מַתִּיר אֲסוּרִים.

Zokeif K'fufim: Blessing for Standing Up

> **Kavanah:** *I am blessed with the ability to stand and walk upright. Furthermore, Hashem raises those who are immobilized by life's challenges and burdens.*

You, Adonoy our G-d, Source of all blessings, Master of the World, raise those who are bent over.

Baruch atah Adonoy Elo-heinu Melech ha-olam zo-keif k'fu-fim.   בָּרוּךְ אַתָּה יי אֱלֹהֵינוּ מֶלֶךְ הָעוֹלָם זוֹקֵף כְּפוּפִים.

Blessings for Trust in G-d

It is in the nature of a Jew to trust in Hashem. This is perhaps the greatest challenge of our generation when we have so much material and financial wealth. Hashem has been there to support us individually and nationally up to now and He will be there for us today and in the future.

Roka Ha'arets: Blessing for Nature

> **Kavanah:** *Hashem has created an awesome, majestic world filled with the wonders of nature — mountains, flowers, butterflies, oceans, and stars. Hashem's artistry is endless. I am blessed to live in such a beautiful world. And if He creates and runs the whole world with such precision and order, He guides my life in the same way as well.*

You, Adonoy our G-d, Source of all blessings, Master of the World, spread out the earth upon the waters.

Baruch atah Adonoy Elo-heinu Melech ha-olam ro-ka ha-arets al ha-ma-yim.   בָּרוּךְ אַתָּה יי אֱלֹהֵינוּ מֶלֶךְ הָעוֹלָם רוֹקַע הָאָרֶץ עַל הַמָּיִם.

Ha'meichin: Blessing for Hashem's Guidance

> **Kavanah:** *All of our challenges, as well as our opportunities to spread goodness, are determined by Hashem. Everything that occurs during the day is determined by Hashem's guidance — whom we meet, what we see, where we go. What we do with these opportunities is up to us.*

You, Adonoy our G-d, Source of all blessings, Master of the World, prepare a person's footsteps.

Baruch atah Adonoy Elo-heinu Melech ha-olam ha-mei-chin mits-adei ga-ver. בָּרוּךְ אַתָּה יי אֱלֹהֵינוּ מֶלֶךְ הָעוֹלָם הַמֵּכִין מִצְעֲדֵי גָבֶר.

She'asah Li: Blessing for All that Hashem Provides Me

> **Kavanah:** *It is Hashem who provides me with all that I need. Hashem has provided me with everything up to this point in my life, and He will certainly provide me with everything I need today.*

You, Adonoy our G-d, Source of all blessings, Master of the World, provide me with *everything* I need.

Baruch atah Adonoy Elo-heinu Melech ha-olam she-asah li kol tsar-ki. בָּרוּךְ אַתָּה יי אֱלֹהֵינוּ מֶלֶךְ הָעוֹלָם שֶׁעָשָׂה לִי כָּל צָרְכִּי.

Blessings for Strength and Renewal

No matter who we are and what our circumstances might be, life is challenging. Perhaps that is the definition of "life." We remind ourselves that just as Hashem sends us challenges, it is He who gives us the ability to withstand those challenges and to use them for tools of growth and development.

Ozeir Yisrael: Blessing for Inner Strength

> **Kavanah:** *Hashem gives me the strength, fortitude, and determination to stand up proudly and firmly as a Jew, as one of G-d's people, even if this means going against the conventional wisdom or practices of the times or in my particular surroundings.*

You, Adonoy our G-d, Source of all blessings, Master of the World, surround the people of Israel with strength.

Baruch atah Adonoy Elo-heinu Melech ha-olam o-zeir Yisrael bi-g'vu-rah. בָּרוּךְ אַתָּה יי אֱלֹהֵינוּ מֶלֶךְ הָעוֹלָם אוֹזֵר יִשְׂרָאֵל בִּגְבוּרָה.

Oteir Yisrael: Blessing for Inner Beauty

> **Kavanah:** *Being a Jew means experiencing the beauty and meaning of authentic, real Judaism. Hashem, give me the opportunity to experience this today and every day.*

You, Adonoy our G-d, Source of all blessings, Master of the World, crown the people of Israel with inner beauty.

Baruch atah Adonoy Elo-heinu Melech ha-olam o-teir Yisrael b'tif-arah.

בָּרוּךְ אַתָּה יי אֱלֹהֵינוּ מֶלֶךְ הָעוֹלָם עוֹטֵר יִשְׂרָאֵל בְּתִפְאָרָה.

Hanotein Laya'eif Ko'ach: Blessing for Strength

> **Kavanah:** *After my being so tired last night, Hashem has given me renewed strength, hope, determination, and confidence to fulfill my individual purpose.*

You, Adonoy our G-d, Source of all blessings, Master of the World, give renewed strength to the weary.

Baruch atah Adonoy Elo-heinu Melech ha-olam ha-no-tein la-ya-eif ko-ach.

בָּרוּךְ אַתָּה יי אֱלֹהֵינוּ מֶלֶךְ הָעוֹלָם הַנּוֹתֵן לַיָּעֵף כֹּחַ.

Hama'avir Sheinah: Blessing for Renewal

> **Kavanah:** *Hashem has given me renewed awareness, clarity, and inner strength to make the right choices today.*

You, Adonoy our G-d, Source of all blessings, Master of the World, remove sleep from my eyes and drowsiness from my eyelids.

Baruch atah Adonoy Elo-heinu Melech ha-olam ha-ma-avir shei-nah mei-einai u-t'nu-mah mei-af-apai.

בָּרוּךְ אַתָּה יי אֱלֹהֵינוּ מֶלֶךְ הָעוֹלָם הַמַּעֲבִיר שֵׁנָה מֵעֵינַי וּתְנוּמָה מֵעַפְעַפָּי.

Vihi Ratson: Prayer for Positive Influences

> **Kavanah:** *I will make a positive difference in the world today. Whomever and whatever I come in contact with today should have a positive influence upon me and I ask Hashem to help me to overcome all negative influences.*

Adonoy, our G-d and the G-d of our ancestors: Please help us to become accustomed to regular Torah study and to feel attached to Your mitzvot. Help us to stay away from the power of error and of wrongdoing, from difficult tests in life, from shame, from the power of the "Evil Inclination" (i.e., jealousy, lust for money, honor, and the like), from evil people, and from false friends. Instead help us to be connected to the "Good Inclination" and good deeds and help us to channel all of our desires to serve Your wishes. Share with us today and every day Your kindness and compassion, as well as compassion from all those with whom we will come in contact. Let them be kind to us. You, Adonoy our G-d, Source of all blessings, Master of the World, act kindly to His nation, Israel.

Vi-hi ra-tson mil-fa-necha Adonoy Elo-heinu veilo-hei avo-teinu, shetar-gi-leinu b'Tora-techa v'dab-keinu b'mits-vo-techa, v'al t'vi-einu lo li-dei cheit, v'lo li-dei avei-rah va-a-von, v'lo li-dei nisa-yon, v'lo li-dei viza-yon, v'al tash-leit ba-nu yetser ha-ra. V'har-chi-keinu mei-adam ra u-mei-cha-veir ra. V'dab-keinu b'yei-tser ha-tov u-v'ma-asim tovim, v'chof et yits-reinu l'hish-ta-bed lach. U-t'nei-nu ha-yom u-v'chol yom l'chein u-l'che-sed u-l'ra-cha-mim b'ei-necha u-v'ei-nei chol ro-einu, v'tig-m'lei-nu cha-sa-dim to-vim.

Baruch atah Adonoy ha-go-mel cha-sa-dim to-vim l'amo Yisrael.

וִיהִי רָצוֹן מִלְּפָנֶיךָ יי אֱלֹהֵינוּ וֵאלֹהֵי אֲבוֹתֵינוּ, שֶׁתַּרְגִּילֵנוּ בְּתוֹרָתֶךָ וְדַבְּקֵנוּ בְּמִצְוֹתֶיךָ, וְאַל תְּבִיאֵנוּ לֹא לִידֵי חֵטְא, וְלֹא לִידֵי עֲבֵרָה וְעָוֹן, וְלֹא לִידֵי נִסָּיוֹן, וְלֹא לִידֵי בִזָּיוֹן, וְאַל תַּשְׁלֶט בָּנוּ יֵצֶר הָרָע. וְהַרְחִיקֵנוּ מֵאָדָם רָע וּמֵחָבֵר רָע. וְדַבְּקֵנוּ בְּיֵצֶר הַטּוֹב וּבְמַעֲשִׂים טוֹבִים, וְכוֹף אֶת יִצְרֵנוּ לְהִשְׁתַּעְבֶּד לָךְ. וּתְנֵנוּ הַיּוֹם וּבְכָל יוֹם לְחֵן וּלְחֶסֶד וּלְרַחֲמִים בְּעֵינֶיךָ וּבְעֵינֵי כָל רוֹאֵינוּ, וְתִגְמְלֵנוּ חֲסָדִים טוֹבִים.

בָּרוּךְ אַתָּה יי הַגּוֹמֵל חֲסָדִים טוֹבִים לְעַמּוֹ יִשְׂרָאֵל.

Hareini M'kabel: The Mitzvah to Love Other Jews

> **Kavanah:** *All Jewish people are part of one family — our family, my family. I will try to show them concern, compassion, and empathy today. In return, may Hashem treat me with similar compassion and kindness.*

[NOTE: The custom to recite this blessing at this point in the daily prayer is prevalent among some Chassidic groups. As it is not a custom among all groups, it does not appear in every siddur.]

I accept upon myself the obligation to perform the mitzvah of loving my fellow Jews.

Ha-rei-ni m'ka-bel alai mits-vat asei shel v'a-hav-ta l'rei-acha ka-mo-cha. הֲרֵינִי מְקַבֵּל עָלַי מִצְוַת עֲשֵׂה שֶׁל וְאָהַבְתָּ לְרֵעֲךָ כָּמוֹךָ.

On each weekday, at this point, put some money, even one coin, into a charity box. In the merit of you assisting others, you can ask Hashem to act charitably towards you. After all, you are doing what Hashem put you on this Earth to do — mitzvot and good deeds! (For Shabbat, put the money aside for charity before Shabbat.)

L'olam: Prayer for Jewish Pride

> **Kavanah:** *In a world that is often filled with non-Jewish and even anti-Jewish ideas and ideals, I am proud to be part of the Jewish People who are loyal to Hashem, just as our ancestors have been for almost 4,000 years.*

One should always be G-d fearing, whether in private or in the company of others. One should acknowledge the truth and be reminded of this always. When we arise, we should say: Master of the World, it is not because of our great righteousness that we ask You to fulfill all of our needs, but because of *your* compassion. For indeed, what are we, what is our life, our strength, our bravery, our great acts of kindness? What can we say to You, our G-d, the G-d of our ancestors? We are not heroes or famous or wise or understanding compared to You. Most of our actions and much of our days are filled with emptiness — except for my pure soul, which will eventually stand before You to judge my life's actions.

While the other nations are insignificant before You, *we* are your People, the People of the Covenant, the children of the forefathers: Avraham, to whom you gave an everlasting oath, Yitzchak, who was prepared to give his life in loyalty to you, and Yaakov, whom you named Yisrael (meaning "those who overcome challenges") and Yeshurun (meaning "dedication to what is right") because of your love for him. Therefore, we are obliged to thank You. How fortunate are we! How wonderful, how pleasant, how beautiful is our Jewish heritage!

L'olam y'hei adam y'rei sha-mayim b'sei-ter uva-galu-i, u-modeh al ha-emet, v'do-veir emet bil-va-vo, v'yash-keim v'yo-mar: Ri-bon kol ha-ola-mim, lo al tsid-ko-teinu a-nach-nu ma-pilim tacha-nu-neinu l'fa-nechah, ki al ra-cha-mecha ha-ra-bim.

Mah a-nach-nu, meh cha-yeinu, meh chas-deinu, mah tsid-ko-teinu, mah y'shu-a-teinu, mah ko-cheinu, mah g'vura-teinu.

Mah no-mar l'fa-necha, Adonoy Elo-heinu vei-lo-hei avo-teinu, ha-lo kol ha-gi-bo-rim k'a-yin l'fa-necha, v'an-shei ha-sheim k'lo ha-yu, va-cha-chamim ki-v'li mada, u-n'vonim ki-v'li has-keil.

Ki rov ma-asei-hem to-hu, vi-mei cha-yei-hem hevel l'fa-necha, u-mo-tar ha-adam min ha-b'hei-mah a-yin, ki ha-kol ha-vel.

L'vad ha-n'sha-mah ha-t'horah she-hi ati-dah li-tein din v'chesh-bon lif-nei chi-sei ch'vo-decha.

V'chol ha-goyim k'ayin neg-decha, she-ne-emar "hein goyim k'mar mid-li u-ch'sha-chak moz-nayim nech-shavu hein i-yim ka-dak yi-tol."

לְעוֹלָם יְהֵא אָדָם יְרֵא שָׁמַיִם בְּסֵתֶר וּבַגָּלוּי, וּמוֹדֶה עַל הָאֱמֶת, וְדוֹבֵר אֱמֶת בִּלְבָבוֹ, וְיַשְׁכֵּם וְיֹאמַר: רִבּוֹן כָּל הָעוֹלָמִים, לֹא עַל צִדְקוֹתֵינוּ אֲנַחְנוּ מַפִּילִים תַּחֲנוּנֵינוּ לְפָנֶיךָ, כִּי עַל רַחֲמֶיךָ הָרַבִּים.

מָה אֲנַחְנוּ, מֶה חַיֵּינוּ, מֶה חַסְדֵּנוּ, מַה צִּדְקוֹתֵינוּ, מַה יְּשׁוּעָתֵנוּ, מַה כֹּחֵנוּ, מַה גְּבוּרָתֵנוּ.

מַה נֹּאמַר לְפָנֶיךָ, יְיָ אֱלֹהֵינוּ וֵאלֹהֵי אֲבוֹתֵינוּ, הֲלֹא כָּל הַגִּבּוֹרִים כְּאַיִן לְפָנֶיךָ, וְאַנְשֵׁי הַשֵּׁם כְּלֹא הָיוּ, וַחֲכָמִים כִּבְלִי מַדָּע, וּנְבוֹנִים כִּבְלִי הַשְׂכֵּל.

כִּי רֹב מַעֲשֵׂיהֶם תֹּהוּ, וִימֵי חַיֵּיהֶם הֶבֶל לְפָנֶיךָ, וּמוֹתַר הָאָדָם מִן הַבְּהֵמָה אָיִן, כִּי הַכֹּל הָבֶל.

לְבַד הַנְּשָׁמָה הַטְּהוֹרָה שֶׁהִיא עֲתִידָה לִתֵּן דִּין וְחֶשְׁבּוֹן לִפְנֵי כִסֵּא כְבוֹדֶךָ.

וְכָל הַגּוֹיִם כְּאַיִן נֶגְדֶּךָ, שֶׁנֶּאֱמַר הֵן גּוֹיִם כְּמַר מִדְּלִי וּכְשַׁחַק מֹאזְנַיִם נֶחְשָׁבוּ הֵן אִיִּים כַּדַּק יִטּוֹל.

Step 2: Contemplating Hashem's Impact on the World (Who is G-d?)

Baruch She'amar: Recognizing G-d

> **Kavanah:** *Before I reaffirm my acceptance of Hashem in the* Shema *and before I ask Hashem to give us so many things in the* Shemoneh Esrei, *I focus on whom I am speaking to, namely Hashem, the Source of all creation, who wishes a relationship with the people He created and who has a special relationship with the Jewish People.*

[NOTE: This is a free translation, not a literal one.]

Hashem is the Source of all blessings: He who spoke at the time of creation and the world came into being; He who speaks and acts, who decrees and fulfills, who maintains the world, who has compassion on the earth and upon those who were created, who rewards those who follow and who have awe of Hashem; He who lives forever, who redeems and rescues people from moral and physical danger. I acknowledge that You, Hashem, our G-d, Source of all blessing, is praised and thanked by the Jewish People. We shall thank You with words and song, You who are the One and only source of life. You, Adonoy, whom we praise and thank, are indeed the Source of all blessings.

Baruch she-amar v'ha-ya ha-olam, Baruch Hu. Baruch oseh v'rei-sheet, Baruch o-meir v'oseh, Baruch go-zeir u-m'ka-yeim, Baruch m'ra-cheim al ha-arets, Baruch m'ra-cheim al ha-bri-yot, Baruch m'sha-leim sa-char tov li-rei-av, Baruch chai la-ad v'ka-yam l'ne-tsach, Baruch po-deh u-ma-tsil, Baruch sh'mo. Baruch atah Adonoy Elo-heinu Melech ha-olam, ha-El ha-Av ha-Ra-cha-man ha-m'hu-lal b'feh amo, m'shu-bach u-m'fo-ar bi-l'shon cha-si-dav va-ava-dav, u-v'shi-rei Da-vid av-decha. N'ha-le-l'cha Adonoy Elo-heinu bish'va-chot u-vi-z'mi-rot. N'ga-del-cha u-n'sha-beicha-cha u-n'fa-ercha v'naz-kir shim-cha v'nam-li-ch'cha, Mal-keinu Elo-heinu. Ya-chid, chei ha-ola-mim, Melech m'shu-bach u-m'fo-ar a-dei ad sh'mo ha-gadol.

Baruch atah Adonoy Melech m'hu-lal ba-tish-ba-chot.

בָּרוּךְ שֶׁאָמַר וְהָיָה הָעוֹלָם, בָּרוּךְ הוּא. בָּרוּךְ עוֹשֶׂה בְרֵאשִׁית, בָּרוּךְ אוֹמֵר וְעוֹשֶׂה, בָּרוּךְ גּוֹזֵר וּמְקַיֵּם, בָּרוּךְ מְרַחֵם עַל הָאָרֶץ, בָּרוּךְ מְרַחֵם עַל הַבְּרִיּוֹת, בָּרוּךְ מְשַׁלֵּם שָׂכָר טוֹב לִירֵאָיו, בָּרוּךְ חַי לָעַד וְקַיָּם לָנֶצַח, בָּרוּךְ פּוֹדֶה וּמַצִּיל, בָּרוּךְ שְׁמוֹ. בָּרוּךְ אַתָּה יְיָ אֱלֹהֵינוּ מֶלֶךְ הָעוֹלָם, הָאֵל הָאָב הָרַחֲמָן הַמְהֻלָּל בְּפֶה עַמּוֹ, מְשֻׁבָּח וּמְפֹאָר בִּלְשׁוֹן חֲסִידָיו וַעֲבָדָיו, וּבְשִׁירֵי דָוִד עַבְדֶּךָ. נְהַלֶּלְךָ יְיָ אֱלֹהֵינוּ בִּשְׁבָחוֹת וּבִזְמִירוֹת. נְגַדֶּלְךָ וּנְשַׁבֵּחֲךָ וּנְפָאֶרְךָ וְנַזְכִּיר שִׁמְךָ וְנַמְלִיכְךָ, מַלְכֵּנוּ אֱלֹהֵינוּ. יָחִיד, חֵי הָעוֹלָמִים, מֶלֶךְ מְשֻׁבָּח וּמְפֹאָר עֲדֵי עַד שְׁמוֹ הַגָּדוֹל.

בָּרוּךְ אַתָּה יְיָ מֶלֶךְ מְהֻלָּל בַּתִּשְׁבָּחוֹת.

Ashrei: A poem authored by King David — Psalm 145

> **Kavanah:** *Hashem is good to everyone and takes care of us all, even if we don't see or understand the good in a particular situation. We all can have a close relationship with Hashem if we sincerely wish to.*

[NOTE: This is a free translation, not a literal one. There are two themes in this Psalm, as noted below.]

Introductory Theme: Happiness and Thanks

Happy are those who live in spiritual places. It is right for them to thank You.
Happy is the nation who practices this and whose G-d is Hashem.

Theme: The Jewish People and I will always appreciate all that You do for us

A psalm of praise by David.
I will always thank You, Hashem, the Master of the World.
Every day I will acknowledge my appreciation for all of Your blessings.
Hashem's divine deeds are the epitome of greatness and beyond human comprehension.
Each generation will praise Your works and Your acts of strength to their children.
I will tell of Your power and Your wonders.
They will speak about Your awesome power and I will tell of Your great deeds.
They will remember all the good You have done and will join in song to You.
Hashem is compassionate and patient with us. He shows us great kindness.
Hashem is good to everyone and has compassion on all that He creates.
All should thank Hashem and those who are dearest should acknowledge Your blessings.
They will speak of Your mastery of the world and of Your power… so they can tell this to others.
You are the Master of the entire World for all time and for every generation.
Hashem gives support to all who have fallen and to those who are "bent over" due to life's hardships.
The eyes of all look to You in hope and You feed them in the proper time.

Special *Kavanah* is required when reciting this next verse:

You open Your hand and give what is needed to every living thing.
Hashem is right in all His ways and kind in all that He does.
Hashem is close to all who call out to Him sincerely.
Hashem will fulfill the wishes of those who have awe of Hashem and He will hear their call and save them.

Hashem protects all those who have love of Hashem and He will destroy all of the evil people.
I will always thank Hashem and may all of Humanity appreciate Hashem now and forever.

Introduction:

Ash-rei yo-sh'vei vei-techa.	אַשְׁרֵי יוֹשְׁבֵי בֵיתֶךָ,
Od y'ha-l'lu-cha selah.	עוֹד יְהַלְלוּךָ סֶּלָה.
Ash-rei ha-am sheka-cha lo,	אַשְׁרֵי הָעָם שֶׁכָּכָה לּוֹ,
ash-rei ha-am she-Adonoy Elo-hav.	אַשְׁרֵי הָעָם שֶׁיְיָ אֱלֹהָיו.

Psalm 145:

Thi-lah l'Da-vid:	תְּהִלָּה לְדָוִד,
A-ro-mim-cha Elo-hai ha-melech,	אֲרוֹמִמְךָ אֱלוֹהַי הַמֶּלֶךְ,
va-a-var-cha shim-cha l'olam va-ed.	וַאֲבָרְכָה שִׁמְךָ לְעוֹלָם וָעֶד.
B'chol yom a-var-checha,	בְּכָל יוֹם אֲבָרְכֶךָּ,
va-a-ha-l'la shim-cha l'olam va-ed.	וַאֲהַלְלָה שִׁמְךָ לְעוֹלָם וָעֶד.
Ga-dol Adonoy u-m'hu-lal m'od,	גָּדוֹל יְיָ וּמְהֻלָּל מְאֹד,
v'lig-dula-to ein chei-ker.	וְלִגְדֻלָּתוֹ אֵין חֵקֶר.
Dor l'dor y'sha-bach ma-a-secha,	דּוֹר לְדוֹר יְשַׁבַּח מַעֲשֶׂיךָ,
u-g'vu-ro-techa ya-gi-du.	וּגְבוּרֹתֶיךָ יַגִּידוּ.
Ha-dar k'vod ho-decha,	הֲדַר כְּבוֹד הוֹדֶךָ,
v'di-vrei nif-l'o-techa a-sichah.	וְדִבְרֵי נִפְלְאֹתֶיךָ אָשִׂיחָה.
Ve-ezuz nor-o-techa yo-mei-ru,	וֶעֱזוּז נוֹרְאֹתֶיךָ יֹאמֵרוּ,
u-g'dula-t'cha a-sa-p'renah.	וּגְדֻלָּתְךָ אֲסַפְּרֶנָּה.
Zei-cher rav tu-v'cha ya-bi-u,	זֵכֶר רַב טוּבְךָ יַבִּיעוּ,
v'tsid-ka-t'cha y'ra-nei-nu.	וְצִדְקָתְךָ יְרַנֵּנוּ.
Cha-nun v'ra-chum Adonoy,	חַנּוּן וְרַחוּם יְיָ,
erech a-pa-yim u-g'dal cha-sed.	אֶרֶךְ אַפַּיִם וּגְדָל חָסֶד.
Tov Adonoy la-kol,	טוֹב יְיָ לַכֹּל,
v'ra-cha-mav al kol ma-asav.	וְרַחֲמָיו עַל כָּל מַעֲשָׂיו.
Yo-du-cha Adonoy kol ma-a-secha,	יוֹדוּךָ יְיָ כָּל מַעֲשֶׂיךָ,
va-cha-si-decha y'var-chu-chah.	וַחֲסִידֶיךָ יְבָרְכוּכָה.
K'vod mal-chu-t'cha yo-mei-ru,	כְּבוֹד מַלְכוּתְךָ יֹאמֵרוּ,
u-g'vu-ra-t'cha y'da-bei-ru.	וּגְבוּרָתְךָ יְדַבֵּרוּ.
L'ho-di-a liv-nei ha-adam g'vu-ro-tav,	לְהוֹדִיעַ לִבְנֵי הָאָדָם גְּבוּרֹתָיו,
u-ch'vod ha-dar mal-chu-to.	וּכְבוֹד הֲדַר מַלְכוּתוֹ.
Mal-chu-t'cha mal-chut kol ola-mim,	מַלְכוּתְךָ מַלְכוּת כָּל עוֹלָמִים,
u-mem-shal-t'cha b'chol dor va-dor.	וּמֶמְשַׁלְתְּךָ בְּכָל דּוֹר וָדֹר.
So-meich Adonoy l'chol ha-nof-lim,	סוֹמֵךְ יְיָ לְכָל הַנֹּפְלִים,
v'zo-keif l'chol ha-k'fu-fim.	וְזוֹקֵף לְכָל הַכְּפוּפִים.
Ei-nei chol ei-lecha y'sa-bei-ru,	עֵינֵי כֹל אֵלֶיךָ יְשַׂבֵּרוּ,
v'atah no-tein lahem et ach-lam b'i-to.	וְאַתָּה נוֹתֵן לָהֶם אֶת אָכְלָם בְּעִתּוֹ.
Po-tei-ach et ya-decha,	**פּוֹתֵחַ אֶת יָדֶךָ,**

u-mas-bi-a l'chol chai ra-tson.	וּמַשְׂבִּיעַ לְכָל חַי רָצוֹן:
Tsa-dik Adonoy b'chol d'ra-chav,	צַדִּיק יְיָ בְּכָל דְּרָכָיו,
v'cha-sid b'chol ma-asav.	וְחָסִיד בְּכָל מַעֲשָׂיו.
Ka-rov Adonoy l'chol kor-av,	קָרוֹב יְיָ לְכָל קֹרְאָיו,
l'chol asher yikra-u-hu ve-emet.	לְכֹל אֲשֶׁר יִקְרָאֻהוּ בֶאֱמֶת.
R'tson y'rei-av ya-aseh,	רְצוֹן יְרֵאָיו יַעֲשֶׂה,
v'et shav-atam yish-ma v'yo-shi-eim.	וְאֶת שַׁוְעָתָם יִשְׁמַע וְיוֹשִׁיעֵם.
Sho-meir Adonoy et kol o-ha-vav,	שׁוֹמֵר יְיָ אֶת כָּל אֹהֲבָיו,
v'eit kol ha-r'sha-im yash-mid.	וְאֵת כָּל הָרְשָׁעִים יַשְׁמִיד.
T'hi-lat Adonoy y'da-ber pi, vi-va-reich	תְּהִלַּת יְיָ יְדַבֶּר פִּי,
kol ba-sar sheim kod-sho l'olam va-ed.	וִיבָרֵךְ כָּל בָּשָׂר שֵׁם קָדְשׁוֹ לְעוֹלָם וָעֶד.
Va-a-nach-nu n'va-reich Yah,	וַאֲנַחְנוּ נְבָרֵךְ יָהּ,
mei-atah v'ad olam. Ha-l'lu-Yah.	מֵעַתָּה וְעַד עוֹלָם, הַלְלוּיָהּ.

Halleluyahs: Psalms of Praise

Halleluyah I: Psalm 146

> **Kavanah:** *We have so many things to thank Hashem for. He provides so much for us and takes care of those who cannot take care of themselves. We should rely on Hashem, rather than on people in positions of power. We should try to emulate Hashem and help those who have difficulties in their life.*

Halleluyah. My soul, praise Hashem! I will praise Hashem and sing to my G-d as long as I live. Do not depend on prominent people or on any person, for they cannot provide salvation. When their spirit departs, they return to the earth and, on that day, all of their plans come to an end. One who turns to Hashem, the G-d of our forefather Yaakov, for help, is happy. Hashem is the creator of heaven and earth, the seas and all that live within them.

Hashem guards the truth forever. He does justice for the exploited, gives bread to the hungry, releases those who are imprisoned, provides sight for the blind, straightens those who are bent, and loves the righteous. Hashem protects strangers and righteous converts to Judaism and provides encouragement to orphans and widows. But Hashem bends the way of the wicked.

Hashem, the G-d of Zion, shall reign forever, from one generation to another. Halleluyah.

Ha-l'lu-yah, Ha-l'li naf-shi et Adonoy	הַלְלוּיָהּ, הַלְלִי נַפְשִׁי אֶת יי.
Aha-l'lah Adonoy b'cha-ya,	אֲהַלְלָה יי בְּחַיָּי,
azam-rah lei-lo-hai b'o-di.	אֲזַמְּרָה לֵאלֹהַי בְּעוֹדִי.
Al tiv-t'chu vin-di-vim,	אַל תִּבְטְחוּ בִנְדִיבִים,
b'ven adam she-ein lo t'shu-ah.	בְּבֶן אָדָם שֶׁאֵין לוֹ תְשׁוּעָה.
Tei-tsei ru-cho, ya-shuv l'ad-ma-to,	תֵּצֵא רוּחוֹ, יָשֻׁב לְאַדְמָתוֹ,
ba-yom ha-hu av-du esh-to-no-tav.	בַּיּוֹם הַהוּא אָבְדוּ עֶשְׁתֹּנֹתָיו.
Ashrei she-El Ya'akov b'ez-ro,	אַשְׁרֵי שֶׁאֵל יַעֲקֹב בְּעֶזְרוֹ,
si-v'ro al Adonoy Elo-hav.	שִׂבְרוֹ עַל יי אֱלֹהָיו.
Oseh sha-ma-yim va-arets,	עֹשֶׂה שָׁמַיִם וָאָרֶץ,
et ha-yam v'et kol asher bam,	אֶת הַיָּם וְאֶת כָּל אֲשֶׁר בָּם,
ha-sho-meir emet l'olam.	הַשֹּׁמֵר אֱמֶת לְעוֹלָם.
Oseh mish-pat la-a-su-kim,	עֹשֶׂה מִשְׁפָּט לָעֲשׁוּקִים,
no-tein lechem la-r'ei-vim,	נֹתֵן לֶחֶם לָרְעֵבִים, יי מַתִּיר אֲסוּרִים.
Adonoy ma-tir a-su-rim.	
Adonoy po-kei-ach ivrim,	יי פֹּקֵחַ עִוְרִים,
Adonoy zo-keif k'fu-fim,	יי זֹקֵף כְּפוּפִים,
Adonoy o-heiv tsa-di-kim.	יי אֹהֵב צַדִּיקִים.
Adonoy sho-meir et gei-rim,	יי שֹׁמֵר אֶת גֵּרִים, יָתוֹם וְאַלְמָנָה יְעוֹדֵד,
ya-tom v'al-ma-nah y'o-deid,	
v'derech r'sha-im y'a-veit.	וְדֶרֶךְ רְשָׁעִים יְעַוֵּת.
Yim-loch Adonoy l'olam,	יִמְלֹךְ יי לְעוֹלָם,
Elo-ha-yich Tsi-yon,	אֱלֹהַיִךְ צִיּוֹן,
l'dor va-dor, Ha-l'lu-yah.	לְדֹר וָדֹר, הַלְלוּיָהּ.

Halleluyah II: Psalm 148 ("The G-d of Nature")

> **Kavanah:** *One way to come to recognition of Hashem is through observation of the natural world. All of humanity will one day recognize that Hashem alone runs the world. They will thank Him and will come to praise His special people, the Jewish People.*

Halleluyah. Praise Hashem from the heavens and the heights. Praise Him, angels and heavenly beings. Praise Him, sun, moon, and the bright stars. Praise Him, highest heavens and the waters above the heavens. Let them all praise Hashem since He commanded and created them. He established them forever. He decreed how they should operate and that will never change.

Praise Hashem, Earth, sea creatures, and all in the watery depths. Fire, hail, snow, vapor, and storm winds fulfill Hashem's direction. Mountains and hills, fruit trees and cedars, wild and domestic animals, creeping creatures and birds, kings and governments, princes and judges, young men and women, elders and youth; let them all praise Hashem for He alone rules earth and heaven. He will lift up the pride of His nation, the Children of Israel, his closest nation, causing praise to be showered upon His devout people. *Halleluyah.*

Ha-l'lu-yah, ha-l'lu et Adonoy min ha-sha-ma-yim, ha-l'lu-hu ba-m'ro-mim.	הַלְלוּיָהּ, הַלְלוּ אֶת יי מִן הַשָּׁמַיִם, הַלְלוּהוּ בַּמְּרוֹמִים.
Ha-l'lu-hu chol mal-achav, ha-l'lu-hu kol ts'va-av.	הַלְלוּהוּ כָל מַלְאָכָיו, הַלְלוּהוּ כָּל צְבָאָיו.
Ha-l'lu-hu shemesh v'ya-rei-ach, ha-l'lu-hu kol koch-vei or.	הַלְלוּהוּ שֶׁמֶשׁ וְיָרֵחַ, הַלְלוּהוּ כָּל כּוֹכְבֵי אוֹר.
Ha-l'lu-hu sh'mei ha-sha-ma-yim, v'ha-ma-yim asher mei-al ha-sha-ma-yim.	הַלְלוּהוּ שְׁמֵי הַשָּׁמָיִם, וְהַמַּיִם אֲשֶׁר מֵעַל הַשָּׁמָיִם.
Y'ha-l'lu et sheim Adonoy, ki Hu tsi-va v'niv-ra-u.	יְהַלְלוּ אֶת שֵׁם יי, כִּי הוּא צִוָּה וְנִבְרָאוּ.
Va-ya-ami-deim la-ad l'olam, chak na-tan v'lo ya-avor.	וַיַּעֲמִידֵם לָעַד לְעוֹלָם, חָק נָתַן וְלֹא יַעֲבוֹר.
Ha-l'lu et Adonoy min ha-arets, ta-ni-nim v'chol t'ho-mot.	הַלְלוּ אֶת יי מִן הָאָרֶץ, תַּנִּינִים וְכָל תְּהֹמוֹת.
Eish u-va-rad, sheleg v'ki-tor, ru-ach s'a-rah osah d'va-ro.	אֵשׁ וּבָרָד שֶׁלֶג וְקִיטוֹר, רוּחַ סְעָרָה עֹשָׂה דְבָרוֹ.
He-ha-rim v'chol g'va-ot, eits pri v'chol ara-zim.	הֶהָרִים וְכָל גְּבָעוֹת, עֵץ פְּרִי וְכָל אֲרָזִים.
Ha-cha-yah v'chol b'hei-mah, remes v'tsi-por ka-naf.	הַחַיָּה וְכָל בְּהֵמָה, רֶמֶשׂ וְצִפּוֹר כָּנָף.
Mal-chei erets v'chol l'u-mim, sa-rim v'chol shof-tei arets.	מַלְכֵי אֶרֶץ וְכָל לְאֻמִּים, שָׂרִים וְכָל שֹׁפְטֵי אָרֶץ.
Ba-chu-rim v'gam b'tu-lot, z'kei-nim im n'arim.	בַּחוּרִים וְגַם בְּתוּלוֹת, זְקֵנִים עִם נְעָרִים.
Y'ha-l'lu et sheim Adonoy, ki nis-gav sh'mo l'va-do, ho-do al erets v'sha-ma-yim.	יְהַלְלוּ אֶת שֵׁם יי, כִּי נִשְׂגָּב שְׁמוֹ לְבַדּוֹ, הוֹדוֹ עַל אֶרֶץ וְשָׁמָיִם.
Va-ya-rem keren l'amo, t'hi-lah l'chol cha-si-dav, liv-nei Yisrael am k'rovo. Ha-l'lu-yah.	וַיָּרֶם קֶרֶן לְעַמּוֹ, תְּהִלָּה לְכָל חֲסִידָיו, לִבְנֵי יִשְׂרָאֵל עַם קְרֹבוֹ, הַלְלוּיָהּ.

98 STAIRWAY TO HEAVEN

Va-y'varech David: Hashem Directs the World

NOTE: It is customary to stand when saying this prayer.

> **Kavanah:** *Hashem can do anything. All things come from Hashem. Only Hashem determines who receives wealth and power. I will trust in Hashem. I will strive to be his partner by sharing my success with those who are less fortunate and those who are trying to share goodness with others.*

And King David blessed Hashem in front of the entire assembly. He said, "To You, Hashem, the Source of all blessings, the G-d of Israel (i.e., Jacob), our forefather, in this world and the World to Come, belongs the greatness, the strength, the beauty, the glory, and everything in the heavens and earth. To You, Hashem, is the kingship and the sovereignty over every leader."

Before you say this phrase, it is customary, on a regular weekday, to put three coins into a charity box.

Wealth and honor come from You and You rule everything. In Your hand is the power and the strength and You are able to make anyone great or strong. And now, our G-d, we thank You and praise Your name.

Va-y'va-rech Da-vid et Adonoy l'ei-nei kol ha-kahal. Va-yo-meir Da-vid, Baruch atah Adonoy Elo-hei Yisroel avi-nu, mei-olam v'ad olam. L'cha Adonoy ha-g'du-lah v'ha-g'vu-rah v'ha-tif-eret v'ha-nei-tsach v'ha-hod, ki chol ba-sha-ma-yim u-va-arets. L'cha Adonoy ha-mam-lachah, v'ha-mit-na-sei l'chol l'rosh. V'ha-osher v'ha-kavod mil-fa-necha, v'atah mo-shel ba-kol. U-v'ya-d'cha ko-ach u-g'vu-rah, u-v'ya-d'cha l'ga-del u-l'cha-zeik la-kol. V'atah Elo-heinu mo-dim a-nach-nu lach, u-m'ha-l'lim l'sheim tif-ar-techa.

וַיְבָרֶךְ דָּוִיד אֶת יי לְעֵינֵי כָּל הַקָּהָל, וַיֹּאמֶר דָּוִיד: בָּרוּךְ אַתָּה יי אֱלֹהֵי יִשְׂרָאֵל אָבִינוּ, מֵעוֹלָם וְעַד עוֹלָם. לְךָ יי הַגְּדֻלָּה וְהַגְּבוּרָה וְהַתִּפְאֶרֶת וְהַנֵּצַח וְהַהוֹד, כִּי כֹל בַּשָּׁמַיִם וּבָאָרֶץ. לְךָ יי הַמַּמְלָכָה, וְהַמִּתְנַשֵּׂא לְכֹל לְרֹאשׁ. וְהָעֹשֶׁר וְהַכָּבוֹד מִלְּפָנֶיךָ, וְאַתָּה מוֹשֵׁל בַּכֹּל. וּבְיָדְךָ כֹּחַ וּגְבוּרָה, וּבְיָדְךָ לְגַדֵּל וּלְחַזֵּק לַכֹּל. וְעַתָּה אֱלֹהֵינוּ מוֹדִים אֲנַחְנוּ לָךְ, וּמְהַלְלִים לְשֵׁם תִּפְאַרְתֶּךָ.

Kri'at Yam Suf: Remember the Splitting of the Red Sea ("G-d in History")

> **Kavanah:** *Hashem chose Israel from all other nations to be His special people — to be His messengers on earth. He changed nature for the Jewish People in Egypt and at the Red Sea and destroyed their Egyptian enemies. He does the same for us today. I will trust in Hashem and in our great Torah leaders.*

And on that day, Hashem saved Israel from the hand of Egypt and Israel saw the Egyptians dead on the seashore. Israel saw the great hand that Hashem inflicted upon Egypt and the people feared Hashem, and they had faith in Hashem and in His servant, Moshe.

Va-yo-sha Adonoy ba-yom ha-hu et Yisrael mi-yad Mits-ra-yim va-yar Yisrael et Mits-ra-yim meit al s'fat ha-yam. Va-yar Yisrael et ha-yad ha-g'do-lah asher asah Adonoy b'Mits-ra-yim, va-yir-u ha-am et Adonoy, va-ya-ami-nu ba-Adonoy u-v'Mosheh av-do.

וַיּוֹשַׁע יְיָ בַּיּוֹם הַהוּא אֶת יִשְׂרָאֵל מִיַּד מִצְרָיִם וַיַּרְא יִשְׂרָאֵל אֶת מִצְרַיִם מֵת עַל שְׂפַת הַיָּם. וַיַּרְא יִשְׂרָאֵל אֶת הַיָּד הַגְּדֹלָה אֲשֶׁר עָשָׂה יְיָ בְּמִצְרַיִם וַיִּירְאוּ הָעָם אֶת יְיָ וַיַּאֲמִינוּ בַּיְיָ וּבְמֹשֶׁה עַבְדּוֹ.

Yishtabach:

This is the concluding blessing of Part II of the daily morning prayers, in which we remind ourselves who G-d is and what He does every moment of every day.

> **Kavanah:** *I recognize that Hashem creates everything and is the Source of Life and I should remember to thank Hashem, always.*

Hashem, our G-d, who is great and holy, may Your Name be praised forever in the heavens and on earth. Because for You, Adonoy, our G-d and the G-d of our ancestors, all forms of praise and thanks are fitting in this world and in the world to come.

Adonoy, the Source of all blessings, is one whom we ought to thank, the one who performs wonders, who creates all souls and is the Master of all that is created, who is the unique One, the Source of life in the world.

Yish-ta-bach shim-cha la-ad mal-keinu, ha-El ha-Melech ha-gadol v'ha-kadosh ba-sha-ma-yim u-va-arets.

יִשְׁתַּבַּח שִׁמְךָ לָעַד מַלְכֵּנוּ, הָאֵל הַמֶּלֶךְ הַגָּדוֹל וְהַקָּדוֹשׁ בַּשָּׁמַיִם וּבָאָרֶץ.

Ki l'cha na-eh Adonoy Elo-heinu vei-lo-hei avo-tei-nu, shir u-sh'va-chah, ha-lel v'zim-rah, oz u-mem-sha-lah, netsach g'du-lah u-g'vu-rah, t'hi-lah v'tif-eret k'du-shah u-mal-chut, b'ra-chot v'ho-da-ot mei-atah v'ad olam.

כִּי לְךָ נָאֶה יְיָ אֱלֹהֵינוּ וֵאלֹהֵי אֲבוֹתֵינוּ, שִׁיר וּשְׁבָחָה, הַלֵּל וְזִמְרָה, עֹז וּמֶמְשָׁלָה, נֶצַח גְּדֻלָּה וּגְבוּרָה, תְּהִלָּה וְתִפְאֶרֶת, קְדֻשָּׁה וּמַלְכוּת, בְּרָכוֹת וְהוֹדָאוֹת מֵעַתָּה וְעַד עוֹלָם.

Baruch atah Adonoy, El Melech gadol ba-tish-ba-chot, El ha-ho-da-ot, Adon ha-nif-la-ot, ha-bo-cheir b'shi-rei zim-rah, Melech El chei ha-ola-mim.

בָּרוּךְ אַתָּה יְיָ, אֵל מֶלֶךְ גָּדוֹל בַּתִּשְׁבָּחוֹת, אֵל הַהוֹדָאוֹת, אֲדוֹן הַנִּפְלָאוֹת, הַבּוֹחֵר בְּשִׁירֵי זִמְרָה, מֶלֶךְ אֵל חֵי הָעוֹלָמִים.

Step 3: Reaffirming Hashem's Oneness and Our Connection to Him

Shema Yisrael (Three Parts)
[See Page 59 for an extended explanation of this prayer and of this mitzvah.]

Part I. *Shema* Meditation: The Oneness of Hashem

NOTE: You can choose to say this line more slowly and think as you say each word or you can say the line more quickly as it appears on the next page.

Cover your eyes with your right hand while saying the opening line of the *Shema*.

שְׁמַע יִשְׂרָאֵל, יי אֱלֹהֵינוּ, יי אֶחָד:

שְׁמַע *Shema* Understand (I "hear" you).

יִשְׂרָאֵל *Yisrael* The Jew, one who struggles with G-d, with the world, and with one's self and is victorious.

יי *Adonoy* God of compassion.

אֱלֹהֵינוּ *Eloheinu* Our G-d and the G-d of judgement.

יי *Adonoy* God of compassion.

אֶחָד *Echad* is the One and Only.

Three meanings:

• The One who creates and runs the world (past and present). The Source of everything. We cover our eyes because we see separation and difference. Hashem is the one unifying life force.

• Hashem is One with me. My soul contains a part of G-d within me.

• Hashem and *Eloheinu* are both One. Both compassion and judgement are ultimately compassion. Like a good parent.

בָּרוּךְ שֵׁם כְּבוֹד מַלְכוּתוֹ לְעוֹלָם וָעֶד (whisper)
(whisper) *Baruch sheim k'vod mal-chu-to l'olam va-ed.*
(whisper) **May Hashem be acknowledged as the Source of blessing forever.**

NOTE: Please continue with the rest of Shema on the next page, starting with "V'a-hav-ta."

> **Kavanah:** *Hashem is the one life force behind all things. Everything that Hashem does is for the good. Part of Hashem is within me. I am one with Hashem and He is one with me. I will try to follow Hashem's directions and connect with Him by utilizing the forces of love and awe that Hashem has put in my soul.*

 Cover your eyes with your right hand while saying the opening line of the *Shema*.

שְׁמַע יִשְׂרָאֵל, יְיָ אֱלֹהֵינוּ, יְיָ אֶחָד:

(whisper)

בָּרוּךְ שֵׁם כְּבוֹד מַלְכוּתוֹ לְעוֹלָם וָעֶד

Shema Yisrael, Adonoy Elo-heinu, Adonoy Echad.

(whisper)

Baruch sheim k'vod mal-chu-to l'olam va-ed.

Listen Israel, Adonoy is our G-d, Adonoy is One.

(whisper)

May Hashem be acknowledged as the Source of blessing forever.

(from *Devarim* (Deuteronomy), Chapter 6, verses 5 to 9)

וְאָהַבְתָּ אֵת יְיָ אֱלֹהֶיךָ, בְּכָל לְבָבְךָ, וּבְכָל נַפְשְׁךָ, וּבְכָל מְאֹדֶךָ. וְהָיוּ הַדְּבָרִים הָאֵלֶּה, אֲשֶׁר אָנֹכִי מְצַוְּךָ הַיּוֹם, עַל לְבָבֶךָ. וְשִׁנַּנְתָּם לְבָנֶיךָ, וְדִבַּרְתָּ בָּם, בְּשִׁבְתְּךָ בְּבֵיתֶךָ, וּבְלֶכְתְּךָ בַדֶּרֶךְ, וּבְשָׁכְבְּךָ וּבְקוּמֶךָ. וּקְשַׁרְתָּם לְאוֹת עַל יָדֶךָ, וְהָיוּ לְטֹטָפֹת בֵּין עֵינֶיךָ. וּכְתַבְתָּם עַל מְזֻזוֹת בֵּיתֶךָ, וּבִשְׁעָרֶיךָ.

V'a-hav-ta eit Adonoy Elo-hecha, b'chol l'va-v'cha, u-v'chol naf-sh'cha, u-v'chol mo-decha. V'ha-yu ha-d'va-rim ha-eileh, asher ano-chi m'tsa-v'cha ha-yom, al l'va-vecha. V'shi-nan-tam l'va-necha, v'di-bar-ta bam, b'shiv-t'cha b'vei-techa, u-v'lech-t'cha va-derech, u-v'shach-b'cha u-v'ku-mecha. U-k'shar-tam l'ot al ya-decha, v'ha-yu l'to-ta-fot bein ei-necha. U-ch'tav-tam al m'zu-zot bei-techa u-vish-a-recha.

And you shall love Hashem, your G-d, with all your heart, with all your soul, and with all that is dear to you. These words which I command you today shall always be in your heart. Teach them to your children. Speak about them when you are at home, when you travel, when you lay down, and when you arise. Bind them as a sign on your arm (i.e., *tefillin* on the arm) and as *tefillin* upon the center of your head and write them as *mezuzot* for the doorposts of your house and your gates.

Part II. *V'hayah Im Shamo'a*
Cause and Effect: The Results of the Jewish People's Choices and Behavior

> **Kavanah:** *What I do matters to me and to the Jewish People.*
> *All of my actions are recorded and evaluated.*
> *Each action has an effect upon me and on the Jewish Nation.*
> *There is cause and effect and consequence to my actions,*
> *words, thoughts, and decisions.*

(from *Devarim* (Deuteronomy), Chapter 11, Verses 13 to 21)

And if you are careful to listen to My commandments, which I am commanding you today, and if you love Hashem, your G-d, and serve Him with all your heart and all your soul, then I, Hashem, have made this promise: I (Hashem) will provide rain to your land in its proper times so that you can harvest grain, wine, and olive oil. I will provide grass in your fields for your cattle and you will have sufficient food to eat and be satiated. Be careful not to be led astray by your heart's temptations to worship other gods or to bow to them. If you do follow other gods, Hashem will be angry with you and will restrain the heavens and there will be no rain and the earth will not yield produce. And you will vanish quickly from the good land which Hashem is giving you. Place these words of Mine upon your heart and soul. Bind them (for *tefillin*) as a sign on your arm and let them be *tefillin* in the center of your head. Teach these words to your children. Discuss them at home, when you travel, when you lay down, and when you get up. And write them on *mezuzot* for the doorposts of your homes and gates. If you do this, you and your children will endure for a long time upon the land that Hashem swore to your ancestors, that He would to give them, for as long as the heavens remain above the earth (i.e., forever).

V'ha-yah, im sha-mo-a tish-m'u el mits-vo-tai, asher a-no-chi m'tsa-veh et-chem ha-yom, l'a-ha-vah et Adonoy Elo-heichem u-l'av-do, b'chol l'vav-chem u-v'chol naf-sh'chem. V'na-ta-ti m'tar ar-ts'chem b'i-to, yo-reh u-mal-kosh, v'a-saf-ta d'ga-necha v'ti-ro-sh'cha v'yits-ha-recha. V'na-ta-ti ei-sev b'sa-d'cha liv-hem-techa, v'a-chal-ta v'sa-va-ta. Hi-sham-ru la-chem, pen yif-teh l'vav-chem, v'sar-tem va-ava-d'tem Elo-him achei-rim, v'hish-ta-cha-vitem la-hem. V'cha-rah af Adonoy ba-chem, v'a-tsar et ha-sha-ma-yim, v'lo yi-h'yeh ma-tar,

וְהָיָה, אִם שָׁמֹעַ תִּשְׁמְעוּ אֶל מִצְוֹתַי, אֲשֶׁר אָנֹכִי מְצַוֶּה אֶתְכֶם הַיּוֹם, לְאַהֲבָה אֶת יְיָ אֱלֹהֵיכֶם וּלְעָבְדוֹ, בְּכָל לְבַבְכֶם וּבְכָל נַפְשְׁכֶם. וְנָתַתִּי מְטַר אַרְצְכֶם בְּעִתּוֹ, יוֹרֶה וּמַלְקוֹשׁ, וְאָסַפְתָּ דְגָנֶךָ וְתִירֹשְׁךָ וְיִצְהָרֶךָ. וְנָתַתִּי עֵשֶׂב בְּשָׂדְךָ לִבְהֶמְתֶּךָ, וְאָכַלְתָּ וְשָׂבָעְתָּ. הִשָּׁמְרוּ לָכֶם, פֶּן יִפְתֶּה לְבַבְכֶם, וְסַרְתֶּם וַעֲבַדְתֶּם אֱלֹהִים אֲחֵרִים, וְהִשְׁתַּחֲוִיתֶם לָהֶם. וְחָרָה אַף יְיָ בָּכֶם, וְעָצַר אֶת הַשָּׁמַיִם, וְלֹא יִהְיֶה מָטָר, וְהָאֲדָמָה לֹא תִתֵּן אֶת יְבוּלָהּ, וַאֲבַדְתֶּם

v'ha-ada-mah lo ti-tein et y'vu-lah, va-ava-d'tem m'hei-rah mei-al ha-arets ha-tovah asher Adonoy no-tein la-chem. V'sam-tem et d'va-rai ei-leh, al l'vav-chem v'al naf-sh'chem, u-k'shar-tem otam l'ot al yed-chem, v'ha-yu l'to-ta-fot bein ei-nei-chem. V'li-ma-d'tem otam et b'nei-chem, l'da-beir bam b'shiv-t'cha b'vei-techa, u-v'lech-t'cha va-derech, u-v'shach-b'cha u-v'ku-mecha. U-ch'tav-tam al m'zu-zot bei-techa, u-vish-arecha.

מְהֵרָה מֵעַל הָאָרֶץ הַטֹּבָה אֲשֶׁר יְיָ נֹתֵן לָכֶם. וְשַׂמְתֶּם אֶת דְּבָרַי אֵלֶּה, עַל לְבַבְכֶם וְעַל נַפְשְׁכֶם, וּקְשַׁרְתֶּם אֹתָם לְאוֹת עַל יֶדְכֶם, וְהָיוּ לְטוֹטָפֹת בֵּין עֵינֵיכֶם. וְלִמַּדְתֶּם אֹתָם אֶת בְּנֵיכֶם, לְדַבֵּר בָּם בְּשִׁבְתְּךָ בְּבֵיתֶךָ, וּבְלֶכְתְּךָ בַדֶּרֶךְ, וּבְשָׁכְבְּךָ וּבְקוּמֶךָ. וּכְתַבְתָּם עַל מְזוּזוֹת בֵּיתֶךָ, וּבִשְׁעָרֶיךָ.

L'ma-an yir-bu y'mei-chem vi-mei v'nei-chem, al ha-ada-mah asher nish-ba Adonoy la-avo-tei-chem la-teit la-hem, ki-mei ha-sha-ma-yim al ha-arets.

לְמַעַן יִרְבּוּ יְמֵיכֶם וִימֵי בְנֵיכֶם, עַל הָאֲדָמָה אֲשֶׁר נִשְׁבַּע יְיָ לַאֲבֹתֵיכֶם לָתֵת לָהֶם, כִּימֵי הַשָּׁמַיִם עַל הָאָרֶץ.

Part III. *Vayomeir*
Remember the Exodus from Egypt and Be Careful to Do the Right Thing

> **Kavanah:** *I will strive to be constantly aware that I am part of the Jewish People and its mission in the world.*
> *Hashem helps us to break through our perceived barriers and limitations to achieve personal growth.*

Identify those issues that are holding you back from growing, achieving, and being the best you can be today. Ask yourself, "Am I sad, angry, lazy, self-focused?" Ask Hashem to help you break out of your personal "Egypt," i.e., your personal barriers and limitations.

(from *Bamidbar* (Numbers), Chapter 15, verses 37 to 41)
And Hashem spoke to Moshe and instructed him to speak to the Jewish People and have them make *tzitzit* (special tassels) on the corners of four-cornered garments for all generations. These should include a thread of sky-blue wool (dyed from a source that is no longer available today). These shall be your *tzitzit*. When you see them, you will remember all of Hashem's commandments and keep and follow them. Thus, you will not be led astray by the desires of your heart and eyes, which have a tendency to lead you astray. You will remember and keep all of My commandments and will be holy to your G-d. I am Hashem, your G-d, who brought you out of Egypt to be your G-d. I am Hashem, your G-d. This is truth.

Va-yo-meir Adonoy el Mosheh lei-mor:

וַיֹּאמֶר יְיָ אֶל מֹשֶׁה לֵּאמֹר:

Da-beir el b'nei Yisrael, v'a-mar-ta alei-hem, v'a-su la-hem tsi-tsit, al kan-fei vig-dei-hem l'doro-tam, v'nat-nu al tsi-tsit ha-kanaf, p'til t'chei-let. V'ha-yah la-chem l'tsi-tsit, u-r'item oto, u-z'char-tem et kol mits-vot Adonoy, va-asi-tem otam, v'lo ta-tu-ru acha-rei l'vav-chem v'a-cha-rei ei-nei-chem, asher atem zo-nim acha-rei-hem. L'ma-an tiz-k'ru, va-asi-tem et kol mits-vo-tai, vi-h'yi-tem k'do-shim lei-lo-hei-chem. Ani Adonoy Elo-hei-chem, asher ho-tsei-ti et-chem mei-erets Mits-ra-yim, li-h'yot la-chem lei-lo-him; Ani Adonoy Elo-hei-chem. Emet.

דַּבֵּר אֶל בְּנֵי יִשְׂרָאֵל, וְאָמַרְתָּ אֲלֵהֶם, וְעָשׂוּ לָהֶם צִיצִת, עַל כַּנְפֵי בִגְדֵיהֶם לְדֹרֹתָם, וְנָתְנוּ עַל צִיצִת הַכָּנָף, פְּתִיל תְּכֵלֶת. וְהָיָה לָכֶם לְצִיצִת, וּרְאִיתֶם אֹתוֹ, וּזְכַרְתֶּם אֶת כָּל מִצְוֹת יְיָ, וַעֲשִׂיתֶם אֹתָם, וְלֹא תָתוּרוּ אַחֲרֵי לְבַבְכֶם וְאַחֲרֵי עֵינֵיכֶם, אֲשֶׁר אַתֶּם זֹנִים אַחֲרֵיהֶם. לְמַעַן תִּזְכְּרוּ, וַעֲשִׂיתֶם אֶת כָּל מִצְוֹתָי, וִהְיִיתֶם קְדֹשִׁים לֵאלֹהֵיכֶם. אֲנִי יְיָ אֱלֹהֵיכֶם, אֲשֶׁר הוֹצֵאתִי אֶתְכֶם מֵאֶרֶץ מִצְרַיִם, לִהְיוֹת לָכֶם לֵאלֹהִים, אֲנִי יְיָ אֱלֹהֵיכֶם. אֱמֶת.

Ezrat Avoteinu: Hashem, the One who helps me

Introduction: Hashem has always been faithful to the Jewish People. He answers our prayers and redeems us from our personal difficulties. He helps us to break free from whatever holds us back from achieving greater spiritual achievements. This gives us confidence and makes us happy. And that is the way to begin speaking to Hashem. With joy. With confidence. With happiness.

> **Kavanah:** *I am not alone.*
> *I will never have to face life without Hashem's help. Hashem is there for me.*
> *Hashem will help me to do the right thing and to become a better person.*
> *It makes me happy to know that I am not alone;*
> *that Hashem watches over me and protects me.*

Hashem, You alone helped our forefathers, forever protecting and saving them and their descendants in every generation. You live in the highest place and Your justice and righteousness spread to all ends of the earth.

Ez-rat avo-teinu atah hu mei-olam, ma-gein u-mo-shi-a liv-nei-hem acha-rei-hem b'chol dor va-dor. B'rum olam mo-sha-vecha, u-mish-pa-techa v'tsid-ka-t'cha ad af-sei arets.

עֶזְרַת אֲבוֹתֵינוּ אַתָּה הוּא מֵעוֹלָם, מָגֵן וּמוֹשִׁיעַ לִבְנֵיהֶם אַחֲרֵיהֶם בְּכָל דּוֹר וָדוֹר. בְּרוּם עוֹלָם מוֹשָׁבֶךָ, וּמִשְׁפָּטֶיךָ וְצִדְקָתְךָ עַד אַפְסֵי אָרֶץ.

It is true that those who listen to Your mitzvot and take Your teachings to heart are happy. It is true that You are the Master of Your people and the mighty King who fights their battles for both parents and children. It is true that You are first and last and, aside from You, we have no other King, no other redeemer, no other savior.

Ash-rei ish she-yish-ma l'mits-vo-techa v'Tora-t'cha u-d'var-cha ya-sim al libo. Emet atah hu Adon l'a-mecha u-Melech gi-bor la-riv ri-vam. Emet atah hu ri-shon v'atah hu a-cha-ron, u-mi-bal-a-decha ein la-nu Melech go-el u-mo-shi-a.

אַשְׁרֵי אִישׁ שֶׁיִּשְׁמַע לְמִצְוֹתֶיךָ וְתוֹרָתְךָ וּדְבָרְךָ יָשִׂים עַל לִבּוֹ. אֱמֶת אַתָּה הוּא אָדוֹן לְעַמֶּךָ וּמֶלֶךְ גִּבּוֹר לָרִיב רִיבָם. אֱמֶת אַתָּה הוּא רִאשׁוֹן וְאַתָּה הוּא אַחֲרוֹן, וּמִבַּלְעָדֶיךָ אֵין לָנוּ מֶלֶךְ גּוֹאֵל וּמוֹשִׁיעַ.

It is true that You, Hashem, redeemed us from the corruption of Egypt and liberated us from slavery. You killed all of the firstborn Egyptians but redeemed Your firstborn, Israel. For them You split the Red Sea. You drowned the evil sinners and, while Your dear ones crossed through the Sea, the waters engulfed their enemies. Not even one of them remained alive. For this, those who loved You gave thanks and praise with songs, prayers, and blessings to the living and enduring G-d; who is great and awesome; who knocks the conceited down to the ground and lifts the lowly ones up high; who frees the imprisoned, liberates the humble ones, and helps the poor; who answers His people, Israel, whenever they call to Him.

Mi-Mits-ra-yim g'al-ta-nu Adonoy Elo-heinu, u-mi-beit ava-dim p'di-ta-nu. Kol b'cho-rei-hem ha-rag-ta, u-v'chor-cha ga-al-ta, v'Yam Suf ba-ka-ta, v'zei-dim ti-ba-ta, vi-di-dim he-evar-ta, va-y'cha-su ma-yim tsa-rei-hem, echad mei-hem lo no-tar. Al zot shi-b'chu a-hu-vim v'ro-m'mu El, v'nat-nu y'di-dim z'mirot shirot v'tish-ba-chot, b'ra-chot v'ho-da-ot l'melech El chai v'ka-yam. Ram v'nisa, ga-dol v'nora, mash-pil gei-im, u-mag-bi-ha sh'fa-lim, mo-tsi a-si-rim, u-fo-deh ana-vim, vo-zeir da-lim, vo-neh l'amo Yisrael b'eit shav-am ei-lav.

מִמִּצְרַיִם גְּאַלְתָּנוּ יְיָ אֱלֹהֵינוּ, וּמִבֵּית עֲבָדִים פְּדִיתָנוּ. כָּל בְּכוֹרֵיהֶם הָרַגְתָּ, וּבְכוֹרְךָ גָּאָלְתָּ, וְיַם סוּף בָּקַעְתָּ, וְזֵדִים טִבַּעְתָּ, וִידִידִים הֶעֱבַרְתָּ, וַיְכַסּוּ מַיִם צָרֵיהֶם, אֶחָד מֵהֶם לֹא נוֹתָר. עַל זֹאת שִׁבְּחוּ אֲהוּבִים וְרוֹמְמוּ אֵל, וְנָתְנוּ יְדִידִים זְמִירוֹת שִׁירוֹת וְתִשְׁבָּחוֹת, בְּרָכוֹת וְהוֹדָאוֹת לְמֶלֶךְ אֵל חַי וְקַיָּם. רָם וְנִשָּׂא, גָּדוֹל וְנוֹרָא, מַשְׁפִּיל גֵּאִים, וּמַגְבִּיהַּ שְׁפָלִים, מוֹצִיא אֲסִירִים, וּפוֹדֶה עֲנָוִים, וְעוֹזֵר דַּלִּים, וְעוֹנֶה לְעַמּוֹ בְּעֵת שַׁוְּעָם אֵלָיו.

In praise of G-d, their Redeemer, the Source of all blessings, Moshe and the children of Israel sang a song with great joy and said, "Who is like You, Hashem, in the heavens? Who is like You with such mighty holiness, doing great wonders, too awesome to praise?" Those who were redeemed from Egypt sang a new song in unison at the seashore. They gave thanks, acknowledged Your sovereignty, and said, "Hashem will reign forever."

Hashem, upon whom Israel relies, rise up to help Israel and redeem Judah and Israel as You promised. As it is said (in the book of Isaiah), "Our redeemer, whose name is Hashem, the Master of the world, is the Holy One of Israel." You, Hashem, Source of all blessings, redeemed Israel.

T'hi-lot l'El el-yon, baruch hu u-m'vo-rach. Mo-sheh u-v'nei Yisrael l'cha anu shi-rah b'sim-chah ra-bah v'am-ru chu-lam:

תְּהִלּוֹת לְאֵל עֶלְיוֹן, בָּרוּךְ הוּא וּמְבֹרָךְ. מֹשֶׁה וּבְנֵי יִשְׂרָאֵל לְךָ עָנוּ שִׁירָה בְּשִׂמְחָה רַבָּה וְאָמְרוּ כֻלָּם:

"Mi cha-mo-cha ba-ei-lim Adonoy! Mi ka-mo-cha nedar ba-kodesh! Nora t'hi-lot, oseh fe-le!"

מִי כָמֹכָה בָּאֵלִים יְיָ, מִי כָּמֹכָה נֶאְדָּר בַּקֹּדֶשׁ, נוֹרָא תְהִלֹּת, עֹשֵׂה פֶלֶא.

Shi-rah cha-da-shah shi-b'chu g'u-lim l'shim-cha al s'fat ha-yam, ya-chad ku-lam ho-du v'him-li-chu, v'am-ru: "Adonoy yim-loch l'olam va-ed!"

שִׁירָה חֲדָשָׁה שִׁבְּחוּ גְאוּלִים לְשִׁמְךָ עַל שְׂפַת הַיָּם, יַחַד כֻּלָּם הוֹדוּ וְהִמְלִיכוּ וְאָמְרוּ: יְיָ יִמְלֹךְ לְעֹלָם וָעֶד.

Tsur Yisrael, kuma b'ez-rat Yisrael, u-f'dei chi-n'u-mecha Yehudah v'Yisrael. Go-alei-nu Adonoy ts'va-ot sh'mo, K'dosh Yisrael.

צוּר יִשְׂרָאֵל, קוּמָה בְּעֶזְרַת יִשְׂרָאֵל, וּפְדֵה כִנְאֻמֶךָ יְהוּדָה וְיִשְׂרָאֵל. גֹּאֲלֵנוּ יְיָ צְבָאוֹת שְׁמוֹ, קְדוֹשׁ יִשְׂרָאֵל.

Baruch atah Adonoy, ga-al Yisrael.

בָּרוּךְ אַתָּה יְיָ, גָּאַל יִשְׂרָאֵל.

On Shabbat morning, continue with the Shabbat *Shemoneh Esrei* on the next page.

On a regular weekday, please turn to page 128 for the Weekday *Shemoneh Esrei*.

THE SHABBAT MORNING *SHEMONEH ESREI*

Step 4. A Personal Conversation with G-d

The Shabbat morning *Shemoneh Esrei*, also called the *Amidah*, is the central prayer for this morning. It contains the same introduction, introductory request, First Three Blessings, Three Closing Blessings, the Request for Help in controlling negative traits, and Final Stanza as the weekday *Amidah*. However, no personal requests are said on Shabbat. Instead, the main theme of the *Amidah* is the Central Blessing, which discusses the special nature of Shabbat. Each Shabbat *Amidah* blessing addresses a different aspect of Shabbat.

This prayer is said standing, with our feet together, facing Jerusalem, from where our prayers are taken by angels (i.e., spiritual messengers) to the heavens. In Jerusalem, one faces the Temple Mount, the original point of creation upon which the two Jewish Temples stood in ancient times.

If one cannot stand for whatever reason, this prayer can be recited while sitting or lying down. In any case, the words should be whispered so that they become real (i.e., sound waves), yet still approach the closest thing to pure, focused thought.

Take three steps back and then three steps forward, as if you are approaching Hashem directly to talk to Him.

Introductory Request

> **Kavanah:** *It is difficult to* daven.
> *Hashem, please help me to* daven *and get closer to You.*

Hashem, please help me to overcome my limitations, so that I can say Your praises.

Adonoy s'fa-tai tif-tach, u-fi ya-gid t'hi-la-techa.   אֲדֹנָי שְׂפָתַי תִּפְתָּח, וּפִי יַגִּיד תְּהִלָּתֶךָ.

Beginning the Deepest Dialogue
The First Three Blessings: To Whom Are We Speaking?

The First Blessing: The Blessing of the Fathers

> **Kavanah:** *We are not strangers to Hashem nor is He to us.
> We are the children and the living legacy of those in the world who first
> recognized Hashem and stood up for this belief.
> Hashem shielded them from all their trials in life and
> made an eternal covenant with them and their children, including me.*

Bend knees on *Baruch*. Bend at waist on *atah*. Stand upright on *Adonoy*.

You, Hashem, who are the Source of all blessing, are our G-d and the G-d of our forefathers, the G-d of Avraham, the G-d of Yitzchak, and the G-d of Yaakov. The great, powerful, and awesome G-d who is beyond our comprehension, You bestow kindness and create all things. You remember the kindness of our forefathers and send loving redemption to their children, for His name's sake.

Baruch atah Adonoy Elo-heinu vei-lo-hei avo-tei-nu, Elo-hei Avra-ham, Elo-hei Yits-chak, vei-lo-hei Ya-akov, ha-El ha-Ga-dol ha-Gi-bor v'ha-No-ra, El El-yon, go-mel cha-sa-dim to-vim v'ko-nei ha-kol, v'zo-cheir chas-dei avot, u-mei-vi go-el liv-nei v'nei-hem, l'ma-an sh'mo b'a-ha-vah.

בָּרוּךְ אַתָּה יְיָ אֱלֹהֵינוּ וֵאלֹהֵי אֲבוֹתֵינוּ, אֱלֹהֵי אַבְרָהָם, אֱלֹהֵי יִצְחָק, וֵאלֹהֵי יַעֲקֹב, הָאֵל הַגָּדוֹל הַגִּבּוֹר וְהַנּוֹרָא, אֵל עֶלְיוֹן, גּוֹמֵל חֲסָדִים טוֹבִים וְקוֹנֵה הַכֹּל, וְזוֹכֵר חַסְדֵי אָבוֹת, וּמֵבִיא גוֹאֵל לִבְנֵי בְנֵיהֶם, לְמַעַן שְׁמוֹ בְּאַהֲבָה.

NOTE: From Rosh Hashanah to Yom Kippur there are five special inserts or substitutions in the Shabbat *Shemoneh Esrei*. The first one is the following line:

Remember us for life Master of the World, who wants life. Inscribe us in the Book of Life for Your sake, oh Living G-d.

Zach-reinu l'chayim, Melech cha-fetz ba-cha-yim, v'chat-vei-nu b'sei-fer ha-chayim, l'ma-an-cha Elo-him cha-yim.

זָכְרֵנוּ לְחַיִּים, מֶלֶךְ חָפֵץ בַּחַיִּים, וְכָתְבֵנוּ בְּסֵפֶר הַחַיִּים, לְמַעַנְךָ אֱלֹהִים חַיִּים.

Bend knees on *Baruch*, bow on *atah*, stand upright on *Adonoy*.

You are the Master of the World, who helps us, saves us, and protects us. You, Adonoy, Source of all blessing, are the protector of Avraham (and the children of Avraham).

Melech o-zeir u-mo-shi-a u-ma-gein.
Baruch atah Adonoy, ma-gein Avra-ham.

מֶלֶךְ עוֹזֵר וּמוֹשִׁיעַ וּמָגֵן.
בָּרוּךְ אַתָּה יְיָ, מָגֵן אַבְרָהָם.

The Second Blessing: Hashem's Power

Kavanah: *Hashem is the source of life and determines who will live and who will die and, indeed, who will live again in the future.*

You, Hashem, have the power of life and death. You have the power to revive those who are deceased and to save again and again.

Atah gi-bor l'olam Adonoy, m'cha-yei mei-tim atah rav l'ho-shi-a.

אַתָּה גִּבּוֹר לְעוֹלָם אֲדֹנָי, מְחַיֵּה מֵתִים אַתָּה רַב לְהוֹשִׁיעַ.

NOTE: Between Sh'mini Atzeret (the day before Simchat Torah) and Pesach, add this phrase:

Who makes the wind blow and the rain fall,

Ma-shiv ha-ru-ach u-mo-rid ha-ga-shem.

מַשִּׁיב הָרוּחַ וּמוֹרִיד הַגֶּשֶׁם.

Sustains us with kindness, revives the deceased with compassion (e.g., people who sleep, plants that wither), supports those who have fallen, provides healing for the sick, freedom for the imprisoned, and is faithful to those who sleep below the earth. Who is like You who does such powerful things? Who else can cause death, restore life, and send great help?

M'chal-kel cha-yim b'chesed, m'cha-yei mei-tim b'ra-cha-mim ra-bim, so-meich no-f'lim, v'ro-fei cho-lim, u-ma-tir a-su-rim, u-m'ka-yeim emu-na-to li-shei-nei afar. Mi cha-mo-cha ba-al g'vu-rot, u-mi do-meh lach, melech mei-mit u-m'cha-yeh u-mats-mi-ach y'shu-ah.

מְכַלְכֵּל חַיִּים בְּחֶסֶד, מְחַיֵּה מֵתִים בְּרַחֲמִים רַבִּים, סוֹמֵךְ נוֹפְלִים, וְרוֹפֵא חוֹלִים, וּמַתִּיר אֲסוּרִים, וּמְקַיֵּם אֱמוּנָתוֹ לִישֵׁנֵי עָפָר. מִי כָמוֹךָ בַּעַל גְּבוּרוֹת, וּמִי דוֹמֶה לָּךְ, מֶלֶךְ מֵמִית וּמְחַיֶּה וּמַצְמִיחַ יְשׁוּעָה.

NOTE: From Rosh Hashanah to Yom Kippur we add in the following line:

Who is like You, Compassionate Father, Who remembers with compassion those He has created for life.

Mi cha-mo-cha Av Ha-racha-mim, zo-cheir y'tsu-rav l'cha-yim b'ra-cha-mim.

מִי כָמוֹךָ אַב הָרַחֲמִים, זוֹכֵר יְצוּרָיו לְחַיִּים בְּרַחֲמִים.

You are trustworthy to restore life to the deceased. You, Adonoy, Source of all blessing, revive the deceased.

V'ne-eman atah l'ha-cha-yot mei-tim. Baruch atah Adonoy, m'cha-yei ha-mei-tim.

וְנֶאֱמָן אַתָּה לְהַחֲיוֹת מֵתִים. בָּרוּךְ אַתָּה יי, מְחַיֵּה הַמֵּתִים.

The Third Blessing: Hashem's Holiness

> *Kavanah: Holiness means achieving closeness to Hashem and imbuing everything we do with a higher purpose, G-d's purpose. Hashem, help me to be holy today.*

You, Hashem, are holy and Your name is holy. We, the holy People, praise You every day, for You are great and holy. ***You, Adonoy, Source of all blessings, are the holy G-d.

Atah ka-dosh v'shim-cha ka-dosh u-k'do-shim b'chol yom y'ha-l'lu-cha selah.
***Baruch atah Adonoy, ha-El ha-ka-dosh.

אַתָּה קָדוֹשׁ וְשִׁמְךָ קָדוֹשׁ וּקְדוֹשִׁים בְּכָל יוֹם יְהַלְלוּךָ סֶּלָה.
***בָּרוּךְ אַתָּה יי, הָאֵל הַקָּדוֹשׁ.

 NOTE: *** From Rosh Hashanah to Yom Kippur, substitute the following concluding blessing instead.

You, Adonoy, Source of all blessings, are the Holy Master of the World.

Baruch atah Adonoy, ha-Melech ha-ka-dosh.

בָּרוּךְ אַתָּה יי, הַמֶּלֶךְ הַקָּדוֹשׁ.

The Central Blessing for Shabbat Morning: The Holiness of Shabbat

Kavanah: *Shabbat is Hashem's special gift to the Jewish people. We keep the Shabbat and the Shabbat "keeps" us. It reminds us of whom we are and that we are Hashem's special people, chosen from all others for a special purpose, just like the Shabbat.*

Moshe rejoiced in his gift (for he was chosen to receive the tablets). **You, Hashem, called him Your faithful servant. You placed a crown of splendor on his head when he stood before You on Mount Sinai. He brought the two sapphire tablets down from the mountain** (on Shabbat Morning) **and upon them was written the commandment to observe the Shabbat.**

So it is written in Your Torah (Exodus 31:16-17), **"And the Children of Israel shall observe the Shabbat, to make the Shabbat an eternal covenant** (between them and G-d) **for all generations. Between Me** (i.e., Hashem) **and the Children of Israel, it is an eternal sign that in six days Hashem made the heavens and the Earth and on the Seventh Day He rested and infused it with the spirituality of an extra soul and additional spirituality."**

Yis-mach Mosheh b'mat-nat chel-ko, ki eved ne-eman ka-ra-ta lo. K'lil tif-eret b'ro-sho na-ta-ta lo, b'am-do l'fa-necha al Har Sinai u-sh'nei lu-chot ava-nim ho-rid b'ya-do, v'cha-tuv ba-hem sh'mi-rat Shabbat. V'chein ka-tuv b'Tora-techa.	יִשְׂמַח מֹשֶׁה בְּמַתְּנַת חֶלְקוֹ, כִּי עֶבֶד נֶאֱמָן קָרָאתָ לוֹ. כְּלִיל תִּפְאֶרֶת בְּרֹאשׁוֹ נָתַתָּ לוֹ, בְּעָמְדוֹ לְפָנֶיךָ עַל הַר סִינַי. וּשְׁנֵי לוּחוֹת אֲבָנִים הוֹרִיד בְּיָדוֹ, וְכָתוּב בָּהֶם שְׁמִירַת שַׁבָּת. וְכֵן כָּתוּב בְּתוֹרָתֶךָ׃
"V'sham-ru v'nei Yisrael et ha-Shabat, la-asot et ha-Shabat l'do-ro-tam brit olam. Bei-ni u-vein b'nei Yisrael ot hi l'olam, ki shei-shet ya-mim asah Adonoy et ha-sha-mayim v'et ha-arets, u-va-yom ha-sh'vi-i sha-vat va-yi-na-fash."	וְשָׁמְרוּ בְנֵי יִשְׂרָאֵל אֶת הַשַּׁבָּת, לַעֲשׂוֹת אֶת הַשַּׁבָּת לְדֹרֹתָם בְּרִית עוֹלָם. בֵּינִי וּבֵין בְּנֵי יִשְׂרָאֵל אוֹת הִיא לְעוֹלָם, כִּי שֵׁשֶׁת יָמִים עָשָׂה יי אֶת הַשָּׁמַיִם וְאֶת הָאָרֶץ, וּבַיּוֹם הַשְּׁבִיעִי שָׁבַת וַיִּנָּפַשׁ׃

And You, Adonoy our G-d, did not give the Shabbat to the other nations on Earth, nor, Our King, did You give it to those who worship idolatry. The gentiles may not keep the special laws of the Day of Rest, for You have given it with love to Your People, Israel, the offspring of our forefather Yaakov, whom you have chosen from all others.

All who observe the Shabbat and call it a delight rejoice in Your Kingship. Those who make the seventh day holy shall find satisfaction and be delighted with Your goodness. You, Hashem, made the seventh day special and holy. You called it "the most coveted of days," for we remember the time of Creation.

V'lo n'ta-to Adonoy Elo-heinu l'go-yei ha-ara-tsot, v'lo hin-chal-to mal-kei-nu l'ov-dei f'si-lim, v'gam bi-m'nu-cha-to lo yish-k'nu a-rei-lim. Ki l'Yisrael am-cha n'ta-to b'a-ha-vah, l'zera Ya-akov asher bam ba-char-ta.

וְלֹא נְתַתּוֹ יי אֱלֹהֵינוּ לְגוֹיֵי הָאֲרָצוֹת, וְלֹא הִנְחַלְתּוֹ מַלְכֵּנוּ לְעוֹבְדֵי פְסִילִים, וְגַם בִּמְנוּחָתוֹ לֹא יִשְׁכְּנוּ עֲרֵלִים. כִּי לְיִשְׂרָאֵל עַמְּךָ נְתַתּוֹ בְּאַהֲבָה, לְזֶרַע יַעֲקֹב אֲשֶׁר בָּם בָּחָרְתָּ.

Am m'ka-d'shei sh'vi-i, ku-lam yis-b'u v'yit-an-gu mi-tu-vecha, u-va-sh'vi-i ra-tsi-ta bo v'ki-dash-to chem-dat ya-mim oto ka-ra-ta, zei-cher l'ma-asei v'rei-sheet.

עַם מְקַדְּשֵׁי שְׁבִיעִי, כֻּלָּם יִשְׂבְּעוּ וְיִתְעַנְּגוּ מִטּוּבֶךָ. וּבַשְּׁבִיעִי רָצִיתָ בּוֹ וְקִדַּשְׁתּוֹ חֶמְדַּת יָמִים אוֹתוֹ קָרָאתָ, זֵכֶר לְמַעֲשֵׂה בְרֵאשִׁית.

Our G-d and the G-d of our ancestors, be pleased with our Shabbat rest. Make us holy with Your mitzvot and make the Torah the center of our lives. Satisfy us with Your goodness and gladden us with Your help. Give us purity of heart to serve You sincerely.

Adonoy, our G-d, with love and with deep desire, give us Your holy Shabbat as our special heritage. May all of Israel, who sanctifies Your name, rest on Shabbat. You, Adonoy, Source of all blessings, make the Shabbat holy.

Elo-heinu vei-lo-hei avo-teinu, r'tsei na bi-m'nu-cha-teinu, ka-d'shei-nu b'mits-vo-techa, v'tein chel-kei-nu b'Tora-techa. Sa-bei-nu mi-tu-vecha, v'sam-chei-nu bi-shu-a-techa, v'ta-heir li-bei-nu l'av-d'cha ve-emet. V'han-chi-lei-nu Adonoy Elo-heinu b'a-ha-vah u-v'ra-tson Shabat ka-d'shecha, v'ya-nu-chu vo Yisrael m'ka-d'shei sh'mecha. Baruch atah Adonoy, m'ka-deish ha-Shabat.

אֱלֹהֵינוּ וֵאלֹהֵי אֲבוֹתֵינוּ, רְצֵה נָא בִמְנוּחָתֵנוּ, קַדְּשֵׁנוּ בְּמִצְוֹתֶיךָ, וְתֵן חֶלְקֵנוּ בְּתוֹרָתֶךָ, שַׂבְּעֵנוּ מִטּוּבֶךָ, וְשַׂמְּחֵנוּ בִּישׁוּעָתֶךָ, וְטַהֵר לִבֵּנוּ לְעָבְדְּךָ בֶּאֱמֶת, וְהַנְחִילֵנוּ יי אֱלֹהֵינוּ בְּאַהֲבָה וּבְרָצוֹן שַׁבַּת קָדְשֶׁךָ, וְיָנוּחוּ בוֹ יִשְׂרָאֵל מְקַדְּשֵׁי שְׁמֶךָ. בָּרוּךְ אַתָּה יי, מְקַדֵּשׁ הַשַּׁבָּת.

The Three Closing Blessings
Prayers of Thanks and Hope

First Closing Blessing: A Return of the Temple Service

> **Kavanah:** *We use prayer as a substitute for the Temple service of old.*
> *I am so far removed from the Temple that I can't even begin*
> *to understand what the service meant or how it worked.*
> *But I know that all who went to the Temple felt so close to Hashem.*
> *They felt tangible feelings of forgiveness and clarity of spirit and of purpose.*
> *I long for that closeness and that clarity and*
> *I know that You want this closeness, too.*

Adonoy, our G-d, please look with favor toward Your people, Israel, and listen to their prayers. Quickly restore the service to the Holy of Holies of Your Temple. Accept the offerings and prayers of Israel with love and always accept the service of Your people, Israel.

R'tsei Adonoy Elo-heinu b'am-cha Yisrael u-li-t'fi-la-tam, v'ha-sheiv et ha-avo-dah li-d'vir bei-techa. V'ishei Yisrael u-t'fi-la-tam b'ahavah t'ka-bel b'ra-tson, u-t'hi l'ra-tson ta-mid avo-dat Yisrael a-mecha.

רְצֵה יי אֱלֹהֵינוּ בְּעַמְּךָ יִשְׂרָאֵל וּלִתְפִלָּתָם, וְהָשֵׁב אֶת הָעֲבוֹדָה לִדְבִיר בֵּיתֶךָ. וְאִשֵּׁי יִשְׂרָאֵל וּתְפִלָּתָם בְּאַהֲבָה תְקַבֵּל בְּרָצוֹן, וּתְהִי לְרָצוֹן תָּמִיד עֲבוֹדַת יִשְׂרָאֵל עַמֶּךָ.

NOTE: Say this special paragraph on Rosh Chodesh, the first day(s) of the new Jewish month. The "first day" may be one day or two, depending on the month. See a Jewish calendar or check on the Internet to see the appropriate dates on the secular calendar.

🗣 Our G-d and the G-d of our ancestors, may your remembrance of us and our ancestors, and of the Mashiach, the offspring of King David Your servant, and of Jerusalem, Your holy city, and of all of your people, the House of Israel, rise up and reach, be noticed, accepted, heard, and remembered before You for deliverance, well-being, grace, kindness, and mercy, for life and peace on this day of Rosh Chodesh (the beginning of the new month).

Remember us today, Adonoy our G-d, for good, for blessings, and help provide us with good life. And with an act of redemption and compassion, have mercy on us, be gracious and merciful, and save us. For our eyes are looking to You, for You are the kind and compassionate Master of the World.

Elo-heinu vei-lo-hei avo-teinu, ya-a-le, v'ya-vo, v'ya-gi-a, v'yei-ra-eh, v'yei-ra-tseh, v'yi-sha-ma, v'yi-pa-keid, v'yi-za-cheir zich-ro-neinu u-fik-do-neinu, v'zich-ron avo-teinu, v'zich-ron Ma-shi-ach ben Da-vid av'decha, v'zich-ron Y'ru-shala-yim ir kad-she-cha, v'zich-ron kol am-cha Beit Yisrael l'fa-necha, lif-lei-tah l'to-vah, l'chein u-l'chesed u-l'ra-cha-mim, l'cha-yim u-l'sha-lom, b'yom Rosh ha-Cho-desh ha-zeh.

אֱלֹהֵינוּ וֵאלֹהֵי אֲבוֹתֵינוּ, יַעֲלֶה, וְיָבוֹא, וְיַגִּיעַ, וְיֵרָאֶה, וְיֵרָצֶה, וְיִשָּׁמַע, וְיִפָּקֵד, וְיִזָּכֵר זִכְרוֹנֵנוּ וּפִקְדוֹנֵנוּ, וְזִכְרוֹן אֲבוֹתֵינוּ, וְזִכְרוֹן מָשִׁיחַ בֶּן דָּוִד עַבְדֶּךָ, וְזִכְרוֹן יְרוּשָׁלַיִם עִיר קָדְשֶׁךָ, וְזִכְרוֹן כָּל עַמְּךָ בֵּית יִשְׂרָאֵל לְפָנֶיךָ, לִפְלֵיטָה לְטוֹבָה, לְחֵן וּלְחֶסֶד וּלְרַחֲמִים, לְחַיִּים וּלְשָׁלוֹם בְּיוֹם רֹאשׁ הַחֹדֶשׁ הַזֶּה.

Zach-reinu Adonoy Elo-heinu bo l'to-vah, u-fa-k'dei-nu vo livra-cha, v'ho-shi-einu vo l'cha-yim, u-vid-var y'shu-ah v'ra-cha-mim, chus v'cha-neinu v'ra-cheim alei-nu v'ho-shi-einu, ki ei-lecha ei-neinu, ki Eil Melech cha-nun v'ra-chum atah.

זָכְרֵנוּ יְיָ אֱלֹהֵינוּ בּוֹ לְטוֹבָה, וּפָקְדֵנוּ בוֹ לִבְרָכָה, וְהוֹשִׁיעֵנוּ בוֹ לְחַיִּים, וּבִדְבַר יְשׁוּעָה וְרַחֲמִים, חוּס וְחָנֵּנוּ וְרַחֵם עָלֵינוּ וְהוֹשִׁיעֵנוּ, כִּי אֵלֶיךָ עֵינֵינוּ, כִּי אֵל מֶלֶךְ חַנּוּן וְרַחוּם אָתָּה.

Let us see Your return to Zion (the Temple) with compassion. You, Adonoy, Source of all blessings, restore His presence to Zion.

V'te-che-zenah ei-neinu b'shu-v'cha l'Tsi-yon b'ra-cha-mim. Baruch atah Adonoy, hama-cha-zir sh'chi-nato l'Tsi-yon.

וְתֶחֱזֶינָה עֵינֵינוּ בְּשׁוּבְךָ לְצִיּוֹן בְּרַחֲמִים. בָּרוּךְ אַתָּה יְיָ, הַמַּחֲזִיר שְׁכִינָתוֹ לְצִיּוֹן.

Second Closing Blessing: Thank You, Hashem

Take a minute or two to review the following list and focus on the things for which you feel especially thankful today. Say, "Thank you, Hashem, for…."

- Life
- Health
- Intellect
- Sight
- Hearing
- Speech
- Movement
- Memories
- Freedom of Choice
- Making Me a Jew

- Parents
- Teachers
- Friends
- Grandparents
- Spouse
- Children
- Grandchildren
- Family
- Israel
- Peace

- My Jewish Soul
- Mitzvot
- Torah (which provides me with direction in life)
- The Ability to Talk to You
- Watching Over Me
- Making Me Your Partner in Creation
- A Place in the Next World (*Olam HaBa*)
- Wonders of Nature
- Material Possessions (home, car, clothes, furniture, heirlooms, books, etc.)
- Forgiveness
- Respect and Honor
- Personal Growth
- Meaning and Purpose
- The Desire to Be Good
- The Power to Change Things
- My Favorite Things
- A Way to Pay Expenses
- Personal Pleasure (physical, intellectual, emotional, and spiritual)
- Add in your own personal thoughts...

> **Kavanah:** *I have so much to be thankful for, every second of the day. I can't even begin to enumerate all the things that I have to be thankful for. And I know that Hashem gives it all to me.*

Bow at *Modim* and stand upright on *lach*.

We thank You, Adonoy, our eternal G-d and the G-d of our ancestors. You are the One we depend on in our lives, who shields us from one generation to the next. We thank You for our lives, which are in Your hands, for our souls, which are watched by You, for the miracles that You do for us every day, and for the wonders and good things that you do for us all the time — every evening, morning, and afternoon. You are the Source of goodness and compassion whose kindness never ends. We always put our hope in You.

Mo-dim a-nach-nu *lach* sha-atah hu Adonoy Elo-heinu vei-lo-hei avo-teinu l'olam va-ed.

Tsur cha-yeinu, ma-gein yish-einu atah hu l'dor va-dor. No-deh l'cha u-n'sa-peir t'hi-la-techa al cha-yeinu ha-m'su-rim b'ya-decha, v'al nish-mo-teinu ha-p'ku-dot lach, v'al ni-secha she-b'chol yom ima-nu, v'al nif-l'o-techa v'to-vo-techa she-b'chol eit, erev va-vo-ker v'tso-ha-ra-yim. Ha-tov ki lo cha-lu ra-cha-mecha v'ha-m'ra-cheim ki lo ta-mu cha-sa-decha mei-olam ki-vi-nu lach.

מוֹדִים אֲנַחְנוּ לָךְ שָׁאַתָּה הוּא יי אֱלֹהֵינוּ וֵאלֹהֵי אֲבוֹתֵינוּ לְעוֹלָם וָעֶד.

צוּר חַיֵּינוּ, מָגֵן יִשְׁעֵנוּ אַתָּה הוּא לְדוֹר וָדוֹר. נוֹדֶה לְּךָ וּנְסַפֵּר תְּהִלָּתֶךָ עַל חַיֵּינוּ הַמְּסוּרִים בְּיָדֶךָ, וְעַל נִשְׁמוֹתֵינוּ הַפְּקוּדוֹת לָךְ, וְעַל נִסֶּיךָ שֶׁבְּכָל יוֹם עִמָּנוּ, וְעַל נִפְלְאוֹתֶיךָ וְטוֹבוֹתֶיךָ שֶׁבְּכָל עֵת, עֶרֶב וָבֹקֶר וְצָהֳרָיִם. הַטּוֹב כִּי לֹא כָלוּ רַחֲמֶיךָ, וְהַמְרַחֵם כִּי לֹא תַמּוּ חֲסָדֶיךָ, מֵעוֹלָם קִוִּינוּ לָךְ.

For all of this, may You be acknowledged forever.

V'al ku-lam yit-ba-rach v'yit-ro-mam shim-cha Mal-keinu ta-mid l'olam va-ed.

וְעַל כֻּלָּם יִתְבָּרַךְ וְיִתְרוֹמַם שִׁמְךָ מַלְכֵּנוּ תָּמִיד לְעוֹלָם וָעֶד.

NOTE: Between Rosh Hashanah and Yom Kippur ADD the line:

Inscribe all of the children of Your covenant (i.e., all of the Jewish People) for good life.

U-ch'tov l'cha-yim tovim kol b'nei v'ri-techa.

וּכְתֹב לְחַיִּים טוֹבִים כָּל בְּנֵי בְרִיתֶךָ.

Bend knees on *Baruch*, bow on *atah*, and stand upright on *Adonoy*.

And all that lives will acknowledge You and will thank, praise, and bless You forever, for that is a good thing to do. Hashem, You are our help and salvation, the G-d of goodness. Adonoy, it is You, whose name is "The Good One," whom we should thank.

V'chol ha-cha-yim yo-du-cha selah,
vi-ha-l'lu et shim-cha be-emet.

Ha-El y'shu-a-teinu v'ez-ra-teinu selah.
Baruch atah Adonoy,
ha-tov shim-cha u-l'cha na-eh l'ho-dot.

וְכֹל הַחַיִּים יוֹדוּךָ סֶּלָה,
וִיהַלְלוּ אֶת שִׁמְךָ בֶּאֱמֶת.

הָאֵל יְשׁוּעָתֵנוּ וְעֶזְרָתֵנוּ סֶלָה.
בָּרוּךְ אַתָּה יְיָ,
הַטּוֹב שִׁמְךָ וּלְךָ נָאֶה לְהוֹדוֹת.

Third Closing Blessing: For Inner Peace and a Life of Goodness

> **Kavanah:** *Inner turmoil and strife within our Jewish family are the greatest blocks to a life of happiness and fulfillment. Help me to use the Torah and its values to achieve a life of inner and outer peace. I want to be a peaceful, kind person who brings goodness and peace to my people and to my world.*

Hashem, give us and all of Israel, Your people, peace, goodness, blessing, life, good favor, kindness, and compassion. Our Father, bless us all as one with Your special light. For with Your special light, You have given us the Torah, our instructions for living, and a love of kindness, righteousness, blessing, compassion, life, and peace. May You find it good to bless us and all of Israel,

Shabbat Morning Shemoneh Esrei

Your People, at all times with Your peace. *** You, Adonoy, Source of all blessings, bless Israel, His People, with peace.

Sim shalom, to-vah, u-v'ra-chah, chein, va-che-sed, v'ra-cha-mim alei-nu v'al kol Yisrael a-mecha. Bar-cheinu avi-nu, ku-la-nu k'echad b'or pa-necha. Ki v'or pa-necha na-ta-ta la-nu, Adonoy Elo-heinu, Torat cha-yim v'a-ha-vat che-sed, u-ts'da-kah, u-v'ra-chah, v'ra-cha-mim, v'cha-yim, v'sha-lom. V'tov b'ei-necha l'va-reich et kol am-cha Yisrael, b'chol eit u-v'chol sha-ah bi-sh'lo-mecha.

שִׂים שָׁלוֹם, טוֹבָה, וּבְרָכָה, חֵן, וָחֶסֶד, וְרַחֲמִים עָלֵינוּ וְעַל כָּל יִשְׂרָאֵל עַמֶּךָ. בָּרְכֵנוּ אָבִינוּ, כֻּלָּנוּ כְּאֶחָד בְּאוֹר פָּנֶיךָ. כִּי בְאוֹר פָּנֶיךָ נָתַתָּ לָּנוּ, יְיָ אֱלֹהֵינוּ, תּוֹרַת חַיִּים וְאַהֲבַת חֶסֶד, וּצְדָקָה, וּבְרָכָה, וְרַחֲמִים, וְחַיִּים, וְשָׁלוֹם. וְטוֹב בְּעֵינֶיךָ לְבָרֵךְ אֶת כָּל עַמְּךָ יִשְׂרָאֵל, בְּכָל עֵת וּבְכָל שָׁעָה בִּשְׁלוֹמֶךָ.

 NOTE: ***From Rosh Hashanah to Yom Kippur we conclude this blessing with the following paragraph, instead of the usual concluding blessing:

In the Book of Life, Blessing, Peace, and Good Livelihood, may we and all of the People of Israel, be remembered and inscribed for good life and peace. You, Adonoy, the Source of all Blessing, makes peace.

B'sei-fer chayim brachah v'shalom, u-far-nassah tovah, ni-za-cheir v'ni-ka-teiv l'fa-necha, a-nach-nu v'chol am-cha Beit Yisrael, l'chayim tovim, u-l'shalom. Baruch atah Adonoy, oseh ha-shalom.

בְּסֵפֶר חַיִּים בְּרָכָה וְשָׁלוֹם, וּפַרְנָסָה טוֹבָה, נִזָּכֵר וְנִכָּתֵב לְפָנֶיךָ, אֲנַחְנוּ וְכָל עַמְּךָ בֵּית יִשְׂרָאֵל, לְחַיִּים טוֹבִים וּלְשָׁלוֹם. בָּרוּךְ אַתָּה יְיָ, עֹשֵׂה הַשָּׁלוֹם.

On a regular day the Blessing for Peace concludes with this statement:

You, Adonoy, Source of all blessings, bless Israel, His people, with peace.

Baruch atah Adonoy, ha-m'va-reich et amo Yisrael ba-shalom.

בָּרוּךְ אַתָּה יְיָ, הַמְבָרֵךְ אֶת עַמּוֹ יִשְׂרָאֵל בַּשָּׁלוֹם.

A Request for Hashem's Help to Control Speech, Jealousy, and Anger

> **Kavanah:** *I have just used the power of speech that Hashem has given me to speak to Hashem ... to request His help, to pray for me and my people, to remember who I am, and to bring me closer to Hashem.*
> *But that same power, if used improperly, can be so damaging. Help me to channel the awesome power of speech only for good and not for slander, gossip, lying, or other words that are unbefitting for me.*
> *Help me to be humble, and not to be jealous or angry. And help me to be open to Hashem's Torah and mitzvot.*

My G-d, please guard my tongue from improper speech and my lips from lying. To those who curse me, let me keep silent and let me be like dust to everyone. Open my heart to Your Torah so that my soul will perform Your mitzvot. And, as for those who wish to harm me, quickly erase their ideas and their advice. Hashem, my G-d and the G-d of my ancestors, may it be Your will that none should be jealous of me, nor I of them; that I should not get angry today, nor should I do something to cause You to be angry with me. Save me from the Evil Inclination and put in my heart the desire for humility and submission. Hashem, our King and G-d, cause the entire world to recognize Your name, rebuild Your city (Jerusalem), build Your home (the Temple), gather Your exiled nation, and fill them with joy. Do this for Your sake, for Your Torah's sake, and for the sake of Your holiness. As the verse in Psalms says, "So that Your beloved ones may rest, let Your hand of kindness save us and respond to me."

Elo-hai, n'tsor l'sho-ni mei-ra, u-s'fa-tai mi-da-beir mir-mah, v'lim-ka-l'lai naf-shi ti-dom, v'naf-shi ke-a-far la-kol ti-h'yeh. P'tach li-bi b'Tora-techa, u-v'mits-vo-techa tir-dof naf-shi. V'chol ha-chosh-vim a-lai ra-ah, m'hei-rah ha-feir atsa-tam v'kal-kel ma-cha-shav-tam.

אֱלֹהַי, נְצוֹר לְשׁוֹנִי מֵרָע, וּשְׂפָתַי מִדַּבֵּר מִרְמָה, וְלִמְקַלְלַי נַפְשִׁי תִדֹּם, וְנַפְשִׁי כֶּעָפָר לַכֹּל תִּהְיֶה. פְּתַח לִבִּי בְּתוֹרָתֶךָ, וּבְמִצְוֹתֶיךָ תִּרְדּוֹף נַפְשִׁי. וְכָל הַחוֹשְׁבִים עָלַי רָעָה, מְהֵרָה הָפֵר עֲצָתָם וְקַלְקֵל מַחֲשַׁבְתָּם.

Asei l'ma-an sh'mecha, asei l'ma-an y'mi-necha, asei l'ma'an k'du-sha-techa, asei l'ma-an Tora-techa. L'ma-an yei-chal-tsun y'di-decha, ho-shi-ah y'min-cha va-anei-ni.

עֲשֵׂה לְמַעַן שְׁמֶךָ, עֲשֵׂה לְמַעַן יְמִינֶךָ, עֲשֵׂה לְמַעַן קְדֻשָּׁתֶךָ, עֲשֵׂה לְמַעַן תּוֹרָתֶךָ. לְמַעַן יֵחָלְצוּן יְדִידֶיךָ, הוֹשִׁיעָה יְמִינְךָ וַעֲנֵנִי.

Let my words and the thoughts in my heart be acceptable to You, G-d, my Redeemer, upon whom I rely. May He, who makes peace in the heavens, make peace upon us and upon all of Israel; and let us say, Amein (that is, I believe this to be the truth).

Yi-h'yu l'ra-tson im-rei fi v'he-g'yon li-bi l'fa-necha. Adonoy tsu-ri v'go-ali.

יִהְיוּ לְרָצוֹן אִמְרֵי פִי וְהֶגְיוֹן לִבִּי לְפָנֶיךָ. יְיָ צוּרִי וְגוֹאֲלִי.

Oseh shalom bi-m'ro-mav, hu ya-aseh shalom alei-nu, v'al kol Yisrael. V'im-ru, Amein.

עֹשֶׂה שָׁלוֹם בִּמְרוֹמָיו, הוּא יַעֲשֶׂה שָׁלוֹם עָלֵינוּ, וְעַל כָּל יִשְׂרָאֵל. וְאִמְרוּ: אָמֵן.

 Take three steps back and bow slightly to the left, right, and center as if taking leave from the king.

The Final Stanza — Rebuild the Temple

> **Kavanah:** *The prayer that I have just finished takes the place of the Temple service. But it is merely a temporary replacement.*
> *We ask you, Hashem, to rebuild the Temple where we will achieve clarity of purpose and of truth and where we will achieve a real and everlasting closeness to You.*
> *Help us to learn Torah and fulfill the mitzvot.*

Adonoy, our G-d and the G-d of our ancestors, may it be Your will that You rebuild the Temple speedily in our days and make the Torah the center of our lives. Then we will serve You with reverence as we did in previous times. And the offerings of Judah and Jerusalem will be pleasing to You as they were in the days of old.

Y'hi ra-tson mil-fa-necha, Adonoy Elo-heinu vei-lo-hei avo-teinu. She-yiba-neh Beit ha-Mik-dash bim-hei-rah v'ya-meinu. V'tein chel-keinu b'Tora-techa v'sham na-ava-d'cha b'yir-ah ki-mei olam u-ch'sha-nim kad-mo-ni-yot. V'ar-vah lado-noy min-chat Yehudah vi-ru-sha-la-yim, ki-mei olam u-ch'sha-nim kad-mo-ni-yot.

יְהִי רָצוֹן מִלְּפָנֶיךָ יְיָ אֱלֹהֵינוּ וֵאלֹהֵי אֲבוֹתֵינוּ. שֶׁיִּבָּנֶה בֵּית הַמִּקְדָּשׁ בִּמְהֵרָה בְיָמֵינוּ. וְתֵן חֶלְקֵנוּ בְּתוֹרָתֶךָ וְשָׁם נַעֲבָדְךָ בְּיִרְאָה כִּימֵי עוֹלָם וּכְשָׁנִים קַדְמוֹנִיּוֹת. וְעָרְבָה לַיְיָ מִנְחַת יְהוּדָה וִירוּשָׁלָיִם, כִּימֵי עוֹלָם וּכְשָׁנִים קַדְמוֹנִיּוֹת.

Step 5. The Concluding Prayers: Taking the Prayers into Our Daily Lives

Introduction: After a tough workout, all trainers advise people to "cool down" before getting back to their everyday activities. It is the same with a spiritual "workout." Are we simply to step away from an intense conversation with the Master of the World and then hop in our cars and speed off to work? Go to dinner with our friends? Go off to sleep?

So rather than just run, we "cool down" by saying a small number of prayers that give us strength until the next prayer service and enable us to integrate the prayers into our lives. Often these prayers are said in song to keep us vitalized with *simchah* (joy), joy in knowing that we have a relationship with Hashem. The joy of knowing that we have a direction and that we are on the right path to a meaningful life.

First Concluding Prayer: *Ein Keloheinu*

Introduction: We look towards Hashem and see His effect upon our lives in many ways. Each name we give Hashem refers to a specific attribute of His in our world. This song contains four of the many Hebrew names that we use to refer to Hashem.

"G-d" (i.e., *Elohim* ; *Eloheinu*, our G-d) refers to Hashem as the hidden life force of the world. It also means G-d from whom we derive our strength.

"Master" (i.e., *Adonoy* ; *Adoneinu*, our Master) refers to Hashem as the Master over the rules of nature, the orderly nature of the world.

"King" (i.e., *Melech* ; *Malkeinu*, our King) refers to Hashem as the One whom we follow. In return He provides for all our needs.

"The One Who Saves" (i.e., *Moshia*; *Moshieinu*) refers to Hashem as the One we turn to in times of trouble.

> **Kavanah:** *There is nothing even remotely close to Hashem. Why would I ever think that the fulfillment of my hopes and dreams would come from anywhere or anyone else? I just need to remind myself of this. This gives me hope. It keeps me strong.*

There is none like our G-d, none like our Master, none like our King, none like Hashem, the One Who Saves.

Who is like our G-d, who is like our Master, who is like our King, who is like Hashem, the One Who Saves.

Let us thank our G-d, let us thank our Master, let us thank our King, let us thank Hashem, the One Who Saves.

The Source of all blessing is our G-d, the Source of all blessing is our Master, the Source of all blessing is our King, and the Source of all blessing is Hashem, the One Who Saves.

 You are our G-d, You are our Master, You are our King, You, Hashem, are the One Who Saves.

Ein ke-lo-heinu, ein ka-do-neinu, *ein k'mal-keinu, ein k'mo-shi-einu.*	אֵין כֵּאלֹהֵינוּ, אֵין כַּאדוֹנֵינוּ, אֵין כְּמַלְכֵּנוּ, אֵין כְּמוֹשִׁיעֵנוּ.
Mi chei-lo-heinu, mi cha-do-neinu, *mi ch'mal-keinu, mi ch'mo-shi-einu.*	מִי כֵאלֹהֵינוּ, מִי כַאדוֹנֵינוּ, מִי כְמַלְכֵּנוּ, מִי כְמוֹשִׁיעֵנוּ.
No-deh lei-lo-heinu, no-deh la-do-neinu, *no-deh l'mal-keinu, no-deh l'mo-shi-einu.*	נוֹדֶה לֵאלֹהֵינוּ, נוֹדֶה לַאדוֹנֵינוּ, נוֹדֶה לְמַלְכֵּנוּ, נוֹדֶה לְמוֹשִׁיעֵנוּ.
Baruch Elo-heinu, baruch Ado-neinu, *baruch Mal-keinu, baruch Mo-shi-einu.*	בָּרוּךְ אֱלֹהֵינוּ, בָּרוּךְ אֲדוֹנֵינוּ, בָּרוּךְ מַלְכֵּנוּ, בָּרוּךְ מוֹשִׁיעֵנוּ.
Atah hu Elo-heinu, atah hu Ado-neinu, *atah hu Mal-keinu, atah hu Mo-shi-einu.*	אַתָּה הוּא אֱלֹהֵינוּ, אַתָּה הוּא אֲדוֹנֵינוּ, אַתָּה הוּא מַלְכֵּנוּ, אַתָּה הוּא מוֹשִׁיעֵנוּ
Atah hu she-hik-ti-ru avo-teinu l'fa-necha *et k'to-ret ha-sa-mim.*	אַתָּה הוּא שֶׁהִקְטִירוּ אֲבוֹתֵינוּ לְפָנֶיךָ אֶת קְטֹרֶת הַסַּמִּים.

Second Concluding Prayer: *Aleinu*
Hashem is the One and Only True G-d

 Introduction: This prayer was written more than 3,200 years ago by Joshua to help the Jewish People remember that they were different from the seven Canaanite pagan nations that inhabited the Land of Israel at that time. It took on even greater significance as a central prayer in the Rosh Hashanah and Yom Kippur prayers. Throughout history, its significance grew as it served as the "anthem prayer" of the Jews during the Christian Crusades and the terribly difficult times that the Jews of Europe endured under their Christian overlords. As such, parts or all of the prayer were censored from the siddur. It is often sung as a marching song to give strength to the Jewish People.

> **Kavanah:** *We sing for the privilege of being part of the Jewish People, whose mission is to better the world through the knowledge and understanding of Hashem.*

It is our duty to praise Hashem, the Master of all things. He, who created all things, has not made us like the nations of other lands and placed us in the same position as the other families on earth. He has not given us a portion similar to theirs, nor is our lot like that of the large empires. For they bow to nothing but emptiness and pray to gods that do not help.

Bow on *bow* and stand upright on *thank*.

But we bend our knees, bow, and thank the King who reigns over kings, the Holy One, the Source of all blessings, He who created the heavens and laid the earth's foundations. Hashem's seat is in the heavens above and His powerful presence dwells in the highest heights. He is our G-d. There is no other. Ours is the true King. There is nothing beside Hashem, as it is written in His Torah: "And you are to know this day and take it to heart, that Hashem is the only G-d in the heavens above and on the earth below. There is no other." And it is said, "Hashem will be the King over all of the world. On that day Hashem will be One and His name will be One."

Alei-nu l'sha-bei-ach la-a-don ha-kol,   עָלֵינוּ לְשַׁבֵּחַ לַאֲדוֹן הַכֹּל,
la-teit g'du-lah l'yo-tseir b'rei-sheet,   לָתֵת גְּדֻלָּה לְיוֹצֵר בְּרֵאשִׁית,
she-lo asa-nu k'go-yei ha-ara-tsot,   שֶׁלֹּא עָשָׂנוּ כְּגוֹיֵי הָאֲרָצוֹת,
v'lo sa-ma-nu k'mish-p'chot ha-ada-mah,   וְלֹא שָׂמָנוּ כְּמִשְׁפְּחוֹת הָאֲדָמָה,
she-lo sam chel-kei-nu ka-hem   שֶׁלֹּא שָׂם חֶלְקֵנוּ כָּהֶם וְגוֹרָלֵנוּ כְּכָל הֲמוֹנָם.
v'go-ra-lei-nu k'chol ha-mo-nam.
She-heim mish-tacha-vim l'he-vel v'rik,   שֶׁהֵם מִשְׁתַּחֲוִים לְהֶבֶל וָרִיק,
u-mit-pa-l'lim el el lo yo-shi-a.   וּמִתְפַּלְלִים אֶל אֵל לֹא יוֹשִׁיעַ.

Bow on *korim* and stand upright on *u-modim*.

Va-a-nach-nu kor-im u-mish-ta-cha-vim u-mo-dim, lif-nei Melech mal-chei ha-m'la-chim ha-Kadosh Baruch Hu.

וַאֲנַחְנוּ כּוֹרְעִים וּמִשְׁתַּחֲוִים וּמוֹדִים, לִפְנֵי מֶלֶךְ מַלְכֵי הַמְּלָכִים הַקָּדוֹשׁ בָּרוּךְ הוּא.

She-hu no-teh sha-ma-yim v'yo-seid arets, u-mo-shav y'ka-ro ba-sha-ma-yim mi-ma-al, u-sh'chi-nat u-zo b'gav-hei m'ro-mim. Hu Elo-heinu, ein od.

שֶׁהוּא נוֹטֶה שָׁמַיִם וְיוֹסֵד אָרֶץ, וּמוֹשַׁב יְקָרוֹ בַּשָּׁמַיִם מִמַּעַל, וּשְׁכִינַת עֻזּוֹ בְּגָבְהֵי מְרוֹמִים. הוּא אֱלֹהֵינוּ, אֵין עוֹד.

Emet Mal-keinu, efes zu-la-to, ka-ka-tuv b'Tora-to: V'ya-da-ta ha-yom, va-ha-shei-vo-ta el l'va-vecha, ki Adonoy hu ha-Elo-him ba-sha-ma-yim mi-ma-al v'al ha-arets mi-ta-chat, ein od.

אֱמֶת מַלְכֵּנוּ, אֶפֶס זוּלָתוֹ, כַּכָּתוּב בְּתוֹרָתוֹ: וְיָדַעְתָּ הַיּוֹם וַהֲשֵׁבֹתָ אֶל לְבָבֶךָ, כִּי יְיָ הוּא הָאֱלֹהִים בַּשָּׁמַיִם מִמַּעַל וְעַל הָאָרֶץ מִתַּחַת, אֵין עוֹד.

V'ne-emar, v'ha-yah Adonoy l'Melech al kol ha-arets ba-yom ha-hu yi-h'yeh Adonoy echad u-sh'mo echad.

וְנֶאֱמַר: וְהָיָה יְיָ לְמֶלֶךְ עַל כָּל הָאָרֶץ בַּיּוֹם הַהוּא יִהְיֶה יְיָ אֶחָד וּשְׁמוֹ אֶחָד.

Third Concluding Prayer: *Hayom* Counting the Days of the Week

Introduction: In the fourth of the "Ten Commandments" (the actual translation is "The Ten Statements"), we are instructed to "Remember the Shabbat to keep it Holy." There are different ways to remember the Shabbat. One way that has been instituted is to count each day towards the upcoming Shabbat. We also count each day to remind us that each day counts. Each day is unique, one in world history. This day will never occur again. We do this at this point in the morning prayers each day.

> **Kavanah:** *I have important work to do each day* but *still I look forward to Shabbat. The vision of Shabbat gives me strength. But it also tells me that time is short. I have to make every day count. Today will never happen again, so I must make it count. I must make some important difference today, even a small one.*

Today is the Holy Shabbat.

Ha-yom yom Sha-bat ko-desh.

הַיּוֹם יוֹם שַׁבָּת קוֹדֶשׁ.

Mourner's Kaddish

If a mourner is present and there is a *minyan* of ten Jewish men, the mourner leads the congregation in the public declaration of our dreams and aspirations for the world at large. The congregants say the parts in bold or italics in response to the mourner's prayer.

NOTE: If there are multiple mourners, Kaddish should be recited out loud, slowly and *together*, just like a choir would sing together. It is a good idea for the mourners to stand near each other when they lead this prayer and to follow the lead of one designated person, so that they lead this prayer in unison.

> Kavanah: *The mourners bring tremendous merit to the ones whose loss is being mourned by causing the entire congregation to focus on the goals and values of the Jewish People, namely, to lead humanity to its ultimate state of perfection, in peace and harmony with Hashem and with all Creation, with the coming of the era of Mashiach.*

May all people declare the greatness and holiness of Hashem's name (the congregation responds: *Amein*) in the world which He created.

May Hashem speedily cause His kingship and salvation to blossom and bring Mashiach, in your lifetime and in the lifetime of the entire Jewish People. And let us respond: *Amein*.

(All say together: **May Hashem be recognized as the Source of blessing forever**.)

And may all of creation stand in awe of Hashem and praise the Name of the Holy One, Blessed is He. (The congregation responds: **He is the Source of all blessing**.)

With expressions of song and praise beyond all that have ever been uttered on earth. And let us respond: *Amein*.

And may there be peace bestowed from Heaven and good life for us and all of Israel. And let us respond: *Amein*.

May He who makes peace in the Heavens, make peace upon us and all of Israel. And let us respond: *Amein*.

Shabbat Morning Shemoneh Esrei

Yit-ga-dal v'yit-ka-dash sh'mei ra-ba. **Amein.**	יִתְגַּדַּל וְיִתְקַדַּשׁ שְׁמֵהּ רַבָּא. **אָמֵן.**
B'al-ma di v'ra chir-u-tei v'yam-lich mal-chu-tei, b'cha-yei-chon u-v'yo-mei-chon u-v'cha-yei d'chol beit Yisrael, ba-aga-la u-vi-z'man ka-riv. V'imru: **Amein.**	בְּעָלְמָא דִּי בְרָא כִרְעוּתֵהּ וְיַמְלִיךְ מַלְכוּתֵהּ, בְּחַיֵּיכוֹן וּבְיוֹמֵיכוֹן וּבְחַיֵּי דְכָל בֵּית יִשְׂרָאֵל, בַּעֲגָלָא וּבִזְמַן קָרִיב. וְאִמְרוּ: **אָמֵן.**
Y'hei sh'mei ra-ba m'va-rach l'alam u-l'al-mei al-ma-ya.	יְהֵא שְׁמֵהּ רַבָּא מְבָרַךְ לְעָלַם וּלְעָלְמֵי עָלְמַיָּא.
Yit-ba-rach v'yish-ta-bach v'yit-pa-ar v'yit-ro-mam v'yit-na-sei v'yit-ha-dar v'yit-aleh v'yit-ha-lal sh'mei d'ku-d'sha. **B'rich hu. B'rich hu.**	יִתְבָּרַךְ וְיִשְׁתַּבַּח וְיִתְפָּאַר וְיִתְרוֹמַם וְיִתְנַשֵּׂא וְיִתְהַדָּר וְיִתְעַלֶּה וְיִתְהַלָּל שְׁמֵהּ דְּקֻדְשָׁא. **בְּרִיךְ הוּא. בְּרִיךְ הוּא.**
L'ei-la min kol bir-cha-ta v'shi-ra-ta tush-b'cha-ta v'ne-chema-ta da-ami-ran b'al-ma. V'imru: **Amein.**	לְעֵלָּא מִן כָּל בִּרְכָתָא וְשִׁירָתָא תֻּשְׁבְּחָתָא וְנֶחֱמָתָא דַּאֲמִירָן בְּעָלְמָא. וְאִמְרוּ: **אָמֵן.**
Y'hei sh'la-ma ra-ba min sh'ma-ya v'cha-yim alei-nu v'al kol Yisrael. V'imru: **Amein.**	יְהֵא שְׁלָמָא רַבָּא מִן שְׁמַיָּא וְחַיִּים עָלֵינוּ וְעַל כָּל יִשְׂרָאֵל. וְאִמְרוּ: **אָמֵן.**
Oseh shalom bi-m'ro-mav hu ya-aseh shalom alei-nu v'al kol Yisrael v'imru: **Amein.**	עוֹשֶׂה שָׁלוֹם בִּמְרוֹמָיו הוּא יַעֲשֶׂה שָׁלוֹם עָלֵינוּ וְעַל כָּל יִשְׂרָאֵל וְאִמְרוּ: **אָמֵן.**

Fourth Concluding Prayer: *Adon Olam*

Introduction: This is a very deep poem written more than a thousand years ago. It contains the theme that Hashem is so great, so powerful – we cannot even begin to comprehend such greatness. Who can possibly comprehend such concepts as timelessness, infinity, the unlimited All-Powerful One, the concept of creation from nothing? Yet with all this, Hashem is still involved intimately in the details of our daily lives, with all of our personal needs, and walks together with us.

> **Kavanah:** *There are many things that I can't understand*
> *and will never comprehend about Hashem.*
> *But I do know that Hashem is with me in every step that I take.*
> *So I will go out with confidence to do what I have to do.*
> *And I will have no fear.*

Master of the World, who reigned before all creation,
At the time when His Will created all form,
He was then proclaimed as the Ruler.
And after all may cease to be, He, the awesome One, will rule alone.
He was, He is, and He will be forever, in Splendor.
He is One; there is no other who can compare to Hashem.
He is without beginning and without end. He holds all the power.
And He is my G-d, my living redeemer, the one I rely upon in my time of trouble.
Hashem is my banner, a place of refuge for me, my cup's fill when I call to Him.
I will trust my spirit in His hand when I go to sleep and when I awake.
Hashem is with me. I shall not fear.

Adon olam asher ma-lach,
b'te-rem kol y'tsir niv-ra,
l'eit na-asah v'chef-tso kol,
a-zai me-lech sh'mo nik'ra.

V'a-cha-rei kich-lot ha-kol,
l'va-do yim-loch no-ra,
v'hu ha-yah v'hu ho-veh,
v'hu yi-h'yeh b'tif-a-rah.

V'hu echad v'ein shei-ni,
l'ham-shil lo l'hach-bi-rah,
b'li rei-sheet b'li tach-lit,
v'lo ha-oz v'ha-mis-rah.

V'hu ei-li v'chai go-a-li,
v'tsur chev-li b'eit tsa-rah,
v'hu ni-si u-ma-nos li,
m'nat ko-si b'yom ek-ra.

B'ya-do af-kid ru-chi,
b'eit ishan v'a-irah,
v'im ru-chi g'vi-ya-ti,
Adonoy li v'lo i-ra.

אֲדוֹן עוֹלָם אֲשֶׁר מָלַךְ,
בְּטֶרֶם כָּל יְצִיר נִבְרָא.
לְעֵת נַעֲשָׂה בְחֶפְצוֹ כֹּל,
אֲזַי מֶלֶךְ שְׁמוֹ נִקְרָא.

וְאַחֲרֵי כִּכְלוֹת הַכֹּל,
לְבַדּוֹ יִמְלוֹךְ נוֹרָא.
וְהוּא הָיָה וְהוּא הֹוֶה,
וְהוּא יִהְיֶה בְּתִפְאָרָה.

וְהוּא אֶחָד וְאֵין שֵׁנִי,
לְהַמְשִׁיל לוֹ לְהַחְבִּירָה.
בְּלִי רֵאשִׁית בְּלִי תַכְלִית,
וְלוֹ הָעֹז וְהַמִּשְׂרָה.

וְהוּא אֵלִי וְחַי גּוֹאֲלִי,
וְצוּר חֶבְלִי בְּעֵת צָרָה.
וְהוּא נִסִּי וּמָנוֹס לִי,
מְנָת כּוֹסִי בְּיוֹם אֶקְרָא.

בְּיָדוֹ אַפְקִיד רוּחִי,
בְּעֵת אִישָׁן וְאָעִירָה.
וְעִם רוּחִי גְּוִיָּתִי,
יְיָ לִי וְלֹא אִירָא.

  Smile and say, "Shabbat Shalom!"

The Personal Daily Psalm

Some have the tradition of reciting their personal Daily Psalm after the morning prayers each day or at some time during the day. Your personal Psalm is the Psalm number of your age plus one, so someone who is twenty-eight years old recites Psalm 29 every day until his next Jewish birthday. When he turns twenty-nine, he switches to Psalm 30 for every day of the following year, and so on. If you aren't certain of your Jewish birthday, check one of the numerous Jewish calendar converter programs on the Internet, such as the one at chabad.org.

THE WEEKDAY MORNING *SHEMONEH ESREI*

Step 4. A Personal Conversation with G-d

The Weekday *Shemoneh Esrei* is the central part of the weekday prayers. It is said standing, with our feet together, facing Jerusalem, from where our prayers are taken by angels (i.e., spiritual messengers) to the heavens. In Jerusalem, one faces the Temple Mount, the original point of creation upon which the two Jewish Temples stood in ancient times.

If one cannot stand for whatever reason, this prayer can be recited while sitting or lying down. In any case, the words should be whispered so that they become real (i.e., sound waves), but still approach the closest thing to pure, focused thought.

> **Kavanah:** *I am now going to pray the most important part of the prayers. I am about to stand and address Hashem directly. These nineteen blessings, plus a closing prayer, include all of the things that I need and that the Jewish People, my people, need. And when Hashem gives me what I need, I will use these gifts for good.*

Take three small steps backward and then three small steps forward, and bear in mind that you are approaching Hashem directly with a series of requests and acknowledgements.

Introductory Request

> **Kavanah:** *It is difficult to* daven.
> *Hashem, please help me to* daven *and to get closer to You.*

Hashem, please help me overcome my limitations, so that I can say Your praises.

Adonoy s'fa-tai tif-tach, u-fi ya-gid t'hi-la-techa. אֲדֹנָי שְׂפָתַי תִּפְתָּח, וּפִי יַגִּיד תְּהִלָּתֶךָ.

Beginning the Deepest Dialogue – The First Three Blessings: To Whom Are We Speaking?

The First Blessing: The Blessing of the Fathers

> **Kavanah:** *We are not strangers to Hashem nor is He to us. We are the children and the living legacy of those in the world who first recognized Hashem and stood up for this belief. Hashem shielded them from all their trials in life and made an eternal covenant with them and their children, including me.*

Bow on *Baruch*, bend your knees on *atah*, and stand upright on *Adonoy*.

You, Hashem, Source of all blessings, are our G-d and the G-d of our forefathers, the G-d of Avraham, the G-d of Yitzchak, and the G-d of Yaakov. The great, powerful, and awesome G-d who is beyond comprehension, bestows kindness, and creates all things. You remember the kindness of our forefathers and send loving redemption to their children, for His name's sake.

Baruch atah Adonoy Elo-heinu vei-lo-hei avo-tei-nu, Elo-hei Avra-ham, Elo-hei Yits-chak, vei-lo-hei Ya-a-kov, ha-El ha-Gadol ha-Gibor v'ha-Nora, El El-yon, go-mel cha-sa-dim to-vim v'ko-nei ha-kol, v'zo-cheir chas-dei avot, u-mei-vi go-el liv-nei v'nei-hem, l'ma-an sh'mo b'a-ha-vah.

בָּרוּךְ אַתָּה יי אֱלֹהֵינוּ וֵאלֹהֵי אֲבוֹתֵינוּ, אֱלֹהֵי אַבְרָהָם, אֱלֹהֵי יִצְחָק, וֵאלֹהֵי יַעֲקֹב, הָאֵל הַגָּדוֹל הַגִּבּוֹר וְהַנּוֹרָא, אֵל עֶלְיוֹן, גּוֹמֵל חֲסָדִים טוֹבִים וְקוֹנֵה הַכֹּל, וְזוֹכֵר חַסְדֵי אָבוֹת, וּמֵבִיא גוֹאֵל לִבְנֵי בְנֵיהֶם, לְמַעַן שְׁמוֹ בְּאַהֲבָה.

NOTE: On the days between Rosh Hashanah and Yom Kippur ADD the line:

Remember us for life, Master of the World who wants life. Inscribe us in the Book of Life for Your sake, oh living G-d.

Zach-rei-nu l'cha-yim, Melech cha-feits ba-cha-yim, v'chat-veinu b'sei-fer ha-cha-yim, l'ma-an-cha Elo-him cha-yim.

זָכְרֵנוּ לְחַיִּים, מֶלֶךְ חָפֵץ בַּחַיִּים, וְכָתְבֵנוּ בְּסֵפֶר הַחַיִּים, לְמַעַנְךָ אֱלֹהִים חַיִּים.

Bow on *Baruch*, bend your knees on *atah*, and stand upright on *Adonoy*.

You are the Master of the World, who helps us, saves us, and protects us. I acknowledge that You, Adonoy, Source of all blessings, are the protector of our forefather Avraham (and his children).

Melech o-zeir u-mo-shi-a u-ma-gein.
Baruch atah Adonoy, ma-gein Avra-ham.

מֶלֶךְ עוֹזֵר וּמוֹשִׁיעַ וּמָגֵן.
בָּרוּךְ אַתָּה יי, מָגֵן אַבְרָהָם.

The Second Blessing: Hashem's Power

Kavanah: *Hashem is the Source of life and determines who will live, who will die, and who will live again in the future.*

You, Hashem, have the power of life and death. You have the power to revive those who are deceased and to save again and again.

Atah gi-bor l'olam Adonoy, m'cha-yei mei-tim atah rav l'ho-shi-a.

אַתָּה גִּבּוֹר לְעוֹלָם אֲדֹנָי, מְחַיֵּה מֵתִים אַתָּה רַב לְהוֹשִׁיעַ.

 NOTE: Between Sh'mini Atseret (the day before Simchat Torah) and Pesach, add this phrase.

Who makes the wind blow and the rain fall,

Ma-shiv ha-ru-ach u-mo-rid ha-ga-shem.

מַשִּׁיב הָרוּחַ וּמוֹרִיד הַגֶּשֶׁם.

Who sustains us with kindness, who revives the deceased with compassion (e.g., people who sleep, plants that wither), who supports those who have fallen, provides healing for the sick, freedom for the imprisoned, and who is faithful to those who sleep below the earth. Who is like You who does such powerful things? Who else can cause death, restore life, and send great help?

M'chal-kel cha-yim b'che-sed, m'cha-yei mei-tim b'ra-cha-mim ra-bim, so-meich nof-lim, v'ro-fei cho-lim, u-ma-tir asu-rim, u-m'ka-yeim emu-na-to li-shei-nei a-far. Mi cha-mo-cha ba-al g'vu-rot, umi domeh lach, Melech mei-mit u-m'chai-yeh u-mats-mi-ach y'shu-ah.

מְכַלְכֵּל חַיִּים בְּחֶסֶד, מְחַיֵּה מֵתִים בְּרַחֲמִים רַבִּים, סוֹמֵךְ נוֹפְלִים, וְרוֹפֵא חוֹלִים, וּמַתִּיר אֲסוּרִים, וּמְקַיֵּם אֱמוּנָתוֹ לִישֵׁנֵי עָפָר. מִי כָמוֹךָ בַּעַל גְּבוּרוֹת, וּמִי דּוֹמֶה לָּךְ, מֶלֶךְ מֵמִית וּמְחַיֶּה וּמַצְמִיחַ יְשׁוּעָה.

NOTE: From Rosh Hashanah to Yom Kippur we add in the following line:

Who is like You, Compassionate Father, Who remembers with compassion those He has created for life.

Mi cha-mo-cha Av Ha-racha-mim, zo-cheir y'tsu-rav l'chayim b'racha-mim.   מִי כָמוֹךָ אַב הָרַחֲמִים, זוֹכֵר יְצוּרָיו לְחַיִּים בְּרַחֲמִים.

You are trustworthy to restore life to the deceased. I acknowledge that You, Adonoy, Source of all blessings, revive the deceased.

V'ne-eman atah l'ha-cha-yot mei-tim. Baruch atah Adonoy, m'cha-yei ha-mei-tim.   וְנֶאֱמָן אַתָּה לְהַחֲיוֹת מֵתִים. בָּרוּךְ אַתָּה יי, מְחַיֵּה הַמֵּתִים.

The Third Blessing: Hashem's Holiness

> **Kavanah:** *Holiness means achieving closeness to Hashem and imbuing everything we do with a higher purpose, G-d's purpose. Hashem, help me to be holy today.*

You, Hashem, are holy and Your name is holy. We, the Holy People, praise You every day for You are great and holy.***You, Adonoy, Source of all blessings, are the Holy G-d.

Atah ka-dosh v'shim-cha ka-dosh u-k'do-shim b'chol yom y'ha-l'lu-cha selah. Baruch atah Adonoy, ha-El ha-ka-dosh.***   אַתָּה קָדוֹשׁ וְשִׁמְךָ קָדוֹשׁ וּקְדוֹשִׁים בְּכָל יוֹם יְהַלְלוּךָ סֶּלָה. בָּרוּךְ אַתָּה יי, הָאֵל הַקָּדוֹשׁ.***

NOTE: *** In the days between Rosh Hashanah and Yom Kippur subtitute the following concluding blessing instead:

You, Adonoy, Source of all blessings, are the Holy Master of the World.

Baruch atah Adonoy, ha-Melech ha-ka-dosh.   בָּרוּךְ אַתָּה יי, הַמֶּלֶךְ הַקָּדוֹשׁ.

The Dialogue:
Thirteen Requests for Everything
that I and My People Need

First Request: For Insight and Understanding

> **Kavanah:** *Help me to gain knowledge and insight so that I can make the right decisions and lead a meaningful and purposeful life.*

You kindly bestow knowledge upon people and teach them insight. Please grant us wisdom, insight, and knowledge. You, Hashem, Source of all blessings, are the gracious Giver of knowledge.

Atah cho-nein l'adam da-at, u-m'la-meid le-enosh bi-nah. Cha-nei-nu mei-i-t'cha dei-ah bi-nah v'has-kel. Baruch atah Adonoy, cho-nein ha-da-at.

אַתָּה חוֹנֵן לְאָדָם דַּעַת, וּמְלַמֵּד לֶאֱנוֹשׁ בִּינָה. חָנֵּנוּ מֵאִתְּךָ דֵּעָה בִּינָה וְהַשְׂכֵּל. בָּרוּךְ אַתָּה יְיָ, חוֹנֵן הַדָּעַת.

Second Request: For Closeness to Hashem

> **Kavanah:** *Help me to return to my essence, to my G-dly soul, which will bring me closer to Hashem and my life's purpose, which is to fulfill the mitzvot.*

Our Father, bring us back to Your Torah. Our Ruler, bring us closer to our purpose and help us return to You. You, Hashem, Source of all blessings, desire our return.

Ha-shi-veinu Avi-nu l'Tora-techa, v'kar-veinu Mal-keinu la-avoda-techa, v'ha-cha-zi-reinu bi-t'shu-vah sh'lei-mah l'fa-necha. Baruch atah Adonoy, ha-rotseh bi-t'shu-vah.

הֲשִׁיבֵנוּ אָבִינוּ לְתוֹרָתֶךָ, וְקָרְבֵנוּ מַלְכֵּנוּ לַעֲבוֹדָתֶךָ, וְהַחֲזִירֵנוּ בִּתְשׁוּבָה שְׁלֵמָה לְפָנֶיךָ. בָּרוּךְ אַתָּה יְיָ, הָרוֹצֶה בִּתְשׁוּבָה.

Third Request: For Forgiveness

> **Kavanah:** *Forgive me for whatever mistakes and errors in judgment and action I have made. Heal my soul. Help me to be a forgiving and non-judgmental person.*

Father, forgive us for we have made mistakes. Pardon us even for our intentional transgressions and errors in judgment, because You are good and forgiving. You, Hashem, Source of all blessings, are kind and forgive us repeatedly.

S'lach la-nu Avi-nu ki cha-ta-nu, m'chal la-nu Mal-keinu ki fa-shanu, ki mo-chel v'so-lei-ach atah. Baruch atah Adonoy, cha-nun ha-mar-beh lis-lo-ach.

סְלַח לָנוּ אָבִינוּ כִּי חָטָאנוּ, מְחַל לָנוּ מַלְכֵּנוּ כִּי פָשָׁעְנוּ, כִּי מוֹחֵל וְסוֹלֵחַ אָתָּה. בָּרוּךְ אַתָּה יי, חַנּוּן הַמַּרְבֶּה לִסְלֹחַ.

Fourth Request: For Relief of Our Struggles and Our Suffering

> **Kavanah:** *Help me to be released from all my daily difficulties. Then my thoughts and emotions will free me to fulfill the purpose of my creation.*

See our suffering, fight our battles, and provide us with speedy and complete redemption from our daily difficulties, for Your sake. You have the power of redemption. You, Hashem, Source of all blessings, are the redeemer of Israel.

R'ei v'an-yeinu, v'ri-vah ri-veinu, u-g'alei-nu m'hei-rah l'ma-an sh'meh-cha, ki go-el cha-zak atah. Baruch atah Adonoy, go-el Yisrael.

רְאֵה בְעָנְיֵנוּ, וְרִיבָה רִיבֵנוּ, וּגְאָלֵנוּ מְהֵרָה לְמַעַן שְׁמֶךָ, כִּי גּוֹאֵל חָזָק אָתָּה. בָּרוּךְ אַתָּה יי, גּוֹאֵל יִשְׂרָאֵל.

Fifth Request: For Health and Healing

> **Kavanah:** *Please heal the sick and allow me to lead a healthy life. Allow me to help those who are ill in some way, whether physically, emotionally, or spiritually.*

Hashem, please heal us completely and provide a complete recovery for all that ails us.

R'fa-einu Adonoy v'nei-ra-fei, ho-shi-einu v'ni-va-shei-ah, ki t'hi-la-teinu atah, v'ha-a-lei r'fu-ah sh'lei-mah l'chol ma-ko-teinu.

רְפָאֵנוּ יי וְנֵרָפֵא, הוֹשִׁיעֵנוּ וְנִוָּשֵׁעָה, כִּי תְהִלָּתֵנוּ אָתָּה, וְהַעֲלֵה רְפוּאָה שְׁלֵמָה לְכָל מַכּוֹתֵינוּ.

If you know of people who are ill, you can say a special prayer for them at this point. Ideally we use their Hebrew name and their mother's Hebrew name (e.g., Moshe the son of Miriam, Leah the daughter of Esther). If you do not know their mother's Hebrew name, use the mother's English name; if you don't know the mother's name at all, substitute the name Sarah Imeinu (our Mother Sarah), as we are all children of the first of the four Matriarchs of the Jewish People. If you are unaware of the ill person's Hebrew name, just insert the English name (e.g., Joanne bat Sarah Imeinu).

The Special Prayer for Someone Who Is Ill

My G-d and the G-d of my ancestors, may it be Your will, that You send from the heavens, a complete and speedy recovery of both body and spirit to _____ (the ill person's name — Hebrew one, if possible — the son/daughter of their mother's Hebrew name, if you know it.) For You have the power to provide healing with compassion.

Y'hi ra-tson mil-fa-necha Adonoy Elo-hai vei-lo-hei avo-tai, she-tish-lach m'hei-rah r'fu-ah sh'lei-mah min ha-sha-ma-yim, r'fu-at ha-nefesh u-r'fu-at ha-guf l'(the ill person's name, son/daughter of his/her mother's Hebrew name, if you know it) *b'toch sh'ar cho-lei Yisrael.*

יְהִי רָצוֹן מִלְפָנֶיךָ יי אֱלֹהַי וֵאלֹהֵי אֲבוֹתַי, שֶׁתִּשְׁלַח מְהֵרָה רְפוּאָה שְׁלֵמָה מִן הַשָּׁמַיִם, רְפוּאַת הַנֶּפֶשׁ וּרְפוּאַת הַגּוּף (פב״פ) בְּתוֹךְ שְׁאָר חוֹלֵי יִשְׂרָאֵל.

You, Adonoy, Source of all blessings, heal the sick people of Israel.

Ki El Melech ro-fei ne-eman v'ra-cha-man a-tah. Baruch atah Adonoy, ro-fei cho-lei amo Yisrael.

כִּי אֵל מֶלֶךְ רוֹפֵא נֶאֱמָן וְרַחֲמָן אָתָּה. בָּרוּךְ אַתָּה יי, רוֹפֵא חוֹלֵי עַמּוֹ יִשְׂרָאֵל.

Sixth Request: For Prosperity

> **Kavanah:** *Please send me material success and I will use it for spiritual success. Please bless nature and the fruits of the land and the economy, especially in the Land of Israel.*

Hashem, bless us this year and bless our crops. Bless the earth [in winter: with dew and rain] and let us be satisfied with its produce. Bless this year as you have blessed the best of years. For You are Hashem, who is good and does so much good and blesses the years. You, Adonoy, Source of all blessings, bless the years.

Ba-reich alei-nu Adonoy Elo-heinu et ha-sha-nah ha-zot v'et kol mi-nei t'vu-a-tah l'to-vah [From the third night of Passover through the afternoon of December 4th (December 5th if the following February will have 29 days), say: *v'tein b'ra-chah*. From the evening of December 4th (or 5th) through erev Pesach, say: *v'tein tal u-ma-tar li-v'ra-chah*. At all times, continue:] *Al p'nei ha-ada-mah, v'sab-einu mi-tu-vah, u-va-reich sh'na-teinu ka-sha-nim ha-to-vot. Baruch atah Adonoy, m'va-reich ha-sha-nim.*

בָּרֵךְ עָלֵינוּ יי אֱלֹהֵינוּ אֶת הַשָּׁנָה הַזֹּאת וְאֶת כָּל מִינֵי תְבוּאָתָהּ לְטוֹבָה, וְתֵן [From the third night of Passover through the afternoon of December 4th (December 5th if the following February will have 29 days), (בְּרָכָה), From the evening of December 4th (or 5th) through erev Pesach, say: (טַל וּמָטָר לִבְרָכָה) עַל פְּנֵי הָאֲדָמָה, וְשַׂבְּעֵנוּ מִטּוּבָהּ, וּבָרֵךְ שְׁנָתֵנוּ כַּשָּׁנִים הַטּוֹבוֹת. בָּרוּךְ אַתָּה יי, מְבָרֵךְ הַשָּׁנִים.

Seventh Request: For the Return of our Alienated and Persecuted People (First of the Four National Requests)

Kavanah: Hashem, please gather the alienated and captive members of our nation and bring us back once again to the Land of Israel. From there, we will provide spiritual and moral leadership to the entire world.

Sound the great shofar of our freedom, gather our alienated and persecuted exiles and all of us from the Four Corners of the world, and bring us back to our land. You, Adonoy, Source of all blessings, gather the dispersed members of His People, Israel.

T'ka b'sho-far ga-dol l'chei-ru-teinu, v'sa neis l'ka-beits galu-yo-teinu, v'ka-b'tsei-nu ya-chad mei-ar-ba kan-fot ha-arets. Baruch atah Adonoy, m'ka-beits nid-chei amo Yisrael.

תְּקַע בְּשׁוֹפָר גָּדוֹל לְחֵרוּתֵנוּ, וְשָׂא נֵס לְקַבֵּץ גָּלֻיּוֹתֵינוּ, וְקַבְּצֵנוּ יַחַד מֵאַרְבַּע כַּנְפוֹת הָאָרֶץ. בָּרוּךְ אַתָּה יי, מְקַבֵּץ נִדְחֵי עַמּוֹ יִשְׂרָאֵל.

Eighth Request: For Spiritual Leadership (Second National Request)

Kavanah: Hashem, please provide us with spiritual leaders and give them the strength and inspiration to guide us correctly. Please provide me with a spiritual leader who can teach me, direct me, and inspire me.

Hashem, please restore our Jewish judges and our spiritual advisors as they once were. Remove from us all sorrow and turmoil. Re-establish your Kingship with kindness and compassion. Help us do what is right and just. You, Adonoy, Source of all blessings, love what is right and just.

Ha-shi-vah shof-teinu k'va-ri-sho-nah, v'yo-a-tseinu k'va-t'chi-lah, v'ha-seir mi-me-nu ya-gon va-ana-chah, u-m'loch alei-nu atah Adonoy l'va-d'cha b'che-sed u-v'ra-cha-mim, v'tsad-keinu ba-mish-pat.

הָשִׁיבָה שׁוֹפְטֵינוּ כְּבָרִאשׁוֹנָה, וְיוֹעֲצֵינוּ כְּבַתְּחִלָּה, וְהָסֵר מִמֶּנּוּ יָגוֹן וַאֲנָחָה, וּמְלוֹךְ עָלֵינוּ אַתָּה יְיָ לְבַדְּךָ בְּחֶסֶד וּבְרַחֲמִים, וְצַדְּקֵנוּ בַּמִּשְׁפָּט.

on a regular day conclude with the following line:
Baruch atah Adonoy, Melech o-heiv ts'da-kah u-mish-pat.

on a regular day conclude with the following line:
בָּרוּךְ אַתָּה יְיָ, מֶלֶךְ אוֹהֵב צְדָקָה וּמִשְׁפָּט.

NOTE: From Rosh Hashanah to Yom Kippur substitute the following conclusion to this blessing instead of the usual one:

You, Adonoy, Source of all blessings are the just Master of the World.

Baruch atah Adonoy, Melech ha-mish-pat.

בָּרוּךְ אַתָּה יְיָ, הַמֶּלֶךְ הַמִּשְׁפָּט.

Ninth Request: For Protection from Our Enemies (Third National Request)

Kavanah: *Please let those who wish to harm us physically and spiritually fail.*
Give them what is due to them.
Let me be aware of those who wish to harm my people or me.
And let us be protected so that we can fulfill our spiritual destiny.

Let there be no hope for those who slander us and wish to hurt us spiritually. Cut down all the enemies of Your people. Quickly smash them, throw them down, lower them, and humble them. You, Adonoy, Source of all blessings, break our enemies and humble those who are arrogant.

V'la-mal-shi-nim al t'hi tik-vah, v'chol ha-rish-ah k're-ga to-veid, v'chol oi-vei am-cha m'hei-rah yi-ka-reitu, v'ha-zei-dim m'hei-rah t'a-keir u-t'sha-beir u-t'ma-geir v'tach-ni-a bim-hei-rah v'ya-meinu. Baruch atah Adonoy, sho-veir oi-vim u-mach-ni-a zei-dim.

וְלַמַּלְשִׁינִים אַל תְּהִי תִקְוָה, וְכָל הָרִשְׁעָה כְּרֶגַע תֹּאבֵד, וְכָל אוֹיְבֵי עַמְּךָ מְהֵרָה יִכָּרֵתוּ, וְהַזֵּדִים מְהֵרָה תְעַקֵּר וּתְשַׁבֵּר וּתְמַגֵּר וְתַכְנִיעַ בִּמְהֵרָה בְיָמֵינוּ. בָּרוּךְ אַתָּה יְיָ, שׁוֹבֵר אוֹיְבִים וּמַכְנִיעַ זֵדִים.

Tenth Request: For the Righteous People (Fourth National Request)

> Kavanah: *Please give strength and influence to the righteous and holy people.*
> *Let me meet them and be influenced by them.*
> *Help me strive always to be one of them.*

Hashem, please be compassionate to the leaders of Israel, the righteous, the devout, the elders, the scholars, the righteous converts to Judaism, and all of us. Please reward all who sincerely believe in You. Let us always be counted among the sincere believers and let us never feel ashamed. We trust in You and Your great compassion. You, Adonoy, Source of all blessings, are the Source of goodness for the righteous who trust in You.

Al ha-tsa-di-kim v'al ha-cha-si-dim, v'al zik-nei am-cha beit Yisrael, v'al p'lei-tat sof-rei-hem, v'al gei-rei ha-tsedek v'alei-nu, ye-hemu ra-cha-mecha Adonoy Elo-heinu, v'tein sa-char tov l'chol ha-bo-t'chim b'shim-cha be-emet, v'sim chel-keinu i-ma-hem l'olam, v'lo nei-vosh ki v'cha va-tach-nu. Baruch atah Adonoy, mish-an u-miv-tach la-tsa-di-kim.

עַל הַצַּדִּיקִים וְעַל הַחֲסִידִים, וְעַל זִקְנֵי עַמְּךָ בֵּית יִשְׂרָאֵל, וְעַל פְּלֵיטַת סוֹפְרֵיהֶם, וְעַל גֵּרֵי הַצֶּדֶק וְעָלֵינוּ, יֶהֱמוּ רַחֲמֶיךָ יי אֱלֹהֵינוּ, וְתֵן שָׂכָר טוֹב לְכָל הַבּוֹטְחִים בְּשִׁמְךָ בֶּאֱמֶת, וְשִׂים חֶלְקֵנוּ עִמָּהֶם לְעוֹלָם, וְלֹא נֵבוֹשׁ כִּי בְךָ בָּטָחְנוּ. בָּרוּךְ אַתָּה יי, מִשְׁעָן וּמִבְטָח לַצַּדִּיקִים.

Eleventh Request: To Rebuild Jerusalem

> Kavanah: *Hashem, please rebuild Jerusalem as the center of spiritual light and guidance for the world.*
> *We need a place where we can find clarity in all matters and know with complete certainty what is right for us to do.*
> *That was Jerusalem of old.*
> *Let there be such a Jerusalem again!*
> *Let me achieve clarity of purpose.*

Please return to Your city, Jerusalem, and dwell within it for all to see, just as You have promised. Rebuild it now and let it last forever. Set the throne of Mashiach, King David's heir, within Jerusalem very soon. You, Adonoy, Source of all blessings, are the builder of Jerusalem.

V'li-ru-sha-la-yim ir-cha b'ra-cha-mim ta-shuv, v'tish-kon b'to-cha ka-asher di-bar-ta, u-v'nei otah b'ka-rov b'ya-meinu bin-yan olam, v'chi-sei Da-vid m'hei-rah l'to-chah ta-chin. Baruch atah Adonoy, bo-nei Y'ru-sha-la-yim.

וְלִירוּשָׁלַיִם עִירְךָ בְּרַחֲמִים תָּשׁוּב, וְתִשְׁכֹּן בְּתוֹכָהּ כַּאֲשֶׁר דִּבַּרְתָּ, וּבְנֵה אוֹתָהּ בְּקָרוֹב בְּיָמֵינוּ בִּנְיַן עוֹלָם, וְכִסֵּא דָוִד מְהֵרָה לְתוֹכָהּ תָּכִין. בָּרוּךְ אַתָּה יְיָ, בּוֹנֵה יְרוּשָׁלָיִם.

Twelfth Request: For the Arrival of Mashiach

Kavanah: Please send Mashiach to correct the world and all of us in it. Let me witness this era when there will be no more tears of sadness and sorrow. Then, I will spend my whole life spreading goodness, without experiencing any pain or troubles. I will achieve unbelievable closeness to Hashem.

Send Mashiach, the offspring of King David, quickly. We hope and look forward to this all day and every day. You, Adonoy, Source of all blessings, send salvation.

Et tse-mach Da-vid av-d'cha m'hei-rah tats-mi-ach, v'kar-no ta-rum bi-shu-a-techa, ki li-shu-a-t'cha ki-vi-nu kol ha-yom. Baruch atah Adonoy, mats-mi-ach ke-ren y'shu-ah.

אֶת צֶמַח דָּוִד עַבְדְּךָ מְהֵרָה תַצְמִיחַ, וְקַרְנוֹ תָּרוּם בִּישׁוּעָתֶךָ, כִּי לִישׁוּעָתְךָ קִוִּינוּ כָּל הַיּוֹם. בָּרוּךְ אַתָּה יְיָ, מַצְמִיחַ קֶרֶן יְשׁוּעָה.

Thirteenth Request: For Acceptance of Our Prayers

Kavanah: Please answer my prayers and those of all of Israel. No matter how weak and feeble I may be, You know what is in my heart and what is best for me. Please answer me!

Hashem, our G-d and our compassionate Father, have pity and compassion for us and accept our prayers. You hear our prayers and our requests. Do not turn us away empty-handed, but instead be kind to us. Hear our prayers and answer us, for You listen to all of the prayers of Your nation, Israel. You, Adonoy, Source of all blessing, listen to prayers.

Shema ko-leinu Adonoy Elo-heinu, chus v'ra-cheim alei-nu, v'ka-bel b'ra-cha-mim u-v'ra-tson et t'fi-la-teinu, ki El sho-mei-a t'fi-lot v'ta-cha-nu-nim atah. U-mil-fa-necha Mal-keinu rei-kam al t'shi-veinu, ki atah sho-mei-a t'fi-lat am-cha Yisrael b'ra-cha-mim. Baruch atah Adonoy, sho-mei-a t'fi-lah.

שְׁמַע קוֹלֵנוּ יְיָ אֱלֹהֵינוּ, חוּס וְרַחֵם עָלֵינוּ, וְקַבֵּל בְּרַחֲמִים וּבְרָצוֹן אֶת תְּפִלָּתֵנוּ, כִּי אֵל שׁוֹמֵעַ תְּפִלּוֹת וְתַחֲנוּנִים אָתָּה. וּמִלְּפָנֶיךָ מַלְכֵּנוּ רֵיקָם אַל תְּשִׁיבֵנוּ, כִּי אַתָּה שׁוֹמֵעַ תְּפִלַּת עַמְּךָ יִשְׂרָאֵל בְּרַחֲמִים. בָּרוּךְ אַתָּה יְיָ, שׁוֹמֵעַ תְּפִלָּה.

The Three Closing Blessings: Prayers of Thanks and Hope

First Closing Blessing: A Return of the Temple Service

> **Kavanah:** *We use prayer as a substitute for the Temple service of old. I am so far removed from the Temple concept that I can't even begin to understand what the Temple service meant or how it worked. But I know that all who went to the Temple felt so close to Hashem. They felt tangible feelings of forgiveness and clarity of spirit and purpose. I long for that closeness and that clarity and I know that Hashem longs for this closeness, too.*

Hashem, our G-d, please look with favor towards Your People, Israel, and listen to their prayers. Quickly restore the service to the Holy of Holies of Your Temple. Accept the offerings and prayers of Israel with love and always accept the service of Your People, Israel.

R'tsei Adonoy Elo-heinu b'am-cha Yisrael u-vi-t'fi-la-tam, v'ha-sheiv et ha-avo-dah li-d'vir bei-techa. V'i-shei Yisrael u-t'fi-la-tam b'a-ha-vah t'ka-bel b'ra-tson, u-t'hi l'ra-tson ta-mid avo-dat Yisrael a-mecha.

רְצֵה יי אֱלֹהֵינוּ בְּעַמְּךָ יִשְׂרָאֵל וּבִתְפִלָּתָם, וְהָשֵׁב אֶת הָעֲבוֹדָה לִדְבִיר בֵּיתֶךָ. וְאִשֵּׁי יִשְׂרָאֵל וּתְפִלָּתָם בְּאַהֲבָה תְקַבֵּל בְּרָצוֹן, וּתְהִי לְרָצוֹן תָּמִיד עֲבוֹדַת יִשְׂרָאֵל עַמֶּךָ.

 NOTE: Say this special paragraph on Rosh Chodesh, the first day(s) of the new Jewish month. The "first day" may be one or two days, depending on the month. See a Jewish calendar or check on the Internet to see the appropriate dates on the secular calendar.

Our G-d and the G-d of our ancestors, may your remembrance of us and our ancestors, and of the Mashiach, the offspring of King David Your servant, and of Jerusalem, Your holy city, and of all of your people, the House of Israel, rise up and reach, be noticed, accepted, heard and remembered before You; for deliverance, well-being, grace, kindness, and mercy, for life and peace on this day of Rosh Chodesh (the beginning of the new month).

Remember us today, Adonoy our G-d, for good, for blessings, and help provide us with good life. And with an act of redemption and compassion, have mercy on us, be gracious, merciful, and save us. For our eyes are looking to You, for You are the kind and compassionate Master of the World.

Elo-heinu vei-lo-hei avo-teinu, ya-aleh, v'ya-vo, v'ya-gi-a, v'yei-ra-eh, v'yei-ra-tseh, v'yi-sha-ma, v'yi-pa-keid, v'yi-za-cheir zich-ro-neinu u-fik-do-neinu, v'zich-ron avo-teinu, v'zich-ron Ma-shi-ach ben Da-vid av-de-cha, v'zich-ron Y'ru-sha-la-yim ir kad-shecha, v'zich-ron kol am-cha Beit Yisrael l'fa-necha, lif-lei-tah l'to-vah, l'chein u-l'che-sed u-l'ra-cha-mim, l'cha-yim u-l'sha-lom b'yom Rosh ha-Cho-desh ha-zeh.

Zach-reinu Adonoy Elo-heinu bo l'to-vah, u-fa-k'dei-nu vo li-v'ra-chah, v'ho-shi-einu vo l'cha-yim, u-vi-d'var y'shu-ah v'ra-cha-mim, chus v'cha-neinu v'ra-cheim alei-nu v'ho-shi-einu, ki ei-lecha ei-neinu, ki Eil Melech cha-nun v'ra-chum Atah.

אֱלֹהֵינוּ וֵאלֹהֵי אֲבוֹתֵינוּ, יַעֲלֶה, וְיָבוֹא, וְיַגִּיעַ, וְיֵרָאֶה, וְיֵרָצֶה, וְיִשָּׁמַע, וְיִפָּקֵד, וְיִזָּכֵר זִכְרוֹנֵנוּ וּפִקְדוֹנֵנוּ, וְזִכְרוֹן אֲבוֹתֵינוּ, וְזִכְרוֹן מָשִׁיחַ בֶּן דָּוִד עַבְדֶּךָ, וְזִכְרוֹן יְרוּשָׁלַיִם עִיר קָדְשֶׁךָ, וְזִכְרוֹן כָּל עַמְּךָ בֵּית יִשְׂרָאֵל לְפָנֶיךָ, לִפְלֵיטָה לְטוֹבָה, לְחֵן וּלְחֶסֶד וּלְרַחֲמִים, לְחַיִּים וּלְשָׁלוֹם בְּיוֹם רֹאשׁ הַחֹדֶשׁ הַזֶּה.

זָכְרֵנוּ יְיָ אֱלֹהֵינוּ בּוֹ לְטוֹבָה, וּפָקְדֵנוּ בוֹ לִבְרָכָה, וְהוֹשִׁיעֵנוּ בוֹ לְחַיִּים, וּבִדְבַר יְשׁוּעָה וְרַחֲמִים, חוּס וְחָנֵּנוּ וְרַחֵם עָלֵינוּ וְהוֹשִׁיעֵנוּ, כִּי אֵלֶיךָ עֵינֵינוּ, כִּי אֵל מֶלֶךְ חַנּוּן וְרַחוּם אָתָּה.

Let us see Your return to Zion (the Temple) with compassion. You, Adonoy, Source of all blessings, restore His presence to Zion.

V'te-che-zenah ei-neinu b'shu-v'cha l'Tsi-yon b'ra-cha-mim. Baruch atah Adonoy, hama-cha-zir sh'chi-nato l'Tsi-yon.

וְתֶחֱזֶינָה עֵינֵינוּ בְּשׁוּבְךָ לְצִיּוֹן בְּרַחֲמִים. בָּרוּךְ אַתָּה יְיָ, הַמַּחֲזִיר שְׁכִינָתוֹ לְצִיּוֹן.

Second Closing Blessing: Thank You, Hashem

 Take a minute or two to review the following list and focus on the things for which you feel especially thankful today. Say, "Thank you, Hashem, for…."

- Life
- Health
- Intellect
- Sight
- Hearing
- Speech
- Movement
- Memories
- Freedom of Choice
- Making Me a Jew
- My Jewish Soul
- Mitzvot

- Parents
- Teachers
- Friends
- Grandparents
- Spouse
- Children
- Grandchildren
- Family
- Israel
- Peace
- Forgiveness
- Respect and Honor

- Torah (which provides me with direction in life)
- The Ability to Talk to You
- Watching Over Me
- Making Me Your Partner in Creation
- A Place in the Next World (*Olam HaBa*)
- Wonders of Nature
- Material Possessions (home, car, clothes, furniture, dishes, books, etc.)
- Personal Growth
- Meaning and Purpose
- The Desire to Be Good
- The Power to Change Things
- My Favorite Things
- A Way to Pay Expenses
- Pleasure (physical, intellectual, emotional, spiritual, etc.)
- Add in your own personal thoughts…

Kavanah: *I have so much to be thankful for every second of the day. I can't even begin to enumerate all the things that I have to be thankful for. And I know that Hashem gives it all to me.*

Bow on *Modim* and stand upright on *lach*.

We thank You, Hashem, our eternal G-d and the G-d of our ancestors. You are the One we depend on in our lives, who shields us from one generation to the next. We thank You for our lives, which are in Your hands, for our souls, which are watched by You, for the miracles that You do for us every day, and for the wonders and good things that you do for us all the time — every evening, morning, and afternoon. You are the Source of goodness and compassion whose kindness never ends. We always put our hope in You.

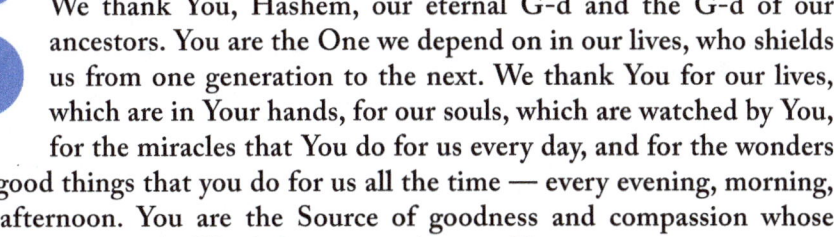

Mo-dim a-nach-nu lach sha-atah hu Adonoy Elo-heinu vei-lo-hei avo-teinu l'olam va-ed. Tsur cha-yeinu, ma-gein yish-einu atah hu l'dor va-dor. No-deh l'cha u-n'sa-peir t'hi-la-techa al cha-yeinu ha-m'su-rim b'ya-decha, v'al nish-mo-teinu ha-p'ku-dot lach, v'al ni-secha she-b'chol yom ima-nu, v'al nif-l'o-techa v'tovo-techa she-b'chol eit, erev va-vo-ker v'tsa-ha-ra-yim. Ha-tov ki lo cha-lu ra-cha-mecha, v'ha-m'ra-cheim ki lo ta-mu cha-sa-decha, mei-olam ki-vi-nu lach.

For all of this, may You be acknowledged forever.

V'al ku-lam yit-ba-rach v'yit-ro-mam shim-cha Mal-keinu ta-mid l'olam va-ed.

> NOTE: Between Rosh Hashanah and Yom Kippur ADD the line:

Inscribe all of the children of Your covenant (i.e., all of the Jewish People) for good life.

U-ch'tov l'cha-yim tovim kol b'nei v'ri-techa.

וּכְתוֹב לְחַיִּים טוֹבִים כָּל בְּנֵי בְרִיתֶךָ.

> Bend knees on *Baruch*, bow on *atah*, stand upright on *Adonoy*.

And all that lives will acknowledge You and will thank, praise, and bless You forever, for that is a good thing to do. Hashem, You are our help and salvation, the G-d of goodness. Adonoy, it is You, whose name is "The Good One," whom we should thank.

V'chol ha-chayim yo-du-cha selah, vi-ha-l'lu et-shim-cha be-emet, ha-El y'shu-a-teinu v'ez-ra-teinu selah.
Baruch atah Adonoy, ha-tov shim-cha u-l'cha na-eh l'ho-dot.

וְכֹל הַחַיִּים יוֹדוּךָ סֶּלָה, וִיהַלְלוּ אֶת שִׁמְךָ בֶּאֱמֶת, הָאֵל יְשׁוּעָתֵנוּ וְעֶזְרָתֵנוּ סֶלָה. בָּרוּךְ אַתָּה יְיָ, הַטּוֹב שִׁמְךָ וּלְךָ נָאֶה לְהוֹדוֹת.

Third Closing Blessing: For Inner Peace and a Life of Goodness

> **Kavanah:** *Inner turmoil and strife within us and within our Jewish family are the greatest blocks to a life of happiness and fulfillment. Help me to use the Torah and the Torah's values to achieve a life of inner and external peace. I want to be a peaceful, kind person who brings goodness and peace to my people and to my world.*

Hashem, give us and all of Your people, Israel, peace, goodness, blessing, life, good favor, kindness, and compassion. Our Father, bless us all as one with Your special light. For with Your special light, You have given us the Torah, our instructions for living, and You have given us a love of kindness, righteousness, blessing, compassion, life, and peace. May You find it good to bless us and all of Israel, Your People, at all times, with Your peace.

Weekday Morning Shemoneh Esrei 143

Sim shalom, tovah, u-v'ra-chah, chein, va-che-sed, v'ra-cha-mim alei-nu v'al kol Yisrael a-mecha. Bar-cheinu avi-nu, ku-lanu k'echad b'or pa-necha, ki v'or pa-necha na-ta-ta la-nu, Adonoy Elo-heinu, Torat cha-yim v'a-ha-vat chesed, u-ts'da-kah, u-v'ra-chah, v'ra-cha-mim, v'cha-yim, v'sha-lom. V'tov b'ei-necha l'va-reich et kol am-cha Yisrael, b'chol eit u-v'chol sha-ah bish-lo-mecha.

שִׂים שָׁלוֹם, טוֹבָה, וּבְרָכָה, חֵן, וָחֶסֶד, וְרַחֲמִים עָלֵינוּ וְעַל כָּל יִשְׂרָאֵל עַמֶּךָ. בָּרְכֵנוּ אָבִינוּ, כֻּלָּנוּ כְּאֶחָד בְּאוֹר פָּנֶיךָ, כִּי בְאוֹר פָּנֶיךָ נָתַתָּ לָּנוּ, יְיָ אֱלֹהֵינוּ, תּוֹרַת חַיִּים וְאַהֲבַת חֶסֶד, וּצְדָקָה, וּבְרָכָה, וְרַחֲמִים, וְחַיִּים, וְשָׁלוֹם. וְטוֹב בְּעֵינֶיךָ לְבָרֵךְ אֶת כָּל עַמְּךָ יִשְׂרָאֵל, בְּכָל עֵת וּבְכָל שָׁעָה בִּשְׁלוֹמֶךָ.

 On a regular day the Blessing for Peace concludes with this statement:

You, Adonoy, Source of all blessings, bless Israel, His people, with peace.

Baruch atah Adonoy, ha-m'va-reich et amo Yisrael ba-shalom.

בָּרוּךְ אַתָּה יְיָ, הַמְבָרֵךְ אֶת עַמּוֹ יִשְׂרָאֵל בַּשָּׁלוֹם.

NOTE: From Rosh Hashanah to Yom Kippur, substitute the following paragraph for the closing blessing:

May we and your People, the entire Nation of Israel, be remembered and inscribed in the Book of Life, blessing, prosperity, good life, and peace. You, Adonoy, Source of all blessings, make peace.

B'sei-fer cha-yim b'rachah v'shalom, u-far-nasah tovah, ni-za-cheir v'ni-ka-teiv l'fa-necha, a-nach-nu v'chol am-cha Beit Yisrael, l'cha-yim to-vim u-l'shalom. Baruch atah Adonoy, oseh ha-shalom.

בְּסֵפֶר חַיִּים בְּרָכָה וְשָׁלוֹם, וּפַרְנָסָה טוֹבָה, נִזָּכֵר וְנִכָּתֵב לְפָנֶיךָ, אֲנַחְנוּ וְכָל עַמְּךָ בֵּית יִשְׂרָאֵל, לְחַיִּים טוֹבִים וּלְשָׁלוֹם. בָּרוּךְ אַתָּה יְיָ, עוֹשֶׂה הַשָּׁלוֹם.

A Request for Hashem's Help to Control Speech, Jealousy, and Anger

Kavanah: *I have just used the power of speech that Hashem has given me to speak to Him… to request His help, to pray for me and my people, to remember who I am, and to bring me closer to Hashem.*
But that same power, if used improperly, can be so damaging.
Help me to channel the awesome power of speech only for good and not for slander, gossip, lying, or other words that are unbefitting for me.
Help me to be humble, and not to be jealous or angry.
And help me to be open to Hashem's Torah and mitzvot.

My G-d, please guard my tongue from improper speech and my lips from lying. To those that curse me, let me keep silent and let me be as humble as dust to everyone. Open my heart to Your Torah so that my soul will perform Your mitzvot. And as for those who wish to harm me, quickly erase their advice and destroy their ideas.

Hashem, my G-d and the G-d of my ancestors, may it be Your will that none should be jealous of me, nor I of them; that I should not get angry today, nor should I do something to make You angry with me. Save me from the Evil Inclination and put in my heart the desire for humility and submission.

Hashem, our King and G-d, cause the entire world to recognize Your name, rebuild Your city (Jerusalem), build Your home (the Temple), gather your exiled nation, and fill them with joy. Do this for Your sake, for Your Torah's sake, and for the sake of Your holiness. As the verse in Psalms says, "So that your beloved ones may rest, let Your hand of kindness save us and respond to me."

Elo-hai, n'tsor l'sho-ni mei-ra, u-s'fa-tai mi-da-beir mir-mah, v'lim-ka-l'lai naf-shi ti-dom, v'naf-shi ke-afar la-kol ti-h'yeh. P'tach li-bi b'Tora-techa, u-v'mits-vo-techa tir-dof naf-shi. V'chol ha-chosh-vim a-lai ra-ah, m'hei-rah ha-feir atsa-tam v'kal-keil ma-cha-shav-tam. Asei l'ma-an sh'mecha, asei l'ma-an y'mi-necha, asei l'ma-an k'du-sha-techa, asei l'ma-an Tora-techa. L'ma-an yei-chal-tsun y'di-decha, ho-shi-ah y'min-cha va-a-nei-ni.

אֱלֹהַי, נְצוֹר לְשׁוֹנִי מֵרָע, וּשְׂפָתַי מִדַּבֵּר מִרְמָה, וְלִמְקַלְלַי נַפְשִׁי תִדֹּם, וְנַפְשִׁי כֶּעָפָר לַכֹּל תִּהְיֶה. פְּתַח לִבִּי בְּתוֹרָתֶךָ, וּבְמִצְוֹתֶיךָ תִּרְדֹּף נַפְשִׁי. וְכָל הַחוֹשְׁבִים עָלַי רָעָה, מְהֵרָה הָפֵר עֲצָתָם וְקַלְקֵל מַחֲשַׁבְתָּם. עֲשֵׂה לְמַעַן שְׁמֶךָ, עֲשֵׂה לְמַעַן יְמִינֶךָ, עֲשֵׂה לְמַעַן קְדֻשָּׁתֶךָ, עֲשֵׂה לְמַעַן תּוֹרָתֶךָ. לְמַעַן יֵחָלְצוּן יְדִידֶיךָ, הוֹשִׁיעָה יְמִינְךָ וַעֲנֵנִי.

Personal Prayer Time

 Add in your personal prayer(s) here, in plain discussion with Hashem, straight from your heart. Who do you want to be today? What do you want to accomplish? How can Hashem help you? Just ask. Hashem will do only what is absolutely best for you. Then say the following:

Let my words and the thoughts in my heart be acceptable to You, Hashem, my personal Redeemer, the One upon whom I rely. May He, who makes peace in the heavens, make peace upon us and all of Israel; and let us say **Amein** (that is, I believe this to be the truth).

Weekday Morning Shemoneh Esrei **145**

Yi-h'yu l'ra-tson im-rei fi v'heg-yon li-bi l'fa-necha, Adonoy tsu-ri v'go-a-li.

יִהְיוּ לְרָצוֹן אִמְרֵי פִי וְהֶגְיוֹן לִבִּי לְפָנֶיךָ, יי צוּרִי וְגוֹאֲלִי.

Oseh shalom bi-m'ro-mav, hu ya-aseh shalom alei-nu, v'al kol Yisrael. V'imru, Amein.

עֹשֶׂה שָׁלוֹם בִּמְרוֹמָיו, הוּא יַעֲשֶׂה שָׁלוֹם עָלֵינוּ, וְעַל כָּל יִשְׂרָאֵל. וְאִמְרוּ: אָמֵן.

 Take three steps back and bow slightly to the right, left, and center as if taking leave from a King.

The Final Stanza: Rebuild the Temple

> **Kavanah:** *The prayer that I have just finished takes the place of the Temple service. But it is merely a temporary replacement. We ask Hashem to rebuild the Temple where we will achieve clarity of purpose and of truth and where we will achieve a real and everlasting closeness to Him. Help us to learn Torah and fulfill the mitzvot.*

Hashem, our G-d and the G-d of our ancestors, may it be Your will that You rebuild the Temple speedily in our days and make the Torah the center of our lives. Then we will serve You with reverence as we did in previous times. And the offerings of Judah and Jerusalem will be pleasing to You as they were in the days of old.

Y'hi ra-tson mil-fa-necha Adonoy Elo-heinu vei-lo-hei avo-teinu, she-yi-ba-neh Beit ha-Mik-dash bim-hei-rah v'ya-meinu, v'tein chel-keinu b'Tora-techa.

יְהִי רָצוֹן מִלְּפָנֶיךָ יי אֱלֹהֵינוּ וֵאלֹהֵי אֲבוֹתֵינוּ, שֶׁיִּבָּנֶה בֵּית הַמִּקְדָּשׁ בִּמְהֵרָה בְיָמֵינוּ, וְתֵן חֶלְקֵנוּ בְּתוֹרָתֶךָ.

V'sham na-ava-d'cha b'yir-ah, ki-mei olam u-ch'sha-nim kad-mo-ni-yot.

וְשָׁם נַעֲבָדְךָ בְּיִרְאָה, כִּימֵי עוֹלָם וּכְשָׁנִים קַדְמוֹנִיּוֹת.

V'ar-vah la-donoy min-chat Y'hudah vi-ru-sha-la-yim, ki-mei olam u-ch'sha-nim kad-mo-ni-yot.

וְעָרְבָה לַיי מִנְחַת יְהוּדָה וִירוּשָׁלָיִם, כִּימֵי עוֹלָם וּכְשָׁנִים קַדְמוֹנִיּוֹת.

Step 5. The Concluding Prayers: Taking the Prayers into Our Daily Lives

Introduction: After a tough workout, all trainers advise people to "cool down" before getting back to their everyday activities. It is the same with a spiritual "workout." Are we simply to step away from an intense conversation with the Master of the World and then hop in our cars and speed off to work? Go to dinner with our friends? Go off to sleep?

Rather than just run, we "cool down" by saying a small number of prayers that give us strength until the next prayer service and enable us to integrate the prayers into our lives. Often these prayers are said in song to keep us vitalized with *simchah* (joy), in knowing that we have a relationship with Hashem. The joy of knowing that we have a direction and that we are on the right path to a meaningful life.

First Concluding Prayer: *Aleinu*
Hashem is the One and Only True G-d

Introduction: This prayer was written more than 3,200 years ago by Joshua to help the Jewish People remember that they were different from the seven Canaanite pagan nations that inhabited the Land of Israel at that time. It took on even greater significance as a central prayer in the Rosh Hashanah and Yom Kippur prayers. Throughout history, its significance grew as it served as the "anthem prayer" of the Jews during the Christian Crusades and the terribly difficult times that the Jews of Europe endured under their Christian overlords. During these times, parts or all of the prayer were censored from the siddur. It is often sung as a marching song to give strength to the Jewish People.

> **Kavanah:** *We sing for the privilege of being part of the Jewish People, whose mission is to better the world through the knowledge and understanding of Hashem.*

It is our duty to praise Hashem, the Master of all things. He, who created all things, has not made us like the nations of other lands and placed us in the same position as the other families on earth. He has not given us a portion similar to theirs, nor is our lot like that of the large empires. For they bow to nothing but emptiness and pray to gods that do not help.

Bow on *bow* and stand upright on *thank*.

But we bend our knees, bow, and thank the King who reigns over kings, the Holy One, the Source of all blessings, He who created the heavens and laid the earth's foundations. Hashem's seat is in the heavens above and His powerful presence dwells in the highest heights. He is our G-d. There is no other. Ours is the true King. There is nothing beside Hashem, as it is written in His Torah: "And you are to know this day and take it to heart, that Hashem is the only G-d in the heavens above and on the earth below. There is no other." And it is said, "Hashem will be the King over all of the world. On that day Hashem will be One and His name will be One."

Alei-nu l'sha-bei-ach la-adon ha-kol, la-teit g'du-lah l'yo-tseir b'rei-sheet, she-lo asa-nu k'go-yei ha-ara-tsot, v'lo sa-ma-nu k'mish-p'chot ha-ada-mah, she-lo sam chel-kei-nu ka-hem v'go-ra-leinu k'chol ha-mo-nam.

עָלֵינוּ לְשַׁבֵּחַ לַאֲדוֹן הַכֹּל, לָתֵת גְּדֻלָּה לְיוֹצֵר בְּרֵאשִׁית, שֶׁלֹּא עָשָׂנוּ כְּגוֹיֵי הָאֲרָצוֹת, וְלֹא שָׂמָנוּ כְּמִשְׁפְּחוֹת הָאֲדָמָה, שֶׁלֹּא שָׂם חֶלְקֵנוּ כָּהֶם וְגוֹרָלֵנוּ כְּכָל הֲמוֹנָם.

She-heim mish-tacha-vim la-hevel v'rik, u-mit-pa-l'lim el el lo yo-shi-a.

שֶׁהֵם מִשְׁתַּחֲוִים לְהֶבֶל וָרִיק, וּמִתְפַּלְּלִים אֶל אֵל לֹא יוֹשִׁיעַ.

 Bow on *korim* and stand upright on *u-modim*.

Va-a-nach-nu kor'im u-mish-tacha-vim u-mo-dim, lif-nei Melech mal-chei ha-m'la-chim ha-Kadosh Baruch Hu.

וַאֲנַחְנוּ כּוֹרְעִים וּמִשְׁתַּחֲוִים וּמוֹדִים, לִפְנֵי מֶלֶךְ מַלְכֵי הַמְּלָכִים הַקָּדוֹשׁ בָּרוּךְ הוּא.

She-hu no-teh sha-ma-yim v'yo-seid arets, u-mo-shav y'karo ba-sha-ma-yim mi-ma-al, u-sh'chi-nat u-zo b'gav-hei m'ro-mim. Hu Elo-heinu, ein od.

שֶׁהוּא נוֹטֶה שָׁמַיִם וְיוֹסֵד אָרֶץ, וּמוֹשַׁב יְקָרוֹ בַּשָּׁמַיִם מִמַּעַל, וּשְׁכִינַת עֻזּוֹ בְּגָבְהֵי מְרוֹמִים. הוּא אֱלֹהֵינוּ, אֵין עוֹד.

Emet mal-keinu, efes zu-la-to, ka-ka-tuv b'Tora-to: V'ya-da-ta ha-yom, va-ha-shei-vo-ta el l'va-vecha, ki Adonoy hu ha-Elo-him ba-sha-ma-yim mi-ma-al v'al ha-arets mi-ta-chat, ein od.

אֱמֶת מַלְכֵּנוּ, אֶפֶס זוּלָתוֹ, כַּכָּתוּב בְּתוֹרָתוֹ: וְיָדַעְתָּ הַיּוֹם וַהֲשֵׁבֹתָ אֶל לְבָבֶךָ, כִּי יְיָ הוּא הָאֱלֹהִים בַּשָּׁמַיִם מִמַּעַל וְעַל הָאָרֶץ מִתָּחַת, אֵין עוֹד.

V'ne-emar, v'ha-yah Adonoy l'Melech al ko ha-arets, ba-yom ha-hu yi-h'yeh Adonoy echad u-sh'mo echad.

וְנֶאֱמַר: וְהָיָה יְיָ לְמֶלֶךְ עַל כָּל הָאָרֶץ בַּיּוֹם הַהוּא יִהְיֶה יְיָ אֶחָד וּשְׁמוֹ אֶחָד.

Second Concluding Prayer: *Ha-Yom*
Counting the Days of the Week

Introduction: In the "Ten Commandments" (the actual translation is "The Ten Statements"), we are instructed to "Remember the Shabbat to keep it Holy." There are different ways to remember the Shabbat. One way that has been instituted is to count each day towards the upcoming Shabbat. We also count each day to remind us that each day counts. Each day is unique, one in world history. This day will never occur again.

> **Kavanah:** *I have important work to do today* but *still I look forward to Shabbat. The vision of Shabbat gives me strength, but it also tells me that time is short. I have to make every day count. Today will never happen again, so I must make it count. I must make some important difference today, even a small one.*

1. **On Sunday:** **Today is the first day towards the coming Shabbat.**

Ha-yom yom ri-shon b'shabat.   הַיוֹם יוֹם רִאשׁוֹן בְּשַׁבָּת.

2. **On Monday:** **Today is the second day towards the coming Shabbat.**

Ha-yom yom shei-ni b'shabat.   הַיוֹם יוֹם שֵׁנִי בְּשַׁבָּת.

3. **On Tuesday:** **Today is the third day towards the coming Shabbat.**

Ha-yom yom sh'li-shi b'shabat.   הַיוֹם יוֹם שְׁלִישִׁי בְּשַׁבָּת.

4. **On Wednesday:** **Today is the fourth day towards the coming Shabbat.**

Ha-yom yom r'vi-i b'shabat.

הַיוֹם יוֹם רְבִיעִי בְּשַׁבָּת.

5. **On Thursday:** **Today is the fifth day towards the coming Shabbat.**

Ha-yom yom cha-mi-shi b'shabat.   הַיוֹם יוֹם חֲמִישִׁי בְּשַׁבָּת.

6. **On Friday:** **Today is the sixth day towards the coming Shabbat.**

Ha-yom yom shi-shi b'shabat.   הַיוֹם יוֹם שִׁשִׁי בְּשַׁבָּת.

Mourner's Kaddish

If a mourner is present and there is a *minyan* of ten Jewish men, the mourner leads the congregation in the public declaration of our dreams and aspirations for the world at large. The congregants say the parts in bold in response to the mourner's prayer.

NOTE: If there are multiple mourners, Kaddish should be recited out loud, slowly and *together*, just like a choir would sing together. It is a good idea for the mourners to stand near each other when they lead this prayer and to follow the lead of one designated person, so that they lead this prayer in unison.

> *Kavanah: The mourners bring tremendous merit to the ones whose loss is being mourned by causing the entire congregation to focus on the goals and values of the Jewish People, namely, to lead humanity to its ultimate state of perfection, in peace and harmony with Hashem and with all Creation, with the coming of the era of Mashiach.*

May all people declare the greatness and holiness of Hashem's name (the congregation responds: *Amein*) in the world which He created.

May Hashem speedily cause His kingship and salvation to blossom and bring Mashiach, in your lifetime and in the lifetime of the entire Jewish People. And let us respond: *Amein*.

(All say together: **May Hashem be recognized as the Source of blessing forever**.)

And may all of creation stand in awe of Hashem and praise the Name of the Holy One, Blessed is He. (The congregation responds: **He is the Source of all blessing**.)

With expressions of song and praise beyond all that have ever been uttered on earth. And let us respond: *Amein*.

And may there be peace bestowed from Heaven and good life for us and all of Israel. And let us respond: *Amein*.

May He who makes peace in the Heavens, make peace upon us and all of Israel. And let us respond: *Amein*.

Yit-ga-dal v'yit-ka-dash sh'mei ra-ba. Amein.

B'al-ma di v'ra chir-u-tei v'yam-lich mal-chu-tei, b'cha-yei-chon u-v'yo-mei-chon u-v'cha-yei d'chol beit Yisrael, ba-aga-la u-vi-z'man ka-riv. V'imru: Amein.

Y'hei sh'mei ra-ba m'va-rach l'alam u-l'al-mei al-ma-ya.

Yit-ba-rach v'yish-ta-bach v'yit-pa-ar v'yit-ro-mam v'yit-na-sei v'yit-ha-dar v'yit-aleh v'yit-ha-lal sh'mei d'ku-d'sha. B'rich hu. B'rich hu.

L'ei-la min kol bir-cha-ta v'shi-ra-ta tush-b'cha-ta v'ne-chema-ta da-ami-ran b'al-ma. V'imru: Amein.

Y'hei sh'la-ma ra-ba min sh'ma-ya v'cha-yim alei-nu v'al kol Yisrael. V'imru: Amein.

Oseh shalom bi-m'ro-mav hu ya-aseh shalom alei-nu v'al kol Yisrael v'imru: Amein.

יִתְגַּדַּל וְיִתְקַדַּשׁ שְׁמֵהּ רַבָּא. אָמֵן.

בְּעָלְמָא דִּי בְרָא כִרְעוּתֵהּ וְיַמְלִיךְ מַלְכוּתֵהּ, בְּחַיֵּיכוֹן וּבְיוֹמֵיכוֹן וּבְחַיֵּי דְכָל בֵּית יִשְׂרָאֵל, בַּעֲגָלָא וּבִזְמַן קָרִיב. וְאִמְרוּ: אָמֵן.

יְהֵא שְׁמֵהּ רַבָּא מְבָרַךְ לְעָלַם וּלְעָלְמֵי עָלְמַיָּא.

יִתְבָּרַךְ וְיִשְׁתַּבַּח וְיִתְפָּאַר וְיִתְרוֹמַם וְיִתְנַשֵּׂא וְיִתְהַדָּר וְיִתְעַלֶּה וְיִתְהַלָּל שְׁמֵהּ דְּקֻדְשָׁא. בְּרִיךְ הוּא. בְּרִיךְ הוּא.

לְעֵלָּא מִן כָּל בִּרְכָתָא וְשִׁירָתָא תֻּשְׁבְּחָתָא וְנֶחֱמָתָא דַּאֲמִירָן בְּעָלְמָא. וְאִמְרוּ: אָמֵן.

יְהֵא שְׁלָמָא רַבָּא מִן שְׁמַיָּא וְחַיִּים עָלֵינוּ וְעַל כָּל יִשְׂרָאֵל. וְאִמְרוּ: אָמֵן.

עוֹשֶׂה שָׁלוֹם בִּמְרוֹמָיו הוּא יַעֲשֶׂה שָׁלוֹם עָלֵינוּ וְעַל כָּל יִשְׂרָאֵל וְאִמְרוּ: אָמֵן.

Fourth Concluding Prayer: *Adon Olam*

Introduction: This is a very deep poem written more than a thousand years ago. It contains the theme that Hashem is so great, so powerful – we cannot even begin to comprehend such greatness. Who can possibly comprehend such concepts as timelessness, infinity, the unlimited All-Powerful One, the concept of creation from nothing? Yet with all this, Hashem is still involved intimately in the details of our daily lives, with all of our personal needs, and walks together with us.

Kavanah: There are many things that I can't understand and will never comprehend about Hashem. But I do know that Hashem is with me in every step that I take. So I will go out with confidence to do what I have to do. And I will have no fear.

Master of the World, who reigned before all creation,
At the time when His Will created all form,
He was then proclaimed as the Ruler.
And after all may cease to be, He, the awesome One, will rule alone.
He was, He is, and He will be forever, in Splendor.
He is One; there is no other who can compare to Hashem.
He is without beginning and without end. He holds all the power.
And He is my G-d, my living redeemer, the one I rely upon in my time of trouble.
Hashem is my banner, a place of refuge for me, my cup's fill when I call to Him.
I will trust my spirit in His hand when I go to sleep and when I awake.
Hashem is with me. I shall not fear.

Adon olam asher ma-lach,
b'te-rem kol y'tsir niv-ra,
l'eit na-asah v'chef-tso kol,
a-zai me-lech sh'mo nik'ra.

אֲדוֹן עוֹלָם אֲשֶׁר מָלַךְ,
בְּטֶרֶם כָּל יְצִיר נִבְרָא.
לְעֵת נַעֲשָׂה בְחֶפְצוֹ כֹּל,
אֲזַי מֶלֶךְ שְׁמוֹ נִקְרָא.

V'a-cha-rei kich-lot ha-kol,
l'va-do yim-loch no-ra,
v'hu ha-yah v'hu ho-veh,
v'hu yi-h'yeh b'tif-a-rah.

וְאַחֲרֵי כִּכְלוֹת הַכֹּל,
לְבַדּוֹ יִמְלֹךְ נוֹרָא.
וְהוּא הָיָה וְהוּא הֹוֶה,
וְהוּא יִהְיֶה בְּתִפְאָרָה.

V'hu echad v'ein shei-ni,
l'ham-shil lo l'hach-bi-rah,
b'li rei-sheet b'li tach-lit,
v'lo ha-oz v'ha-mis-rah.

וְהוּא אֶחָד וְאֵין שֵׁנִי,
לְהַמְשִׁיל לוֹ לְהַחְבִּירָה.
בְּלִי רֵאשִׁית בְּלִי תַכְלִית,
וְלוֹ הָעֹז וְהַמִּשְׂרָה.

V'hu ei-li v'chai go-a-li,
v'tsur chev-li b'eit tsa-rah,
v'hu ni-si u-ma-nos li,
m'nat ko-si b'yom ek-ra.

וְהוּא אֵלִי וְחַי גּוֹאֲלִי,
וְצוּר חֶבְלִי בְּעֵת צָרָה.
וְהוּא נִסִּי וּמָנוֹס לִי,
מְנָת כּוֹסִי בְּיוֹם אֶקְרָא.

B'ya-do af-kid ru-chi,
b'eit ishan v'a-irah,
v'im ru-chi g'vi-ya-ti,
Adonoy li v'lo i-ra.

בְּיָדוֹ אַפְקִיד רוּחִי,
בְּעֵת אִישַׁן וְאָעִירָה.
וְעִם רוּחִי גְּוִיָּתִי,
יְיָ לִי וְלֹא אִירָא.

  Smile and go out with confidence and determination to make at least some small difference today!

The Personal Daily Psalm

Some have the tradition of reciting their personal Daily Psalm after the morning prayers each day or at some time during the day. Your personal Psalm is the Psalm number of your age plus one, so someone who is twenty-eight years old recites Psalm 29 every day until his next Jewish birthday. When he turns twenty-nine, he switches to Psalm 30 for every day of the following year, and so on. If you aren't certain of your Jewish birthday, check one of the numerous Jewish calendar converter programs on the Internet, such as the one at chabad.org.

THE SIX REMEMBRANCES (and then some)

Some have the tradition of reciting and recalling the Six Remembrances every day. Some recite and recall ten incidents from the Torah. See the next page for the particular verses and an explanation of each one.

The Torah instructs us to remember a number of things every day. In Hebrew, the word *kol* means both "every" and "all." This teaches us that the Torah not only tells us to remember these teachings every day but all through the day as well, meaning that these items are to become essential parts of our psyche. They are to form the basis of our subconscious thoughts. They form the essence of how a Jew thinks. They are the "drivers" for the thoughts, actions, and deeds that make up our impact on the world.

There are four views as to how many points it is essential for us to keep in mind constantly. Some (such as the famous Apter Rebbe, the Oheiv Yisrael or "Lover of Israel") held that there are four things to remember, some (like the Alter Rebbe, the "Elder Rebbe" of Lubavitch) stated that there are seven things to remember, while some say we are to keep ten points in mind. Most views hold that there are six points to remember constantly.

Let us examine each of these six points briefly. They are based on specific incidents described in the Torah.

1. The Exodus from Egypt

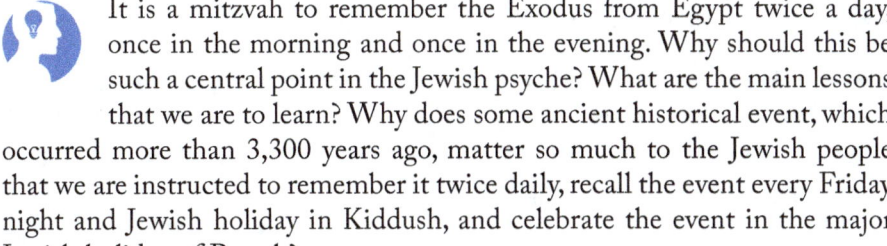

It is a mitzvah to remember the Exodus from Egypt twice a day, once in the morning and once in the evening. Why should this be such a central point in the Jewish psyche? What are the main lessons that we are to learn? Why does some ancient historical event, which occurred more than 3,300 years ago, matter so much to the Jewish people that we are instructed to remember it twice daily, recall the event every Friday night and Jewish holiday in Kiddush, and celebrate the event in the major Jewish holiday of Pesach?

There are two key lessons to recall. The first lesson is that, at the time of the Exodus from Egypt, we were *chosen* by Hashem from all other nations. We are a special people. We have a mission. We are the light to the nations. We are the teachers of the world. We are the living testimony that there is a G-d and that there is morality, goodness, and compassion. We teach the world that we *can* make a difference in the world — that we can make the world a better place.

The second lesson is implied in the Hebrew word for Egypt: *Mitsrayim*. The word is related to the Hebrew word *meitsarim*, which means limitations, constrictions, things that hold you back. The Jews had no rational hope of ever leaving Egypt. It was impossible to escape from Egypt. The Talmud tells us that no slave ever escaped. Furthermore, the society was filled with all the immoral, physically and spiritually enticing pleasures of that world, which attracted the masses and dragged them down. The Talmud explains that even the Jews were dragged down to the forty-ninth level of spiritual impurity. There could be no escape from that either. The Jews were stuck, never to leave. But then, on the night of the fifteenth of the Jewish month of Nissan, the night when we celebrate the first Pesach Seder, Hashem plucked the Jewish People out of Egypt and, within seven weeks, brought them through the Red Sea all the way to Mount Sinai to receive the Torah. At that point, the Jewish people reached the heights of spirituality.

The lesson is that nothing can hold back our Jewish soul. Hashem puts within us the extra strength and ability to break out of anything that holds us back from spiritual growth. We can *all* become holy people. We can all become tzaddikim, people who always strive to do the right thing. When we think we are stuck, when we think we can't go on, when we feel that we can't achieve any more personal growth and refinement, that we have no more strength to battle on, we are compelled to delve into our subconscious and remember that we have a truly supernatural power instilled within us to break out, to always go onwards and upwards.

(from the Book of *Devarim* (Deuteronomy), Chapter 16, Verse 3)

So that you will remember the Exodus from the Land of Egypt all the days of your life.

L'ma-an tiz-kor et yom tsei-t'cha mei-Erets Mitsrayim, kol y'mei cha-yecha.

לְמַעַן תִּזְכֹּר אֶת יוֹם צֵאתְךָ מֵאֶרֶץ מִצְרַיִם, כֹּל יְמֵי חַיֶּיךָ.

2. Receiving the Torah at Mount Sinai

We are instructed to remember the unique event in history of a national revelation of Hashem to the Jewish People at Mount Sinai. Seven weeks after the Exodus from Egypt, Hashem brought the Jewish People to Mount Sinai and gave all those in attendance, approximately three million people, a prophetic vision of G-d. All "heard" the Ten Commandments (literally, the Ten Sayings).

Again there are multiple lessons to learn from this monumental event. Let us focus on only two. The first is that the Torah and the instructions contained within it are directly from Hashem. The Torah is neither man-made nor written by men with special divine guidance and inspiration. It is directly from Hashem. It contains Hashem's thoughts. It is where we find Hashem and Hashem's will. The study of Torah blends our thoughts with Hashem's thoughts. The Torah is Hashem's guidebook for the world.

We must remember that we are never left without divine guidance. The Torah contains within it instructions for every circumstance. The Torah is divine, so every instruction must be considered carefully. These are direct instructions from Hashem to us. Ideally, we should view the Torah as being given to each of us personally every day. It is not that Hashem *gave* us the Torah 3,300 years ago, but rather that Hashem *gives* us the Torah *each* day. We should accept it daily as new and refreshing and exciting and full of meaning and fulfillment.

(from the Book of *Devarim* (Deuteronomy), Chapter 4, Verses 9-10)

Just beware and guard yourself very carefully, so that you should not forget the things your eyes have seen and they should not leave your heart all the days of your life. And you are to teach your children and your grandchildren about the day you stood before Hashem your G-d, at Mount Sinai.

Rak hi-sha-meir l'cha u-sh'mor naf-sh'cha m'od, pen tish-kach et ha-d'va-rim asher ra-u ei-necha u-fen ya-su-ru mil-va-v'cha, kol y'mei cha-yecha. V'ho-da-tam l'va-necha, v'liv-nei va-necha. Yom, asher ama-d'ta lif-nei Hashem Elo-hecha b'cho-reiv.

רַק הִשָּׁמֶר לְךָ וּשְׁמֹר נַפְשְׁךָ מְאֹד, פֶּן תִּשְׁכַּח אֶת הַדְּבָרִים אֲשֶׁר רָאוּ עֵינֶיךָ וּפֶן יָסוּרוּ מִלְּבָבְךָ, כֹּל יְמֵי חַיֶּיךָ. וְהוֹדַעְתָּם לְבָנֶיךָ, וְלִבְנֵי בָנֶיךָ. יוֹם, אֲשֶׁר עָמַדְתָּ לִפְנֵי יְיָ אֱלֹהֶיךָ בְּחֹרֵב.

3. The Attack of Amalek

After the Jews left Egypt, all nations realized that the Jews were a G-dly nation. Then, just as the Jewish People were beginning to develop a passion and commitment towards Hashem and towards goodness, one nation chose to be the arch-enemy of goodness and G-dliness. Amalek, the descendents of Eisav (see the book of Genesis for the complete story), the predecessors of Haman (see the Book of Esther for the complete story), and the assumed predecessors of Nazi Germany (what other nation could be capable of such unspeakable barbarity against the Jews?), attacked the Jewish People at its weakest point.

But Amalek not only represents those external forces that seek to prevent us from fulfilling our mission as Jewish people. Amalek also represents internal psychological forces within each of us that attack us at our weakest moments. The goal of Amalek is to "cool us off" from the passion to perform mitzvot and to spread goodness. Amalek is the feeling that we must be like others, that we must conform to the norms of the society around us. Amalek is going through the motions as we study Torah and perform mitzvot. Amalek means doing mitzvot in a lukewarm fashion, devoid of heart, devoid of meaning. Amalek is the feeling of fatigue, of defeat, of weakness, of giving up.

We must remember to keep going in the face of external forces that seek to prevent us from doing what we are put here to do. More importantly, we must remember to fight the internal psychological forces that push us to just go through the motions without passion and commitment. Mitzvot should be performed with heart. The heart must join with the other parts of the body that are performing that particular mitzvah.

(from the Book of *Devarim* (Deuteronomy), Chapter 25, Verses 17-18)

Remember what Amalek did to you on the way when you were leaving Egypt. How they attacked you (some translate this as "they cooled down your passion") **on the way, and cut down the weakest who were trailing behind you, when you were tired and exhausted. And they** (i.e., Amalek) **did not fear G-d.**

Za-chor eit asher asah l'cha Ama-leik, ba-derech b'tsei-t'chem mi-Mits-ra-yim. Asher kar-cha ba-derech, va-y'za-neiv b'cha kol ha-ne-che-shalim a-cha-recha, v'atah a-yeif v'ya-gei-a, v'lo ya-rei Elo-him.

זָכוֹר אֵת אֲשֶׁר עָשָׂה לְךָ עֲמָלֵק, בַּדֶּרֶךְ בְּצֵאתְכֶם מִמִּצְרָיִם. אֲשֶׁר קָרְךָ בַּדֶּרֶךְ, וַיְזַנֵּב בְּךָ כָּל הַנֶּחֱשָׁלִים אַחֲרֶיךָ, וְאַתָּה עָיֵף וְיָגֵעַ, וְלֹא יָרֵא אֱלֹהִים.

4. The Incident of the Golden Calf

After the Jews experienced the revelation at Mount Sinai, Moshe went up to the mountain, while Hashem (so to speak) came down to the mountain. Heavens met Earth. The heavenly Torah was to be revealed to us here on Earth. Moshe went to learn the Torah and its interpretations directly from Hashem. He was to be on the mountain for a period of forty days.

But some of the Jewish people miscalculated when the period of forty days would end and Moshe would return. When Moshe failed to return at the time they had calculated, they wrongly assumed that he would never return and thus they would be left leaderless and without a spiritual shepherd to bring them closer to Hashem. They felt alone and abandoned. So they fashioned a golden calf to channel spiritual powers and thus serve as an intermediary between the people and Hashem.

This proved to be a tragic mistake with grave consequences. Though they had a real, true, G-dly, spiritual leader, some people seized the moment to worship the golden calf itself. Others, especially the spiritual tribe of Levi, chose to remain faithful to Moshe and to Hashem. A few hours later, Moshe descended with the first set of Tablets, on which Hashem had inscribed the Ten Commandments. When he saw what had happened, he was compelled to shatter the Tablets.

So why remember this event every day? What are the practical implications? The "good news" that came from this event was the concept of *teshuvah*, return. Hashem would forgive the Jewish People once they admitted where they had erred and were sorry for what they had done. Once they resolved never to make the same mistake again, Hashem forgave them.

Moshe carved a new set of sapphire tablets and again ascended Mount Sinai. This time he prayed for forgiveness on behalf of the Jewish people, learned Torah directly from Hashem, and descended 120 days later on the day after the very first Yom Kippur, the Day of Forgiveness.

The incident of the Golden Calf teaches us that Hashem forgives. Hashem always leaves a door open for return. Hashem helps us return. If we honestly contemplate our errors, admit to them, regret them, and make an honest attempt to correct them, Hashem will forgive us. In all likelihood we will stand on a higher spiritual plane than we were on before. We will have used our errors as catalysts for growth and development. The Tablets carved by Hashem were shattered. The ones made by the people in the process of return last forever. They can never be shattered. They are held in trust for us until Mashiach arrives and ushers in the time of worldly return. This is the power of return, of *teshuvah*.

Another lesson to remember is that Hashem never leaves us leaderless. Hashem will never leave his "sheep" without a spiritual "shepherd." The shepherd may be an individual possessing greater or lesser ability and holiness, but Hashem will provide us with leadership.

This is true not only on a national level, but also on an individual level. We are all instructed to find a Torah teacher, a mentor, a spiritual leader. Hashem will help us find this individual or individuals who will bring us closer to Hashem. All we have to do is search and ask Hashem for help. We are guaranteed success.

(from the Book of *Devarim* (Deuteronomy), Chapter 9, Verse 7)

Remember, never forget, how you angered Adonoy, your G-d, in the desert.

Z'chor, al tish-kach, eit asher hik-tsaf-ta et Adonoy Elo-hecha, ba-mid-bar.

זְכֹר, אַל תִּשְׁכַּח, אֵת אֲשֶׁר הִקְצַפְתָּ אֶת יי אֱלֹהֶיךָ, בַּמִּדְבָּר.

5. Miriam's Punishment

As Moshe, the leader of the Jewish People during the Exodus from Egypt, rose in spiritual greatness, he separated himself from his wife. His sister, Miriam, was perturbed by this and informed their elder brother, Aaron. Although her intent was based on her deep concern for her brother, she misused her power of speech. She spoke *lashon hara*, bad talk, words that hurt. In essence, she opened the door for Aaron to lose a measure of respect for his younger brother, Moshe.

Now if you and I had spoken the same words, we would have achieved a new level of greatness. But Miriam was the greatest of all women. She was a prophetess, a spiritual leader of extremely great proportions. Her stature and position compelled her to be held to the highest standards of human behavior. Talking negatively about her brother, Moshe, even though what she was saying was true and even though her intent was good, was deemed by Hashem to be a serious error.

Thus Miriam was afflicted with the spiritual illness of *tsara'at* (improperly translated as leprosy). All of Israel waited for her to be healed and a great lesson was learned by all Jews for all times. We must watch our power of speech. It is what separates us from lower life forms. It is a gift from Hashem.

The power of speech is the power to teach. It is the power to uplift, to inspire, to question and learn, to pray. It is the power to connect to people and to Hashem.

Misused, it is the power to hurt, to destroy, to mislead, to inspire evil. Its negative manifestations are gossip, lies, misleading statements, deception, and spreading true but negative stories that destroy people and their reputations. It can take many, many years to earn a good reputation. It takes only a few words to destroy those years of hard work, and this destruction can never be repaired. Words can never be taken back. Rumors can never be undone. The hurt inflicted by spreading destructive words can never be healed.

We are to be on guard to watch what we say and what we hear every moment.

(from the Book of *Devarim* (Deuteronomy), Chapter 24, Verse 9)

Remember what Adonoy, your G-d, did to Miriam, on the way, when you were leaving Egypt.

Za-chor, eit asher asah Adonoy Elo-hecha l'Miriam, ba-derech, b'tsei-t'chem mi-Mits-ra-yim.

זָכוֹר, אֵת אֲשֶׁר עָשָׂה יי אֱלֹהֶיךָ לְמִרְיָם, בַּדֶּרֶךְ, בְּצֵאתְכֶם מִמִּצְרָיִם.

6. Remember Shabbat

We have already had a discussion of some length about Shabbat in a previous chapter. Recurring references to Shabbat at the end of the daily morning prayers and again in the Six Remembrances confirms its centrality in Jewish life and Jewish thought.

As Ahad Ha'am, the famed Russian-Jewish author, wrote, "More than the Jews have kept Shabbat, Shabbat has kept the Jews." It is the key to our Jewishness. But Shabbat has two seemingly opposing elements. On the one hand, it is called *Shabbat Kodesh*, the Holy Shabbat, the day that is separate from all others, the day to escape from daily life and take refuge in spirituality. It is a day of prayer, of Torah study, of contemplation, of thanksgiving, of greater awareness of Hashem. On the other hand, Shabbat is also the day we eat our finest foods, drink our best wine, and achieve our longest and deepest rest. It is a day of laughter and friendship, a day of love. So which one is it? Is it a spiritual day (i.e., *kodesh*, holy) or is it a day of the finest physical pleasures (i.e., *oneg*, pleasurable)? Aren't these two concepts diametrically opposed to one another?

The answer, of course, is that these two concepts are not in opposition to one another. They work in harmony with one another. Shabbat teaches that we can and we must imbue all daily activities with *kedushah*, holiness. Every day contains the spark, the blessing of Shabbat.

Shabbat teaches that every thing, from food and drink to friendship and love, is a channel through which light and holiness flow into the world. Holiness is not reserved for prayer and Torah study. The domain of holiness is not exclusively in the shuls. Eating can be holy. Work can be holy. Rest can be holy. Laughter can be holy. Love can certainly be holy. So, every day, we remember to infuse our activities, our words, and our thoughts with holiness. That is the lesson of Shabbat. That is the mission that we are to fulfill in our far too short lives here on Earth.

Remember that.

(from the Book of *Shemot* (Exodus), Chapter 20, Verse 8)
Remember the Shabbat day to make it holy (i.e., special).

Za-chor et yom ha-Shabbat l'kad-sho.   זָכוֹר אֶת יוֹם הַשַׁבָּת, לְקַדְּשׁוֹ.

And Then Some . . .

In the writings of the great Sephardic rabbi and mystic known as the Chida, and the kabbalistic siddur *Beit Yaakov* compiled by Rabbi Yaakov Emden in eighteenth-century Germany, an additional four points that we are to recall each day are listed, as follows:

7. Hashem Gives Us *Koach*

Remember that all good things come from Hashem. Food, clothing, shelter, health, and all of the wonderful gifts that we require in order to live productive, meaningful, and purposeful lives, have their source in Hashem and are sent to us by Him. One of the greatest gifts that Hashem gives us is the *koach*, the inner strength, to deal successfully with the daily challenges in life.

(from the Book of *Devarim* (Deuteronomy), Chapter 8, verse 18)
And you should remember Adonoy your G-d, for it is He who gives you the strength to achieve success.

V'za-char-ta, et Adonoy Elo-hecha ki Hu ha-no-tein l'cha koa-ach, la-asot cha-yil.   וְזָכַרְתָּ, אֶת יי אֱלֹהֶיךָ כִּי הוּא הַנֹּתֵן לְךָ כֹּחַ, לַעֲשׂוֹת חָיִל.

8. Remember the *Mahn*

Hashem provides what we need every day. When the Jews left Egypt more than 3,300 years ago and headed into the desert with no food or water, Hashem provided everything they needed, including *mahn* (manna) to eat, for a period of forty years until the Jews reached the Land of Israel. In the same way, He provided for us yesterday, the day before, and the days before that, too. Remember? Hashem will continue provide for us today and tomorrow and the day after that, too. Relax. Enjoy. And appreciate what you have rather than focusing on what you don't have.

(from the book of *Devarim* (Deuteronomy), Chapter 8, verses 2, 3)
And you should always remember the way in which Adonoy, your G-d, led you these forty years in the desert, in order to challenge you, to test you, to know what was in your heart; would you listen to

His mitzvot or not. And He challenged you, made you hungry, and fed you with *mahn*, which you did not know previously and neither did your fathers. So that He will make you understand that man does not live by bread alone, but he lives by what emanates from the mouth of Adonoy.

V'za-char-ta et kol ha-derech, asher ho-li-ch'cha Adonoy Elo-hecha zeh ar-ba-im shanah ba-mid-bar. L'ma-an ano-t'cha l'na-so-t'cha, la-da-at et asher bil-va-v'cha ha-tish-mor mits-vo-tav im lo. Va-y'an-cha, va-yar-i-vecha, va-ya-achil-cha et ha-man asher lo ya-da-ta, v'lo yad-un avo-techa. L'ma-an ho-di-acha, ki lo al ha-lechem l'va-do yich-yeh ha-adam, ki al kol mo-tsa fi Adonoy, yich-yeh ha-adam.

וְזָכַרְתָּ אֶת כָּל הַדֶּרֶךְ, אֲשֶׁר הוֹלִיכְךָ יְיָ אֱלֹהֶיךָ זֶה אַרְבָּעִים שָׁנָה בַּמִּדְבָּר. לְמַעַן עַנֹּתְךָ לְנַסֹּתְךָ, לָדַעַת אֶת אֲשֶׁר בִּלְבָבְךָ הֲתִשְׁמֹר מִצְוֹתָיו אִם לֹא. וַיְעַנְּךָ, וַיַּרְעִבֶךָ, וַיַּאֲכִלְךָ אֶת הַמָּן אֲשֶׁר לֹא יָדַעְתָּ, וְלֹא יָדְעוּן אֲבֹתֶיךָ. לְמַעַן הוֹדִיעֲךָ, כִּי לֹא עַל הַלֶּחֶם לְבַדּוֹ יִחְיֶה הָאָדָם, כִּי עַל כָּל מוֹצָא פִי יְיָ, יִחְיֶה הָאָדָם.

9. Remember Bilam and Balak

When the Jews were about to conclude their journey in the desert and finally enter the Land of Israel, the nation of Midian tried to use all means to destroy the Jewish Nation and prevent it from fulfilling its destiny of being a "light to the nations." Having seen how the Jews defeated mighty armies, Midian prepared to defeat the Jews spiritually. To this end, Balak, the King of Midian, hired the prophet Bilam, the greatest Gentile spiritual personality of his time, to find a way to defeat the Jewish People by exploiting their spiritual weaknesses. However, in the end, it was Balak and Bilam who went down to crushing defeat, and the Jews did indeed enter the Land of Israel and began to achieve their destined role in humanity.

In every generation, indeed in all times, there are those who wish to hurt, defeat, or kill the Jewish People and prevent it from fulfilling its role in humanity. Today, its face is radical Islamist terrorism and extreme liberal antisemitism. But these are just the newest manifestations of Nazism, Communism, early Christendom, radical Islam, and a myriad of other faces of evil.

Hashem saves us from our enemies and turns plans for evil to good outcomes. Our history, past and present, is one filled with wonders and miracles on a daily basis.

(from the Book of *Michah* (Micah), Chapter 6, verse 5)

My Nation, remember how Balak, the king of Moav, devised, and what Bilaam, the son of Beor (the evil prophet), responded to him, from Sheetim all the way to Gilgal, so that you will know the righteous acts of G-d.

Ami, z'char na mah ya-ats Ba-lak melech Mo-av, u-meh anah oto, Bil-am ben B'or, min ha-Shi-tim, ad ha-Gil-gal, l'ma-an, da-at tsid-kot Adonoy.

עַמִּי, זְכָר נָא מַה יָּעַץ בָּלָק מֶלֶךְ מוֹאָב, וּמֶה עָנָה אֹתוֹ, בִּלְעָם בֶּן בְּעוֹר, מִן הַשִּׁטִּים, עַד הַגִּלְגָּל, לְמַעַן, דַּעַת צִדְקוֹת יי.

10. Remember Jerusalem

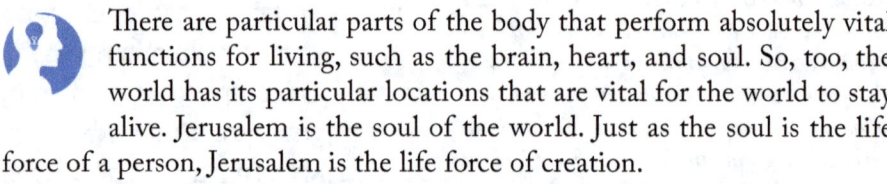

There are particular parts of the body that perform absolutely vital functions for living, such as the brain, heart, and soul. So, too, the world has its particular locations that are vital for the world to stay alive. Jerusalem is the soul of the world. Just as the soul is the life force of a person, Jerusalem is the life force of creation.

It is not simply a city. Jerusalem is a spiritual force that resides in a physical location in Israel. Jerusalem is the source of light, clarity, wisdom, and spirituality for the world. It is the place where heaven and earth connect (just like the center of the hourglass). It is the place from which our prayers ascend to the heavens.

The Holy Temple was the centerpoint of this light. It was destroyed about 2,000 years ago and, as a result, much of the world lives in darkness. Clarity is missing. But Hashem promised that He will indeed rebuild Jerusalem and the Temple, which will once again provide light, clarity, and joy for the entire world. May this happen very soon — perhaps even today!

(from the Book of *Tehillim* (Psalm), 137, verses 5, 6)
If I forget you Jerusalem, let my right hand forget its role,
Let my tongue cleave to my palate, if I do not remember You (Jerusalem),
If I do not place Jerusalem above my greatest joy.

Im esh-kah-cheich Y'ru-sha-la-yim, tish-kach yi-mi-ni. Tid-back l'sho-ni, l'chi-ki, im lo ez-k'rei-chi.

אִם אֶשְׁכָּחֵךְ יְרוּשָׁלָיִם, תִּשְׁכַּח יְמִינִי. תִּדְבַּק לְשׁוֹנִי, לְחִכִּי, אִם לֹא אֶזְכְּרֵכִי.

Im lo a-aleh et Y'ru-sha-la-yim, al rosh sim-cha-ti.

אִם לֹא אַעֲלֶה אֶת יְרוּשָׁלָיִם, עַל רֹאשׁ שִׂמְחָתִי.

MINCHAH: THE WEEKDAY AFTERNOON PRAYERS

This is the prayer that touches Hashem more than any other. Much of the day has passed. It is the time of day when Hashem looks at each of us to see what we have accomplished with our time and our other individual gifts, now that most of our waking hours have passed. Events of the day have reached a feverish pace. And then suddenly, in the midst of all that we are doing, we take some time out to refocus, to recharge, to re-evaluate.

> **Kavanah:** *There is another half of the day left.*
> *There is so much that I can accomplish.*
> *Hashem, help me to do the right things, to make the right decisions.*
> *Show me how to make a difference in the world.*
> *Give me opportunities to do your mitzvot.*
> *Give me faith and trust in You.*
> *Give me patience.*
> *Let me relax, calm down, smile, and enjoy the beauty of life.*

The four elements of the Weekday Afternoon Prayer are as follows:

- *Ashrei* (see pages 93 to 95).

- Weekday *Shemoneh Esrei* (see pages 128 to 145).

- The Concluding Prayer: *Aleinu* (see pages 146 to 147).

- If a mourner is present and there is a *minyan* of ten Jewish men, the mourner recites the Mourner's Kaddish at this point (see pages 124 to 125).

MA'ARIV:
THE WEEKDAY EVENING PRAYERS

NOTE: For Friday night Shabbat prayers, see page 171.

It is near the end of the day. I am tired. I can't even remember waking up this morning. It is time to look back and evaluate the day. What did I accomplish? What mitzvot did I fulfill? Whom did I touch? Let me appreciate all that I did and all that I have. And if I made mistakes, I need forgiveness, as well as the good judgment and strength to stop making those same mistakes tomorrow and in the future. The night is dark. It is a spiritual time, but it can also be scary and lonely and filled with fear of the unknown. What will come tomorrow?

Ma'ariv is the time for quiet resolve. Resolve to continue to be good and to make a difference. It is a time for faith and trust in Hashem. It is a time to seek the strength to keep going no matter what challenges may lay ahead. It is a time for appreciation. It is a time for faith and hope and resolve.

Blessings before the *Shema*:

First Blessing: *Hama'ariv Aravim*
Who Brings on the Evening

> **Kavanah:** *Hashem makes night and day. Everything has a meaning and a purpose. Hashem runs the world and everything is part of His plan. Hashem is with us and with me even in times of darkness. Hashem, help me to trust You.*

You, Hashem, Source of all blessings, are the One who runs the world. With Hashem's word, He brings on the evenings, releases the morning sun, controls the weather, changes the seasons, and sets the stars in their positions. Hashem creates day and night and gradually rolls away the light before the darkness and the darkness before the light. Hashem makes the day pass to bring the night and makes a distinction between day and night. Hashem controls all of the forces of the universe. May Hashem, the living, eternal G-d, rule over us forever.

You, Adonoy, Source of all blessings, bring on the evening.

Baruch atah Adonoy, Elo-heinu Melech ha-olam, a-sher bid-varo ma-ariv ara-vim, b'choch-mah po-tei-ach sh'arim, u-vi-t'vu-nah m'sha-neh i-tim u-ma-cha-lif et ha-z'ma-nim, u-m'sa-deir et ha-ko-cha-vim b'mish-m'ro-tei-hem ba-ra-ki-a kir-tso-no. Bo-rei yom va-lailah, go-lel or mi-p'nei cho-shech v'cho-shech mi-p'nei or. U-ma-a-vir yom u-mei-vi lailah, u-mav-dil bein yom u-vein lailah, Adonoy ts'va-ot sh'mo. El chai v'ka-yam ta-mid yim-loch alei-nu l'olam va-ed.

בָּרוּךְ אַתָּה יְיָ, אֱלֹהֵינוּ מֶלֶךְ הָעוֹלָם, אֲשֶׁר בִּדְבָרוֹ מַעֲרִיב עֲרָבִים, בְּחָכְמָה פּוֹתֵחַ שְׁעָרִים, וּבִתְבוּנָה מְשַׁנֶּה עִתִּים וּמַחֲלִיף אֶת הַזְּמַנִּים, וּמְסַדֵּר אֶת הַכּוֹכָבִים בְּמִשְׁמְרוֹתֵיהֶם בָּרָקִיעַ כִּרְצוֹנוֹ. בּוֹרֵא יוֹם וָלָיְלָה, גּוֹלֵל אוֹר מִפְּנֵי חֹשֶׁךְ וְחֹשֶׁךְ מִפְּנֵי אוֹר. וּמַעֲבִיר יוֹם וּמֵבִיא לָיְלָה, וּמַבְדִּיל בֵּין יוֹם וּבֵין לָיְלָה, יְיָ צְבָאוֹת שְׁמוֹ. אֵל חַי וְקַיָּם תָּמִיד יִמְלוֹךְ עָלֵינוּ לְעוֹלָם וָעֶד.

Baruch atah Adonoy, ha-ma-ariv ara-vim.

בָּרוּךְ אַתָּה יְיָ, הַמַּעֲרִיב עֲרָבִים.

Second Blessing: *Oheiv Amo Yisrael*
Who Loves the Jewish People

> **Kavanah:** *Hashem loves the Jewish People in a special way. As we will say next in the* Shema, *we, the Jewish People, love Hashem. We understand that we are distinct from all others and that we have Hashem's greatest expression of His love, the Torah. The Torah provides the keys to our life in this world and the next world.*

With an everlasting love, You have loved Your People, the People of Israel. You taught us and trained us to keep the Torah with all its mitzvot, including the laws that we understand and those that are beyond our comprehension.

A-ha-vat olam beit Yisrael am-cha a-hav-ta, Torah u-mits-vot chu-kim u-mish-pa-tim, ota-nu li-ma-d'ta.

אַהֲבַת עוֹלָם בֵּית יִשְׂרָאֵל עַמְּךָ אָהָבְתָּ. תּוֹרָה וּמִצְוֹת חֻקִּים וּמִשְׁפָּטִים אוֹתָנוּ לִמַּדְתָּ.

Therefore, Hashem, our G-d, when we wake up and when we go to sleep, we will learn and discuss Your laws and we will find joy in the words of Your Torah and Your mitzvot forever. They are (the keys to) life in this world and to eternal life in the World to Come. And we will think about them during the day and night. And do not remove Your love from us forever. You, Adonoy, Source of all blessings, love His people, Israel.

Al kein Adonoy Elo-heinu b'shach-veinu u-v'ku-meinu na-si-ach b'chu-kecha, v'nis-mach b'div-rei Tora-techa u-v'mits-vo-techa l'o-lam va-ed.

עַל כֵּן יְיָ אֱלֹהֵינוּ בְּשָׁכְבֵנוּ וּבְקוּמֵנוּ נָשִׂיחַ בְּחֻקֶּיךָ, וְנִשְׂמַח בְּדִבְרֵי תוֹרָתֶךָ וּבְמִצְוֹתֶיךָ לְעוֹלָם וָעֶד.

Ki heim cha-yeinu v'o-rech ya-meinu u-va-hem neh-geh yo-mam va-lailah. V'a-ha-va-t'cha al ta-sir mi-me-nu l'ola-mim.

כִּי הֵם חַיֵּינוּ וְאֹרֶךְ יָמֵינוּ וּבָהֶם נֶהְגֶּה יוֹמָם וָלָיְלָה. וְאַהֲבָתְךָ אַל תָּסִיר מִמֶּנּוּ לְעוֹלָמִים.

Baruch atah Adonoy, o-heiv amo Yisrael.

בָּרוּךְ אַתָּה יי, אוֹהֵב עַמּוֹ יִשְׂרָאֵל.

Shema Yisrael (Three Parts)
[See Page 59 for an extended explanation of this prayer and of this mitzvah.]

Part I. *Shema* Meditation: The Oneness of Hashem

NOTE: You can choose to say this line more slowly and think as you say each word or you can say the line more quickly as it appears on the next page.

 Cover your eyes with your right hand while saying the opening line of the *Shema*.

שְׁמַע יִשְׂרָאֵל, יי אֱלֹהֵינוּ, יי אֶחָד:

שְׁמַע *Shema* Understand (I "hear" you).
יִשְׂרָאֵל *Yisrael* The Jew, one who struggles with G-d, with the world, and with one's self and is victorious.
יי *Adonoy* God of compassion.
אֱלֹהֵינוּ *Eloheinu* Our G-d and the G-d of judgement.
יי *Adonoy* God of compassion.
אֶחָד *Echad* is the One and Only.

Three meanings:

• The One who creates and runs the world (past and present). The Source of everything. We cover our eyes because we see separation and difference. Hashem is the one unifying life force.

• Hashem is One with me. My soul contains a part of G-d within me.

• Hashem and *Eloheinu* are both One. Both compassion and judgement are ultimately compassion. Like a good parent.

בָּרוּךְ שֵׁם כְּבוֹד מַלְכוּתוֹ לְעוֹלָם וָעֶד (whisper)
(whisper) *Baruch sheim k'vod mal-chu-to l'olam va-ed.*
(whisper) **May Hashem be acknowledged as the Source of blessing forever.**

> **Kavanah:** *Hashem is the one life force behind all things.*
> *Everything that Hashem does is for the good.*
> *Part of Hashem is within me. I am one with Hashem and He is one with me.*
> *I will try to follow Hashem's directions and connect with Him by utilizing the forces of love and awe that Hashem has put in my soul.*

NOTE: Please continue with the rest of *Shema* below, starting with "V'a-hav-ta."

 Cover your eyes with your right hand while saying the opening line of the *Shema*.

שְׁמַע יִשְׂרָאֵל, יְיָ אֱלֹהֵינוּ, יְיָ אֶחָד:
(whisper)
בָּרוּךְ שֵׁם כְּבוֹד מַלְכוּתוֹ לְעוֹלָם וָעֶד

Shema Yisrael, Adonoy Elo-heinu, Adonoy Echad.
(whisper)
Baruch sheim k'vod mal-chu-to l'olam va-ed.

Listen Israel, Adonoy is our G-d, Adonoy is One.
(whisper)
May Hashem be acknowledged as the Source of blessing forever.

(from *Devarim* (Deuteronomy), Chapter 6, verses 5 to 9)

V'a-hav-ta eit Adonoy Elo-hecha, b'chol l'va-v'cha, u-v'chol naf-sh'cha, u-v'chol mo-decha. V'ha-yu ha-d'va-rim ha-eileh, asher ano-chi m'tsa-v'cha ha-yom, al l'va-vecha. V'shi-nan-tam l'va-necha, v'di-bar-ta bam, b'shiv-t'cha b'vei-techa, u-v'lech-t'cha va-derech, u-v'shach-b'cha u-v'ku-mecha. U-k'shar-tam l'ot al ya-decha, v'ha-yu l'to-ta-fot bein ei-necha. U-ch'tav-tam al m'zu-zot bei-techa u-vish-a-recha.

וְאָהַבְתָּ אֵת יְיָ אֱלֹהֶיךָ, בְּכָל לְבָבְךָ, וּבְכָל נַפְשְׁךָ, וּבְכָל מְאֹדֶךָ. וְהָיוּ הַדְּבָרִים הָאֵלֶּה, אֲשֶׁר אָנֹכִי מְצַוְּךָ הַיּוֹם, עַל לְבָבֶךָ. וְשִׁנַּנְתָּם לְבָנֶיךָ, וְדִבַּרְתָּ בָּם, בְּשִׁבְתְּךָ בְּבֵיתֶךָ, וּבְלֶכְתְּךָ בַדֶּרֶךְ, וּבְשָׁכְבְּךָ וּבְקוּמֶךָ. וּקְשַׁרְתָּם לְאוֹת עַל יָדֶךָ, וְהָיוּ לְטֹטָפֹת בֵּין עֵינֶיךָ. וּכְתַבְתָּם עַל מְזֻזוֹת בֵּיתֶךָ וּבִשְׁעָרֶיךָ.

And you shall love Hashem, your G-d, with all your heart, with all your soul, and with all that is dear to you. These words which I command you today shall always be in your heart. Teach them to your children. Speak about them when you are at home, when you travel, when you lay down, and when you arise. Bind them as a sign on your arm (i.e., *tefillin* on the arm) and as *tefillin* upon the center of your head and write them as *mezuzot* for the doorposts of your house and your gates.

Part II. *V'hayah Im Shamo'a*
Cause and Effect: The Results of the Jewish People's Choices and Behavior

> **Kavanah:** *What I do matters to me and to the Jewish People. All of my actions will be recorded and evaluated. Each action has an effect upon me and on the Jewish Nation. There is cause and effect and consequence to my actions, words, thoughts, and decisions.*

(from *Devarim* (Deuteronomy) Chapter 11, Verses 13 to 21)

V'ha-yah, im sha-mo-a tish-m'u el mits-vo-tai, asher ano-chi m'tsa-veh et-chem ha-yom, l'a-ha-vah et Adonoy Elo-heichem u-l'av-do, b'chol l'vav-chem u-v'chol naf-sh'chem, v'na-ta-ti m'tar ar-ts'chem b'i-to, yo-reh u-mal-kosh, v'a-saf-ta d'ga-necha, v'ti-ro-sh'cha v'yits-ha-recha. V'na-ta-ti eisev b'sa-d'cha liv-hem-techa, v'a-chal-ta v'sa-va-ta. Hi-sham-ru la-chem, pen yif-teh l'vav-chem, v'sar-tem va-ava-d'tem Elo-him achei-rim, v'hish-ta-cha-vitem la-hem. V'cha-rah af Adonoy ba-chem, v'a-tsar et ha-sha-ma-yim, v'lo yi-h'yeh ma-tar, v'ha-ada-mah lo ti-tein et y'vu-lah, va-ava-d'tem m'hei-rah mei-al ha-arets ha-tovah asher Adonoy no-tein la-chem. V'sam-tem et d'va-rei eileh, al l'vav-chem v'al naf-sh'chem, u-k'shar-tem o-tam l'ot al yed-chem, v'ha-yu l'to-ta-fot bein einei-chem. V'li-ma-d'tem o-tam et b'nei-chem, l'da-beir bam b'shiv-t'cha b'vei-techa, u-v'lech-t'cha va-derech, u-v'shach-b'cha u-v'ku-mecha. U-ch'tav-tam al m'zu-zot bei-techa, u-vish-a-recha.

L'ma-an yir-bu y'mei-chem vi-mei v'nei-chem, al ha-ada-mah asher nish-ba Adonoy la-avo-tei-chem la-teit la-hem, ki-mei ha-sha-ma-yim al ha-arets.

וְהָיָה, אִם שָׁמֹעַ תִּשְׁמְעוּ אֶל מִצְוֹתַי, אֲשֶׁר אָנֹכִי מְצַוֶּה אֶתְכֶם הַיּוֹם, לְאַהֲבָה אֶת יְיָ אֱלֹהֵיכֶם וּלְעָבְדוֹ, בְּכָל לְבַבְכֶם וּבְכָל נַפְשְׁכֶם. וְנָתַתִּי מְטַר אַרְצְכֶם בְּעִתּוֹ, יוֹרֶה וּמַלְקוֹשׁ, וְאָסַפְתָּ דְגָנֶךָ וְתִירשְׁךָ וְיִצְהָרֶךָ. וְנָתַתִּי עֵשֶׂב בְּשָׂדְךָ לִבְהֶמְתֶּךָ, וְאָכַלְתָּ וְשָׂבָעְתָּ. הִשָּׁמְרוּ לָכֶם, פֶּן יִפְתֶּה לְבַבְכֶם, וְסַרְתֶּם וַעֲבַדְתֶּם אֱלֹהִים אֲחֵרִים, וְהִשְׁתַּחֲוִיתֶם לָהֶם. וְחָרָה אַף יְיָ בָּכֶם, וְעָצַר אֶת הַשָּׁמַיִם, וְלֹא יִהְיֶה מָטָר, וְהָאֲדָמָה לֹא תִתֵּן אֶת יְבוּלָהּ, וַאֲבַדְתֶּם מְהֵרָה מֵעַל הָאָרֶץ הַטֹּבָה אֲשֶׁר יְיָ נֹתֵן לָכֶם. וְשַׂמְתֶּם אֶת דְּבָרַי אֵלֶּה, עַל לְבַבְכֶם וְעַל נַפְשְׁכֶם, וּקְשַׁרְתֶּם אֹתָם לְאוֹת עַל יֶדְכֶם, וְהָיוּ לְטוֹטָפֹת בֵּין עֵינֵיכֶם. וְלִמַּדְתֶּם אֹתָם אֶת בְּנֵיכֶם, לְדַבֵּר בָּם בְּשִׁבְתְּךָ בְּבֵיתֶךָ, וּבְלֶכְתְּךָ בַדֶּרֶךְ, וּבְשָׁכְבְּךָ וּבְקוּמֶךָ. וּכְתַבְתָּם עַל מְזוּזוֹת בֵּיתֶךָ, וּבִשְׁעָרֶיךָ.

לְמַעַן יִרְבּוּ יְמֵיכֶם וִימֵי בְנֵיכֶם, עַל הָאֲדָמָה אֲשֶׁר נִשְׁבַּע יְיָ לַאֲבֹתֵיכֶם לָתֵת לָהֶם, כִּימֵי הַשָּׁמַיִם עַל הָאָרֶץ.

And if you are careful to listen to My commandments, which I am commanding you today, and if you love Hashem, your G-d, and serve Him with all your heart and all your soul, then I, Hashem, have made this promise: I (Hashem) will provide rain to your land in its proper times so that you can harvest grain, wine, and olive oil. I will provide grass in your fields for your cattle and you will have sufficient food to eat and be satiated. Be careful not to be led astray by your heart's temptations to worship other gods or to bow to them. If you do follow other gods, Hashem will be angry with you and will restrain the heavens and there will be no rain and the earth will not yield produce. And you will vanish quickly from the good land which Hashem is giving you. Place these words of Mine upon your heart and soul. Bind them (for *tefillin*) as a sign on your arm and let them be *tefillin* in the center of your head. Teach these words to your children. Discuss them at home, when you travel, when you lay down, and when you get up. And write them on *mezuzot* for the doorposts of your homes and gates. If you do this, you and your children will endure for a long time upon the land that Hashem swore to your ancestors, that He would to give them, for as long as the heavens remain above the earth (i.e., forever).

Part III. *Vayomeir*
Remember the Exodus from Egypt and Be Careful to Do the Right Thing

> **Kavanah:** *I will strive to be constantly aware that I am part of the Jewish People and its mission in the world. Hashem helps us to break through our perceived barriers and limitations to achieve personal growth.*

 Identify those issues that are holding you back from growing, achieving, and being the best you can be today. Ask yourself, "Am I sad, angry, lazy, self-focused?" Ask Hashem to help you break out of your personal "Egypt," i.e., your personal barriers and limitations.

(from *Bamidbar* (Numbers) Chapter 15, verses 37 to 41)

Va-yo-meir Adonoy el Mosheh lei-mor: Da-beir el b'nei Yisrael, v'a-mar-ta alei-hem, v'a-su la-hem tsi-tsit, al kan-fei vig-dei-hem l'doro-tam, v'nat-nu al tsi-tsit ha-kanaf, p'til t'chei-let. V'ha-yah la-chem l'tsi-tsit, u-r'item oto, u-z'char-tem et kol mits-vot Adonoy, va-asi-tem o-tam, v'lo ta-tu-ru acha-rei l'vav-chem v'a-cha-rei einei-chem, asher a-tem zo-nim acha-rei-hem. L'ma-an tiz-k'ru, va-asi-tem et

וַיֹּאמֶר יי אֶל מֹשֶׁה לֵּאמֹר: דַּבֵּר אֶל בְּנֵי יִשְׂרָאֵל, וְאָמַרְתָּ אֲלֵהֶם, וְעָשׂוּ לָהֶם צִיצִת, עַל כַּנְפֵי בִגְדֵיהֶם לְדֹרֹתָם, וְנָתְנוּ עַל צִיצִת הַכָּנָף, פְּתִיל תְּכֵלֶת. וְהָיָה לָכֶם לְצִיצִת, וּרְאִיתֶם אֹתוֹ, וּזְכַרְתֶּם אֶת כָּל מִצְוֹת יי, וַעֲשִׂיתֶם אֹתָם, וְלֹא תָתוּרוּ אַחֲרֵי לְבַבְכֶם וְאַחֲרֵי עֵינֵיכֶם, אֲשֶׁר אַתֶּם זֹנִים אַחֲרֵיהֶם. לְמַעַן תִּזְכְּרוּ, וַעֲשִׂיתֶם אֶת

kol mits-vo-tai, vi-h'yi-tem k'do-shim lei-lo-heichem. Ani Adonoy Elo-heichem, asher ho-tsei-ti et-chem mei-erets Mits-ra-yim, li-h'yot la-chem lei-lo-him; Ani Adonoy Elo-heichem. Emet.

כָּל מִצְוֹתָי, וִהְיִיתֶם קְדֹשִׁים לֵאלֹהֵיכֶם. אֲנִי יְיָ אֱלֹהֵיכֶם, אֲשֶׁר הוֹצֵאתִי אֶתְכֶם מֵאֶרֶץ מִצְרַיִם, לִהְיוֹת לָכֶם לֵאלֹהִים, אֲנִי יְיָ אֱלֹהֵיכֶם. אֱמֶת.

And Hashem spoke to Moshe and instructed him to speak to the Jewish People and have them make *tzitzit* (special tassels) on the corners of four-cornered garments for all generations. These should include a thread of sky-blue wool (dyed from a source that is no longer available today). These shall be your *tzitzit*. When you see them, you will remember all of Hashem's commandments and keep and follow them. Thus, you will not be led astray by the desires of your heart and eyes, which have a tendency to lead you astray. You will remember and keep all of My commandments and will be holy to your G-d. I am Hashem, your G-d, who brought you out of Egypt to be your G-d. I am Hashem, your G-d. This is truth.

1. Turn to the Central Weekday Prayer, *Shemoneh Esrei* (see pages 128 to 145).

2. Then say the Concluding Prayer, *Aleinu* (see pages 146 to 147).

3. If a mourner is present and if a *minyan* of ten Jewish men is present, the mourner recites the Mourner's Kaddish at this point (see pages 124 to 125).

FRIDAY NIGHT PRAYERS

Take a deep breath, close your eyes, and relax.

Ahhh. The week is over and what a week it was. I can't even remember all the way back to last Saturday night. I was so busy. I did so many things, accomplished a lot, spoke to so many people. But thankfully this week is now over. I can now relax, rest my body and my mind. Think of all the things I am blessed with. Remember Hashem and all that Hashem does for me. I can sit back and smile. Thank G-d, *baruch Hashem*, for it is finally the best day of the week, Shabbat!!

Kabbalat Shabbat: Welcoming Shabbat

Fixing the Six Days of the Past Week

These are parts or all of the six Psalms that remind us that Hashem created and runs the world. When we recite or sing excerpts from each of these Psalms, we should have in mind that we are "fixing" any of the mistakes we made during the past week so that we can enter Shabbat with a clean slate and a renewed spirit.

For those who wish to sing the three Psalms that are usually sung in a "Carlebach-style" service, the Hebrew, transliteration, and translation for those entire psalms are provided.

> **Kavanah:** *Sometimes we get caught up in many silly, insignificant things. We focus too much on material things and material success: silly thoughts, relationships that don't really matter, mistakes that happened, the "small picture." Perhaps we forgot about Hashem and the part Hashem plays in our lives every second of every day. We all likely made some mistakes, said some things we regret saying, and missed some glorious opportunities to perform specific mitzvot and make a difference.*
> *So let us fix up the past week by using the "mystical keys" of the specific Psalms written by King David for this purpose by focusing once again on the "big picture." Let us focus once again on Hashem, on Shabbat, on joy, on being Jewish. Let's rejuvenate our spirit!*

Fixing this past Sunday: An Excerpt from Psalm 95

Theme: Hashem created the world and runs it.

 Come, let us sing to Hashem. Let us call out to the Dependable One who saves us. Let us greet Hashem with thanks and call to Hashem with songs of praise.

L'chu n'ra-n'nah l'Adonoy,	לְכוּ נְרַנְּנָה לַיָי,
na-ri-ah l'tsur yish-einu,	נָרִיעָה לְצוּר יִשְׁעֵנוּ.
N'kad-mah fa-nav b'todah,	נְקַדְּמָה פָנָיו בְּתוֹדָה,
bi-z'mi-rot na-ri-a lo.	בִּזְמִרוֹת נָרִיעַ לוֹ.

Fixing this past Monday: Psalm 96

Theme: When Mashiach comes, all of the world will recognize Hashem and rejoice.

Let us sing a new song to Hashem. Let all people sing to Hashem! Sing to Hashem and recognize that He is the source of all blessings. Tell the people of all the nations of Hashem's glory and His wonders, that Hashem is truly great and is praised very much. He is awesome above all other forces. The gods of the nations are nothing. Hashem is the Creator of the heavens. All of the glory, majesty, might, and beauty in the world comes from Hashem.

Let all the families of man recognize that honor and strength come from Hashem. Give honor to Hashem. Bring a gift and come into His courtyard. Bow before Hashem in His holy place. Let everyone be in awe of Him.

Tell the nations that Hashem rules. He runs the world and it cannot fall. Hashem will judge the nations fairly.

The heavens will be happy, the earth will rejoice, the seas will roar, the fields and all that live in them will celebrate, and the trees of the forests will sing. For Hashem will have arrived to judge the earth. Hashem will judge the world righteously and the nations with His truth.

Shi-ru l'Adonoy shir cha-dash,	שִׁירוּ לַיָי שִׁיר חָדָשׁ, שִׁירוּ לַיָי כָּל הָאָרֶץ.
shi-ru l'Adonoy kol ha-arets.	שִׁירוּ לַיָי בָּרְכוּ שְׁמוֹ.
Shi-ru l'Adonoy bar-chu sh'mo.	
Bas'ru mi-yom l'yom y'shu-ato.	בַּשְּׂרוּ מִיוֹם לְיוֹם יְשׁוּעָתוֹ.

Sa-p'ru va-go-yim k'vo-do, b'chol ha-amim nif-l'o-tav.	סַפְּרוּ בַגּוֹיִם כְּבוֹדוֹ, בְּכָל הָעַמִּים נִפְלְאוֹתָיו.
Ki ga-dol Adonoy u-m'hu-lal m'od, no-ra hu al kol ha-Elo-him.	כִּי גָדוֹל יְיָ וּמְהֻלָּל מְאֹד, נוֹרָא הוּא עַל כָּל אֱלֹהִים.
Ki, kol Elo-hei ha-amim Eli-lim, va-Adonoy sha-ma-yim asah.	כִּי, כָּל אֱלֹהֵי הָעַמִּים אֱלִילִים, וַיְיָ שָׁמַיִם עָשָׂה.
Hod v'ha-dar l'fa-nav, oz v'tif-eret b'mik-da-sho.	הוֹד וְהָדָר לְפָנָיו, עֹז וְתִפְאֶרֶת בְּמִקְדָּשׁוֹ.
Ha-vu l'Adonoy mish-p'chot a-mim, ha-vu l'Adonoy ka-vod va-oz.	הָבוּ לַייָ מִשְׁפְּחוֹת עַמִּים, הָבוּ לַייָ כָּבוֹד וָעֹז.
Ha-vu l'Adonoy, k'vod sh'mo, s'u min-chah u-vo-u l'chats-ro-tav.	הָבוּ לַייָ, כְּבוֹד שְׁמוֹ, שְׂאוּ מִנְחָה וּבֹאוּ לְחַצְרוֹתָיו.
Hish-ta-cha-vu l'Adonoy b'ha-d'rat ko-desh, chi-lu mi-pa-nav kol ha-arets.	הִשְׁתַּחֲווּ לַייָ בְּהַדְרַת קֹדֶשׁ, חִילוּ מִפָּנָיו כָּל הָאָרֶץ.
Im-ru va-goyim Adonoy ma-lach, af ti-kon tei-vel bal ti-mot, ya-din a-mim b'mei-sha-rim.	אִמְרוּ בַגּוֹיִם יְיָ מָלָךְ, אַף תִּכּוֹן תֵּבֵל בַּל תִּמּוֹט, יָדִין עַמִּים בְּמֵישָׁרִים.
Yis-m'chu ha-sha-ma-yim v'ta-gel ha-arets yir-am ha-yam u-m'lo-o.	יִשְׂמְחוּ הַשָּׁמַיִם וְתָגֵל הָאָרֶץ יִרְעַם הַיָּם וּמְלֹאוֹ.
Ya-aloz sa-dai v'chol asher bo, az y'ra-n'nu kol a-tsei ya-ar.	יַעֲלֹז שָׂדַי וְכָל אֲשֶׁר בּוֹ, אָז יְרַנְּנוּ כָּל עֲצֵי יָעַר.
Lif-nei Adonoy ki va, ki va lish-pot ha-arets, yish-pot tei-vel b'tzedek, v'amim be-emuna-to.	לִפְנֵי יְיָ כִּי בָא, כִּי בָא לִשְׁפֹּט הָאָרֶץ, יִשְׁפֹּט תֵּבֵל בְּצֶדֶק, וְעַמִּים בֶּאֱמוּנָתוֹ.

Fixing Tuesday: An Excerpt from Psalm 97

Theme: When Mashiach comes, all people will follow Hashem and righteous people will be rewarded graciously.

Zion will hear and rejoice and the daughters of Judah will be happy because of Your judgments, Hashem. Those who love Hashem hate evil. Hashem guards the lives of the devout ones and saves them from the hands of the evil ones. Great spiritual light awaits the righteous and great happiness for those with an unwavering heart.

Sham-ah va-tis-mach Tsi-yon va-ta-gel-nah b'not Y'hu-dah, l'ma-an mish-pa-techa Adonoy. Ki atah Adonoy el-yon al kol ha-arets, m'od na-alei-ta al kol elo-him. Oha-vei Adonoy sin-u ra, sho-meir naf-shot cha-si-dav, mi-yad r'sha-im ya-tsi-leim. Or za-ru-a la-tsadik, u-l'yish-rei leiv sim-chah. Sim-chu tsa-di-kim ba-Adonoy, v'ho-du l'zei-cher kad-sho.	שָׁמְעָה וַתִּשְׂמַח צִיּוֹן וַתָּגֵלְנָה בְּנוֹת יְהוּדָה, לְמַעַן מִשְׁפָּטֶיךָ יְיָ. כִּי אַתָּה יְיָ עֶלְיוֹן עַל כָּל הָאָרֶץ, מְאֹד נַעֲלֵיתָ עַל כָּל אֱלֹהִים. אֹהֲבֵי יְיָ שִׂנְאוּ רָע, שֹׁמֵר נַפְשׁוֹת חֲסִידָיו, מִיַּד רְשָׁעִים יַצִּילֵם. אוֹר זָרֻעַ לַצַּדִּיק, וּלְיִשְׁרֵי לֵב שִׂמְחָה. שִׂמְחוּ צַדִּיקִים בַּיְיָ, וְהוֹדוּ לְזֵכֶר קָדְשׁוֹ.

Fixing Wednesday: Psalm 98

Theme: When Mashiach comes, all people and all of nature will join in recognition of and thanks to Hashem.

 Sing a new song to Hashem for He has performed powerful wonders. He has the power to enact whatever He wishes. All will know that Hashem saved us. All of the nations will see His righteousness. He remembered His special kindness and faithfulness for Israel. From one end of the earth to the other, all will see how our Hashem saved us.

All people, call to Hashem. Sing and play songs of joy before Hashem. Play music on a harp and sing praises to Hashem. Call to Hashem, the King, with trumpets and with the sound of the shofar. The sea will roar as will the world and all of those who dwell within it. The rivers will clap and the mountains will sing with joy. For Hashem will have come to judge the earth. He will judge the world with righteousness and the nations with fairness.

Miz-mor, shi-ru la-Adonoy shir cha-dash, ki nif-la-ot asah. Ho-shi-ah lo y'mi-no u-z'ro-a kad-sho. Ho-di-a Adonoy y'shu-a-to, l'ei-nei ha-goyim gi-lah tsid-ka-to. Za-char chas-do ve-emuna-to l'veit Yisrael, ra-u chol af-sei arets eit y'shu-at Elo-heinu. Ha-ri-u l'Adonoy kol ha-arets, pits-chu v'ra-n'nu v'za-mei-ru. Zam-ru l'Adonoy b'chi-nor, b'chi-nor v'kol zim-rah. Ba-cha-tso-ts'rot v'kol sho-far, ha-ri-u lif-nei ha-melech Adonoy.	מִזְמוֹר, שִׁירוּ לַייָ שִׁיר חָדָשׁ, כִּי נִפְלָאוֹת עָשָׂה. הוֹשִׁיעָה לּוֹ יְמִינוֹ וּזְרוֹעַ קָדְשׁוֹ. הוֹדִיעַ יְיָ יְשׁוּעָתוֹ, לְעֵינֵי הַגּוֹיִם גִּלָּה צִדְקָתוֹ. זָכַר חַסְדּוֹ וֶאֱמוּנָתוֹ לְבֵית יִשְׂרָאֵל, רָאוּ כָל אַפְסֵי אָרֶץ אֵת יְשׁוּעַת אֱלֹהֵינוּ. הָרִיעוּ לַייָ כָּל הָאָרֶץ, פִּצְחוּ וְרַנְּנוּ וְזַמֵּרוּ. זַמְּרוּ לַייָ בְּכִנּוֹר, בְּכִנּוֹר וְקוֹל זִמְרָה. בַּחֲצֹצְרוֹת וְקוֹל שׁוֹפָר, הָרִיעוּ לִפְנֵי הַמֶּלֶךְ יְיָ.

Yir-am ha-yam u-m'lo-o,	יִרְעַם הַיָּם וּמְלֹאוֹ, תֵּבֵל וְיֹשְׁבֵי בָהּ.
tei-vel v'yosh-vei vah.	נְהָרוֹת יִמְחֲאוּ כָף, יַחַד הָרִים יְרַנֵּנוּ.
N'ha-rot yim-cha-u chaf,	לִפְנֵי יְיָ כִּי בָא לִשְׁפֹּט הָאָרֶץ,
ya-chad ha-rim y'ra-neinu.	יִשְׁפֹּט תֵּבֵל בְּצֶדֶק,
Lif-nei Adonoy ki va lish-pot ha-arets, yish-	וְעַמִּים בְּמֵישָׁרִים.
pot tei-vel b'tse-dek, v'a-mim b'mei-sha-rim.	

Fixing Thursday: An Excerpt from Psalm 99

Theme: When Mashiach comes, justice and fairness will abound. All nations will follow Hashem, whom the Jewish People have followed throughout history.

Moses and Aaron were among His holy people, and the prophet Samuel was among those who called to Him. They called to Hashem and He answered them. In a pillar of clouds He spoke to them. They obeyed his statutes and instructions.

Hashem, our G-d, You answered them. You were a forgiving G-d to them and stood up on behalf of any who would speak against Israel.

Acknowledge Hashem's greatness and bow on His holy mountain, for Hashem, our G-d, is the Holy One.

Mosheh v'Aharon, b'ko-ha-nav,	מֹשֶׁה וְאַהֲרֹן, בְּכֹהֲנָיו, וּשְׁמוּאֵל,
u-Sh'mu-el, b'kor-ei sh'mo,	בְּקֹרְאֵי שְׁמוֹ. קֹרִאִים אֶל יְיָ, וְהוּא יַעֲנֵם.
ko-rim el Adonoy, v'hu ya-a-neim.	בְּעַמּוּד עָנָן יְדַבֵּר אֲלֵיהֶם,
B'a-mud a-nan y'da-beir alei-hem,	שָׁמְרוּ עֵדֹתָיו וְחֹק נָתַן לָמוֹ.
sham-ru ei-do-tav v'chok na-tan la-mo.	יְיָ אֱלֹהֵינוּ, אַתָּה עֲנִיתָם,
Adonoy Elo-heinu, atah a-ni-tam,	אֵל נֹשֵׂא הָיִיתָ לָהֶם, וְנֹקֵם עַל עֲלִילוֹתָם.
El no-sei ha-yi-ta la-hem,	רוֹמְמוּ יְיָ אֱלֹהֵינוּ, וְהִשְׁתַּחֲווּ לְהַר קָדְשׁוֹ, כִּי
v'no-keim al ali-lo-tam.	קָדוֹשׁ יְיָ אֱלֹהֵינוּ.
Ro-m'mu Adonoy Elo-heinu,	
v'hishta-chavu l'har kad-sho,	
ki ka-dosh Adonoy Elo-heinu.	

Fixing Friday: Psalm 29

 Theme: Hashem is the power of the world and will be forever. Hashem blesses His People with strength and peace, which will be everlasting when Mashiach comes.

A Psalm from King David. You, the Jewish People, who are the children of great people, acknowledge that Hashem is the Source of honor and power. Bow to Hashem at the Temple, His holy place.

Hashem's voice is upon the waters. His honor thunders. Hashem's voice is powerful. Hashem's voice is majestic. His voice breaks down evil leaders. It shatters the cedars of Lebanon (that is, those who appear to be impossible to overcome). He makes them dance like baby sheep. Hashem's fiery voice carved the tablets of stone. Hashem's voice spread throughout the desert and the wilderness of Sinai.

The voice of Hashem will make the nations tremble and will strip away power from the strong.

Hashem reigned during the Flood and He will sit on His throne forever.

Hashem will give strength to His People. Hashem will bless His People with peace.

Miz-mor, l'Da-vid.   מִזְמוֹר לְדָוִד׃

Ha-vu la-Adonoy b'nei ei-lim,   הָבוּ לַיי בְּנֵי אֵלִים,
Ha-vu la-Adonoy ka-vod va-oz.   הָבוּ לַיי כָּבוֹד וָעֹז׃

Ha-vu la-Adonoy k'vod sh'mo,   הָבוּ לַיי כְּבוֹד שְׁמוֹ,
hishta-chavu la-Adonoy b'had-rat ko-desh.   הִשְׁתַּחֲווּ לַיי בְּהַדְרַת קֹדֶשׁ׃

Kol Adonoy al ha-ma-yim,   קוֹל יי עַל הַמָּיִם,
el ha-kovod hir-im,   אֵל הַכָּבוֹד הִרְעִים,
Adonoy al ma-yim ra-bim.   יי עַל מַיִם רַבִּים׃

Kol Adonoy ba-ko-ach,   קוֹל יי בַּכֹּחַ,
kol Adonoy be-ha-dar.   קוֹל יי בֶּהָדָר׃

Kol Adonoy sho-veir ara-zim,   קוֹל יי שֹׁבֵר אֲרָזִים,
va-y'sha-beir Adonoy et ar-zei ha-L'vanon.   וַיְשַׁבֵּר יי אֶת אַרְזֵי הַלְּבָנוֹן׃

Va-yar-ki-deim k'mo ei-gel,   וַיַּרְקִידֵם כְּמוֹ עֵגֶל,
L'vanon v'Sir-yon k'mo ven r'ei-mim.   לְבָנוֹן וְשִׂרְיוֹן כְּמוֹ בֶן רְאֵמִים׃

Kol Adonoy cho-tseiv la-ha-vot eish.   קוֹל יי חֹצֵב לַהֲבוֹת אֵשׁ׃

Kol Adonoy ya-chil mid-bar,   קוֹל יי יָחִיל מִדְבָּר,
ya-chil Adonoy Mid-bar Ka-deish.   יָחִיל יי מִדְבַּר קָדֵשׁ׃

Kol Adonoy y'cho-leil aya-lot,	קוֹל יְיָ יְחוֹלֵל אַיָּלוֹת,
va-ye-che-sof y'a-rot, u-v'hei-cha-lo,	וַיֶּחֱשֹׂף יְעָרוֹת, וּבְהֵיכָלוֹ,
ku-lo omeir Ka-vod.	כֻּלּוֹ אוֹמֵר כָּבוֹד.
Adonoy la-ma-bul ya-shav,	יְיָ לַמַּבּוּל יָשָׁב,
va-yei-shev Adonoy melech l'olam.	וַיֵּשֶׁב יְיָ מֶלֶךְ לְעוֹלָם.
Adonoy oz l'amo yi-tein,	יְיָ עֹז לְעַמּוֹ יִתֵּן,
Adonoy y'va-reich et amo va-shalom.	יְיָ יְבָרֵךְ אֶת עַמּוֹ בַשָּׁלוֹם.

L'chah Dodi: Welcoming Shabbat with Song

Introduction: The Talmud teaches that the Jewish People are compared to a groom, while Shabbat is compared to the bride. And so we welcome Shabbat with the love, joy, and anticipation with which a groom welcomes his new bride on their wedding day. Others refer to the Jewish People as the groom and Hashem's closeness as the bride. Thus, we welcome Hashem's closeness on Shabbat and pray for the coming of Mashiach when we will feel Hashem's closeness to us every day. Both interpretations are clearly seen in the song of *L'chah Dodi,* which welcomes Shabbat.

> **Kavanah:** *We feel close to Hashem. Hashem is with us.*
> *Hashem gave us Shabbat as our special gift.*
> *It is when we feel close to Hashem, close to our people, and close to our soul,*
> *the source of our spirituality. This makes us want to sing.*
> *We want this closeness forever!*

Chorus: **Come, my friend, to greet the Bride.**
Let us welcome the Shabbat together.

Hashem, the One and Only G-d,
told us to "keep" the Shabbat and "remember" the Shabbat in one statement (on Mount Sinai at the Giving of the Torah), **and we heard it.**

Let us welcome the Shabbat, for it is the source of all the week's blessings.
From the beginning, Shabbat was honored.
It was created last, but was Hashem's first thought in Creation.

The Holy Temple, the Royal City of Jerusalem, arise from your exile.
You have been in the Valley of Tears too long.
Hashem will have compassion for you.
Jerusalem, arise and shake off your dust.

Let the People of Israel come back through the coming of Mashiach,
the seed of Yishai of Beit Lechem.
For the sake of my soul, bring the redemption.

Jerusalem, wake up, wake up!
Your light has come.
Rise and shine again.
Wake up! Sing a song!
Hashem's glory is revealed upon you.

Don't feel ashamed or humiliated.
Why are you down and discomforted?
Those of our Nation who suffer will find shelter in you,
the city rebuilt on a mountaintop.

Those who oppressed the Jewish People will be driven down.
Those who swallowed you will be cast away.
Hashem, your G-d, will rejoice with you, the Jewish People,
like a groom rejoices for his bride.

You, the Jewish People, will spread out to the right and to the left.
You will tell of Hashem's greatness.
Through the Mashiach, the descendant of Peretz,
you will be happy and filled with joy.

Stand, turn to the door and welcome in the Shabbat.

Dear bride, crown of your beloved husband, come with peace.
Come, enter and join the faithful ones of the treasured People.
Dear bride, come in. Enter with song and with great joy.

 Dance!

Chorus: L'chah Do-di li-k'rat ka-lah, p'nei Sha-bat n'ka-b'lah.	לְכָה דוֹדִי לִקְרַאת כַּלָּה, פְּנֵי שַׁבָּת נְקַבְּלָה.
Sha-mor v'za-chor b'di-bur echad, hi-sh'mi-ani El ha-m'yu-chad, Adonoy Echad u-sh'mo Echad, l'sheim u-l'tif-eret v'li-t'hi-lah.	שָׁמוֹר וְזָכוֹר בְּדִבּוּר אֶחָד, הִשְׁמִיעָנוּ אֵל הַמְיֻחָד, יְיָ אֶחָד וּשְׁמוֹ אֶחָד, לְשֵׁם וּלְתִפְאֶרֶת וְלִתְהִלָּה.
L'chah Do-di li-k'rat ka-lah, p'nei Sha-bat n'ka-b'lah.	לְכָה דוֹדִי לִקְרַאת כַּלָּה, פְּנֵי שַׁבָּת נְקַבְּלָה.
Li-k'rat Sha-bat l'chu v'nel-chah, ki hi m'kor ha-b'ra-chah, mei-rosh mi-ke-dem n'su-chah, sof ma-aseh b'ma-cha-sha-vah t'chi-lah.	לִקְרַאת שַׁבָּת לְכוּ וְנֵלְכָה, כִּי הִיא מְקוֹר הַבְּרָכָה, מֵרֹאשׁ מִקֶּדֶם נְסוּכָה, סוֹף מַעֲשֶׂה בְּמַחֲשָׁבָה תְּחִלָּה.
L'chah Do-di li-k'rat ka-lah, p'nei Sha-bat n'ka-b'lah.	לְכָה דוֹדִי לִקְרַאת כַּלָּה, פְּנֵי שַׁבָּת נְקַבְּלָה.
Mik-dash Melech ir m'lu-chah, ku-mi ts'i mi-toch ha-ha-fei-chah, rav lach she-vet b'ei-mek ha-ba-cha, v'hu ya-cha-mol ala-yich chem-lah.	מִקְדַּשׁ מֶלֶךְ עִיר מְלוּכָה, קוּמִי צְאִי מִתּוֹךְ הַהֲפֵכָה, רַב לָךְ שֶׁבֶת בְּעֵמֶק הַבָּכָא, וְהוּא יַחֲמוֹל עָלַיִךְ חֶמְלָה.
L'chah Do-di li-k'rat ka-lah, p'nei Sha-bat n'ka-b'lah.	לְכָה דוֹדִי לִקְרַאת כַּלָּה, פְּנֵי שַׁבָּת נְקַבְּלָה.
Hit-na-ari mei-afar ku-mi, liv-shi bi-g'dei tif-ar-teich a-mi, Al yad ben Yi-shai beit ha-lach-mi, kar-vah el naf-shi g'alah.	הִתְנַעֲרִי מֵעָפָר קוּמִי, לִבְשִׁי בִּגְדֵי תִפְאַרְתֵּךְ עַמִּי, עַל יַד בֶּן יִשַׁי בֵּית הַלַּחְמִי, קָרְבָה אֶל נַפְשִׁי גְאָלָהּ.
L'chah Do-di li-k'rat ka-lah, p'nei Sha-bat n'ka-b'lah.	לְכָה דוֹדִי לִקְרַאת כַּלָּה, פְּנֵי שַׁבָּת נְקַבְּלָה.
Hit-o-r'ri hit-o-r'ri, ki va o-reich ku-mi o-ri, U-ri u-ri shir da-bei-ri, k'vod Adonoy ala-yich ni-g'lah.	הִתְעוֹרְרִי הִתְעוֹרְרִי, כִּי בָא אוֹרֵךְ קוּמִי אוֹרִי, עוּרִי עוּרִי שִׁיר דַּבֵּרִי, כְּבוֹד יְיָ עָלַיִךְ נִגְלָה.
L'chah Do-di li-k'rat ka-lah, p'nei Sha-bat n'ka-b'lah.	לְכָה דוֹדִי לִקְרַאת כַּלָּה, פְּנֵי שַׁבָּת נְקַבְּלָה.
Lo tei-vo-shi v'lo ti-kal-mi, mah tish-to-cha-chi u-mah te-he-mi, Bach ye-che-si ani-yei ami, v'niv-n'tah ir al ti-lah.	לֹא תֵבוֹשִׁי וְלֹא תִכָּלְמִי, מַה תִּשְׁתּוֹחֲחִי וּמַה תֶּהֱמִי, בָּךְ יֶחֱסוּ עֲנִיֵּי עַמִּי, וְנִבְנְתָה עִיר עַל תִּלָּהּ.

L'chah Do-di li-k'rat ka-lah,
p'nei Sha-bat n'ka-b'lah.

לְכָה דוֹדִי לִקְרַאת כַּלָּה,
פְּנֵי שַׁבָּת נְקַבְּלָה.

V'ha-yu lim-shi-sah sho-sa-yich,
v'ra-cha-ku kol m'val-ayich,
Ya-sis ala-yich Elo-ha-yich,
kim-sos cha-tan al ka-lah.

וְהָיוּ לִמְשִׁסָּה שֹׁאסָיִךְ,
וְרָחֲקוּ כָּל מְבַלְּעָיִךְ,
יָשִׂישׂ עָלַיִךְ אֱלֹהָיִךְ,
כִּמְשׂוֹשׂ חָתָן עַל כַּלָּה.

L'chah Do-di li-k'rat ka-lah,
p'nei Sha-bat n'ka-b'lah.

לְכָה דוֹדִי לִקְרַאת כַּלָּה,
פְּנֵי שַׁבָּת נְקַבְּלָה.

Ya-min u-s'mol tif'ro-tsi,
v'et Adonoy ta-ari-tsi,
Al yad ish ben par-tsi,
v'nis-m'chah v'na-gi-lah.

יָמִין וּשְׂמֹאל תִּפְרוֹצִי,
וְאֶת יי תַּעֲרִיצִי,
עַל יַד אִישׁ בֶּן פַּרְצִי,
וְנִשְׂמְחָה וְנָגִילָה.

L'chah Do-di li-k'rat ka-lah,
p'nei Sha-bat n'ka-b'lah.

לְכָה דוֹדִי לִקְרַאת כַּלָּה,
פְּנֵי שַׁבָּת נְקַבְּלָה.

At this point we stand, turn to the door and welcome in the Shabbat.

Bo-i v'shalom a-teret ba-lah,
gam b'sim-chah u-v'tsa-ha-lah,
Toch emu-nei am s'gu-lah,
bo-i cha-lah, bo-i cha-lah.

בּוֹאִי בְשָׁלוֹם עֲטֶרֶת בַּעְלָהּ,
גַּם בְּשִׂמְחָה וּבְצָהֳלָה,
תּוֹךְ אֱמוּנֵי עַם סְגֻלָּה,
בּוֹאִי כַלָּה, בּוֹאִי כַלָּה.

L'chah Do-di li-k'rat ka-lah,
p'nei Sha-bat n'ka-b'lah.

לְכָה דוֹדִי לִקְרַאת כַּלָּה,
פְּנֵי שַׁבָּת נְקַבְּלָה.

Dance!

The Song for Shabbat: An Excerpt from Psalm 92

Theme: This psalm was written by Adam, the first person ever created, on the first Shabbat in history. He had taken part in the multi-layered error of eating from the Tree of Knowledge of Good and Evil, the single commandment that G-d had given Adam and Eve. He felt a great distance from his Heavenly Parent. But on the first Shabbat eve, this distance was bridged and once again Adam and Eve felt that they were the children of G-d.

Let us sing a song for Shabbat.

It is good to thank Hashem, to sing praises to Your great name, to tell of Your kindness in the morning and Your faithfulness at night . . .

A righteous person will flourish like a palm tree and will grow tall and sturdy like a cedar of Lebanon.

They will flourish, as they are planted in the house of Hashem, in the courtyards of our G-d.

They will still bear fruit in their old age. They will be vigorous and youthful to declare that Hashem is just.

We can always rely on Hashem, in whom there is no wrong.

Miz-mor shir l'yom ha-sha-bat.
Tov l'ho-dot la-Adonoy,
u-l'za-meir l'shim-cha el-yon.
L'ha-gid ba-bo-keir chas-dechah,
ve-emu-na-t'chah ba-lei-lot. . . .

מִזְמוֹר שִׁיר לְיוֹם הַשַּׁבָּת.
טוֹב לְהֹדוֹת לַיְיָ,
וּלְזַמֵּר לְשִׁמְךָ עֶלְיוֹן.
לְהַגִּיד בַּבֹּקֶר חַסְדֶּךָ,
וֶאֱמוּנָתְךָ, בַּלֵּילוֹת.

Tsa-dik ka-ta-mar yif-rach,
k'erez ba-L'vanon yis-geh.
Sh'tu-lim b'veit Adonoy,
b'cha-ts'rot Elo-heinu yaf-ri-chu.

צַדִּיק כַּתָּמָר יִפְרָח,
כְּאֶרֶז בַּלְּבָנוֹן יִשְׂגֶּה.
שְׁתוּלִים בְּבֵית יְיָ,
בְּחַצְרוֹת אֱלֹהֵינוּ יַפְרִיחוּ.

Od y'nu-vun b'sei-vah,
d'shei-nim v'ra-ana-nim yi-h'yu.
L'ha-gid ki ya-shar Adonoy,
tsu-ri v'lo av-la-tah bo.

עוֹד יְנוּבוּן בְּשֵׂיבָה,
דְּשֵׁנִים וְרַעֲנַנִּים יִהְיוּ.
לְהַגִּיד כִּי יָשָׁר יְיָ,
צוּרִי וְלֹא עַוְלָתָה בּוֹ.

Maariv: Friday Night Prayers

For the *Shema*, please see pages 167 to 170. Then return here for *Shemoneh Esrei* below.

The Shabbat Evening *Shemoneh Esrei* or *Amidah*

Note that the Shabbat evening *Amidah* contains the same introduction, introductory request, First Three Blessings, Three Closing Blessings, Request for Hashem's Help in controlling negative traits, and Final Stanza as the weekday *Amidah* (or *Shemoneh Esrei*). However, no personal requests are said on the Shabbat. Instead, the main theme of the *Amidah* is the central blessing, which discusses the special nature of Shabbat. For each Shabbat *Amidah* prayer, the central prayer addresses a different aspect of Shabbat.

This prayer is said standing, with our feet together, facing Jerusalem, from where our prayers are taken by angels (i.e., spiritual messengers) to the heavens. In Jerusalem, one faces the Temple Mount, the original point of creation upon which the two Jewish Temples stood in ancient times.

If one cannot stand for whatever reason, this prayer can be recited while sitting or lying down. In any case, the words should be whispered so that they become real (i.e., sound waves), but still approach the closest thing to pure, focused thought.

> Kavanah: *I am now going to pray the most important part of the prayers. I am about to stand and address Hashem directly.*

Take three small steps backward and then three small steps forward, and bear in mind that you are approaching Hashem directly with a series of requests and acknowledgements.

Introductory Request

> Kavanah: *It is difficult to* daven. *Hashem, please help me to* daven *and to get closer to You.*

Hashem, please help me overcome my limitations, so that I can say Your praises.

Adonoy s'fa-tai tif-tach, u-fi ya-gid t'hi-la-techa.   אֲדֹנָי שְׂפָתַי תִּפְתָּח, וּפִי יַגִּיד תְּהִלָּתֶךָ.

Friday Night Prayers

Beginning the Deepest Dialogue
The First Three Blessings: To Whom Are We Speaking?

The First Blessing: The Blessing of the Fathers

> **Kavanah:** *We are not strangers to Hashem nor is He to us.*
> *We are the children and the living legacy of those in the world who first*
> *recognized Hashem and stood up for this belief.*
> *Hashem shielded them from all their trials in life and made*
> *an eternal covenant with them and their children, including me.*

Bend your knees on *Baruch*, bow at *atah*, and stand upright on *Adonoy*.

You, Hashem, Source of all blessings, are our G-d and the G-d of our forefathers, the G-d of Avraham, the G-d of Yitzchak, and the G-d of Yaakov. The great, powerful, and awesome G-d who is beyond comprehension, bestows kindness, and creates all things. You remember the kindness of our forefathers and send loving redemption to their children, for His name's sake.

Baruch atah Adonoy Elo-heinu vei-lo-hei avo-teinu, Elo-hei Avra-ham, Elo-hei Yits-chak, vei-lo-hei Ya-akov, ha-El ha-Ga-dol ha-Gi-bor v'ha-No-ra, El El-yon, go-mel cha-sa-dim to-vim v'ko-nei ha-kol, v'zo-cheir chas-dei a-vot, u-mei-vi go-el liv-nei v'nei-hem, l'ma-an sh'mo b'a-ha-vah.

בָּרוּךְ אַתָּה יי אֱלֹהֵינוּ וֵאלֹהֵי אֲבוֹתֵינוּ, אֱלֹהֵי אַבְרָהָם, אֱלֹהֵי יִצְחָק, וֵאלֹהֵי יַעֲקֹב, הָאֵל הַגָּדוֹל הַגִּבּוֹר וְהַנּוֹרָא, אֵל עֶלְיוֹן, גּוֹמֵל חֲסָדִים טוֹבִים וְקוֹנֵה הַכֹּל, וְזוֹכֵר חַסְדֵי אָבוֹת, וּמֵבִיא גוֹאֵל לִבְנֵי בְנֵיהֶם, לְמַעַן שְׁמוֹ בְּאַהֲבָה.

NOTE: On the days between Rosh Hashanah and Yom Kippur add the line:

Remember us for life, Master of the World who wants life. Inscribe us in the Book of Life for Your sake, oh living G-d.

Zach-reinu l'cha-yim, Melech cha-feits ba-cha-yim, v'chat-veinu b'sei-fer ha-cha-yim, l'ma-an-cha Elo-him cha-yim.

זָכְרֵנוּ לְחַיִּים, מֶלֶךְ חָפֵץ בַּחַיִּים, וְכָתְבֵנוּ בְּסֵפֶר הַחַיִּים, לְמַעַנְךָ אֱלֹהִים חַיִּים.

Bend your knees on *Baruch*, bow at *atah*, and stand upright on *Adonoy*.

You are the Master of the World, who helps us, saves us, and protects us. I acknowledge that You, Adonoy, Source of all blessings, are the protector of our forefather Avraham (and his children).

Melech o-zeir u-mo-shi-a u-ma-gein.
Baruch atah Adonoy, ma-gein Avra-ham.

מֶלֶךְ עוֹזֵר וּמוֹשִׁיעַ וּמָגֵן.
בָּרוּךְ אַתָּה יְיָ, מָגֵן אַבְרָהָם.

The Second Blessing: Hashem's Power

Kavanah: *Hashem is the Source of life and determines who will live and who will die and who will live again in the future.*

You, Hashem, have the power of life and death. You have the power to revive those who are deceased and to save again and again.

Atah gi-bor l'olam Adonoy,
m'cha-yei mei-tim atah rav l'ho-shi-a.

אַתָּה גִבּוֹר לְעוֹלָם אֲדֹנָי,
מְחַיֵּה מֵתִים אַתָּה רַב לְהוֹשִׁיעַ.

NOTE: Between Sh'mini Atseret (the day before Simchat Torah) and Pesach, add this phrase into this prayer.

Who makes the wind blow and the rain fall,

Ma-shiv ha-ru-achu u-mo-rid ha-ge-shem.

מַשִּׁיב הָרוּחַ וּמוֹרִיד הַגֶּשֶׁם.

Who sustains us with kindness, who revives the deceased with compassion (e.g., people who sleep, plants that wither), who supports those who have fallen, provides healing for the sick, freedom for the imprisoned, and who is faithful to those who sleep below the earth. Who is like You who does such powerful things? Who else can cause death, restore life, and send great help?

M'chal-kel cha-yim b'che-sed, m'cha-yei mei-tim b'ra-cha-mim ra-bim, so-meich no-f'lim, v'ro-fei cho-lim, u-ma-tir a-su-rim, u-m'ka-yeim emu-na-to li-shei-nei afar. Mi cha-mo-cha ba-al g'vu-rot, umi do-meh lach, melech mei-mit u-m'cha-yeh u-mats-mi-ach y'shu-a.

מְכַלְכֵּל חַיִּים בְּחֶסֶד, מְחַיֵּה מֵתִים בְּרַחֲמִים רַבִּים, סוֹמֵךְ נוֹפְלִים, וְרוֹפֵא חוֹלִים, וּמַתִּיר אֲסוּרִים, וּמְקַיֵּם אֱמוּנָתוֹ לִישֵׁנֵי עָפָר. מִי כָמוֹךָ בַּעַל גְּבוּרוֹת, וּמִי דּוֹמֶה לָּךְ, מֶלֶךְ מֵמִית וּמְחַיֶּה וּמַצְמִיחַ יְשׁוּעָה.

NOTE: From Rosh Hashanah to Yom Kippur we add in the following line:

Who is like You, Compassionate Father, Who remembers with compassion those He has created for life.

Mi cha-mo-cha Av Ha-ra-cha-mim, zo-cheir y'tsu-rav l'cha-yim b'ra-cha-mim.	מִי כָמוֹךָ אַב הָרַחֲמִים, זוֹכֵר יְצוּרָיו לְחַיִּים בְּרַחֲמִים.

You are trustworthy to restore life to the deceased. I acknowledge that You, Adonoy, Source of all blessings, revive the deceased.

V'ne-eman atah l'ha-cha-yot mei-tim. Baruch atah Adonoy, m'cha-yei ha-mei-tim.	וְנֶאֱמָן אַתָּה לְהַחֲיוֹת מֵתִים. בָּרוּךְ אַתָּה יְיָ, מְחַיֵּה הַמֵּתִים.

The Third Blessing: Hashem's Holiness

> **Kavanah:** *Holiness means achieving closeness to Hashem and imbuing everything we do with a higher purpose, G-d's purpose. Hashem, help me to be holy today.*

You, Hashem, are holy and Your name is holy. We, the Holy People, praise You every day for You are great and holy.
***You, Adonoy, Source of all blessings, are the Holy G-d.

Atah ka-dosh v'shim-cha ka-dosh u-k'do-shim b'chol yom y'ha-l'lu-cha selah.	אַתָּה קָדוֹשׁ וְשִׁמְךָ קָדוֹשׁ וּקְדוֹשִׁים בְּכָל יוֹם יְהַלְלוּךָ סֶּלָה.
on a regular day:	on a regular day:
Baruch atah Adonoy, ha-El ha-ka-dosh.	בָּרוּךְ אַתָּה יְיָ, הָאֵל הַקָּדוֹשׁ.

NOTE: *** In the days between Rosh Hashanah and Yom Kippur substitute the following concluding blessing instead:

You, Adonoy, Source of all blessings, are the Holy Master of the World.

Baruch atah Adonoy, ha-Melech ha-ka-dosh.	בָּרוּךְ אַתָּה יְיָ, הַמֶּלֶךְ הַקָּדוֹשׁ.

The Central Blessing of the Friday Night *Amidah*

You (Hashem) made the seventh day, the purpose of all of Creation, holy for Your Name's sake. You blessed it more than all the other days and made it the holiest of all times. As it is written in Your Torah:

(from *Breisheet* (Genesis), Chapter 2, verses 1 to 3)
"And so the creation of the heavens and the earth and all of the groups within them was finished. On the seventh day, Hashem completed His work, which He had done, and He rested on the seventh day from all of His work, which He had done. Hashem blessed the seventh day and made it holy, because on it He stopped from all His work, which He created for our use."

Atah ki-dash-ta et yom ha-sh'vi-i lish-mecha, tach-lit ma-asei sha-ma-yim va-arets, u-vei-rach-to mi-kol ha-ya-mim, v'ki-dash-to mi-kol ha-z'ma-nim, v'chein ka-tuv b'tora-techa:

אַתָּה קִדַּשְׁתָּ אֶת יוֹם הַשְּׁבִיעִי לִשְׁמֶךָ, תַּכְלִית מַעֲשֵׂה שָׁמַיִם וָאָרֶץ, וּבֵרַכְתּוֹ מִכָּל הַיָּמִים, וְקִדַּשְׁתּוֹ מִכָּל הַזְּמַנִּים, וְכֵן כָּתוּב בְּתוֹרָתֶךָ:

"Va-y'chu-lu ha-sha-ma-yim v'ha-arets v'chol ts'va-am. Va-y'chal Elo-him ba-yom ha-sh'vi-i m'lach-to asher asah, va-yish-bot ba-yom ha-sh'vi-i mi-kol m'lach-to asher asah. Va-y'va-rech Elo-him et yom ha-sh'vi-i va-y'ka-deish oto, ki vo sha-vat mi-kol m'lach-to asher ba-ra Elo-him la-asot."

וַיְכֻלּוּ הַשָּׁמַיִם וְהָאָרֶץ וְכָל צְבָאָם. וַיְכַל אֱלֹהִים בַּיּוֹם הַשְּׁבִיעִי מְלַאכְתּוֹ אֲשֶׁר עָשָׂה, וַיִּשְׁבֹּת בַּיּוֹם הַשְּׁבִיעִי מִכָּל מְלַאכְתּוֹ אֲשֶׁר עָשָׂה. וַיְבָרֶךְ אֱלֹהִים אֶת יוֹם הַשְּׁבִיעִי וַיְקַדֵּשׁ אֹתוֹ, כִּי בוֹ שָׁבַת מִכָּל מְלַאכְתּוֹ אֲשֶׁר בָּרָא אֱלֹהִים לַעֲשׂוֹת.

All who observe the Shabbat and call it a delight rejoice in Your Kingship. Those who make the seventh day holy shall find satisfaction and be delighted with Your goodness. You, Hashem, made the seventh day special and holy. You called it "the most coveted of days," for we remember the time of Creation.

Yis-m'chu v'mal-chu-t'cha shom-rei Shabat v'kor'ei oneg. Am m'ka-d'shei sh'vi-i, ku-lam yis-b'u v'yit-an-gu mi-tu-vecha, u-va-sh'vi-i ra-tsi-ta bo v'ki-dash-to, chem-dat ya-mim oto ka-ra-ta, zei-cher l'ma-asei v'rei-sheet.

יִשְׂמְחוּ בְמַלְכוּתְךָ שׁוֹמְרֵי שַׁבָּת וְקוֹרְאֵי עֹנֶג. עַם מְקַדְּשֵׁי שְׁבִיעִי, כֻּלָּם יִשְׂבְּעוּ וְיִתְעַנְּגוּ מִטּוּבֶךָ, וּבַשְּׁבִיעִי רָצִיתָ בּוֹ וְקִדַּשְׁתּוֹ, חֶמְדַּת יָמִים אוֹתוֹ קָרָאתָ, זֵכֶר לְמַעֲשֵׂה בְרֵאשִׁית.

Our G-d and the G-d of our ancestors, be pleased with our Shabbat rest. Make us holy with Your mitzvot and make the Torah the center of our lives. Satisfy us with Your goodness and gladden us with Your help. Give us purity of heart to serve You sincerely.

Adonoy, our G-d, with love and with deep desire, give us Your holy Shabbat as our special heritage. May all of Israel, who sanctifies Your name, rest on Shabbat. You, Adonoy, Source of all blessings, make the Shabbat holy.

Elo-heinu vei-lo-hei avo-teinu, r'tsei vi-m'nu-cha-teinu, ka-d'sheinu b'mits-vo-techa, v'tein chel-keinu b'Tora-techa. Sab-einu mi-tu-vecha v'sam-cheinu bi-shu-a-techa, v'ta-heir li-beinu l'av-d'cha be-emet. V'han-chi-leinu Adonoy Elo-heinu b'a-ha-vah u-v'ra-tson Shabat ka-d'shecha, v'ya-nu-chu vo Yisrael m'ka-d'shei sh'me-cha. Baruch atah Adonoy, m'ka-deish ha-Shabat.

אֱלֹהֵינוּ וֵאלֹהֵי אֲבוֹתֵינוּ רְצֵה בִמְנוּחָתֵנוּ. קַדְּשֵׁנוּ בְּמִצְוֹתֶיךָ, וְתֵן חֶלְקֵנוּ בְּתוֹרָתֶךָ. שַׂבְּעֵנוּ מִטּוּבֶךָ וְשַׂמְּחֵנוּ בִּישׁוּעָתֶךָ, וְטַהֵר לִבֵּנוּ לְעָבְדְּךָ בֶּאֱמֶת. וְהַנְחִילֵנוּ יְיָ אֱלֹהֵינוּ בְּאַהֲבָה וּבְרָצוֹן שַׁבַּת קָדְשֶׁךָ, וְיָנוּחוּ בוֹ יִשְׂרָאֵל מְקַדְּשֵׁי שְׁמֶךָ. בָּרוּךְ אַתָּה יְיָ מְקַדֵּשׁ הַשַּׁבָּת.

First Closing Blessing: A Return of the Temple Service

> **Kavanah:** *We use prayer as a substitute for the Temple service of old.*
> *I am so far removed from the Temple that I can't even begin to understand what the service meant or how it worked.*
> *But I know that all who went to the Temple felt so close to Hashem.*
> *They felt tangible feelings of forgiveness and clarity of spirit and of purpose.*
> *I long for that closeness and that clarity and I know that You want this closeness, too.*

Adonoy, our G-d, please look with favor toward Your people, Israel, and listen to their prayers. Quickly restore the service to the Holy of Holies of Your Temple. Accept the offerings and prayers of Israel with love and always accept the service of Your people, Israel. Let us see Your return to Zion (the Temple) with compassion. You, Adonoy, Source of all blessings, restore His presence to Zion.

R'tsei, Adonoy Elo-heinu b'am-cha Yisrael u-vi-t'fi-la-tam, v'ha-sheiv et ha-avo-dah li-d'vir bei-techa. V'i-shei Yisrael u-t'fi-la-tam b'a-ha-vah t'ka-bel b'ra-tson, u-t'hi l'ra-tson ta-mid avo-dat Yisrael a-mecha.

רְצֵה יְיָ אֱלֹהֵינוּ בְּעַמְּךָ יִשְׂרָאֵל וּבִתְפִלָּתָם, וְהָשֵׁב אֶת הָעֲבוֹדָה לִדְבִיר בֵּיתֶךָ. וְאִשֵּׁי יִשְׂרָאֵל וּתְפִלָּתָם בְּאַהֲבָה תְקַבֵּל בְּרָצוֹן, וּתְהִי לְרָצוֹן תָּמִיד עֲבוֹדַת יִשְׂרָאֵל עַמֶּךָ.

Say this special paragraph on Rosh Chodesh, the first day(s) of the new Jewish month. The "first day" may be one or two days, depending on the month. See a Jewish calendar or check on the Internet to see the appropriate dates on the secular calendar.

Our G-d and the G-d of our ancestors, may your remembrance of us and our ancestors, and of the Mashiach, the offspring of King David Your servant, and of Jerusalem, Your holy city, and of all of your people, the House of Israel, rise up and reach, be noticed, accepted, heard and remembered before You; for deliverance, well-being, grace, kindness, and mercy, for life and peace on this day of Rosh Chodesh (the beginning of the new month).

Remember us today, Adonoy our G-d, for good, for blessings, and help provide us with good life. And with an act of redemption and compassion, have mercy on us, be gracious, merciful, and save us. For our eyes are looking to You, for You are the kind and compassionate Master of the World.

Elo-heinu vei-lo-hei avo-teinu, ya-aleh, v'ya-vo, v'ya-gi-a, v'yei-ra-eh, v'yei-ra-tseh, v'yi-sha-ma, v'yi-pa-keid, v'yi-za-cheir zich-ro-neinu u-fik-do-neinu, v'zich-ron avo-teinu, v'zich-ron Ma-shi-ach ben Da-vid av-decha, v'zich-ron Y'ru-sha-la-yim ir kad-she-cha, v'zich-ron kol am-cha Beit Yisrael l'fa-necha, lif-lei-tah l'to-vah, l'chein u-l'che-sed u-l'ra-cha-mim, l'cha-yim u-l'shalom b'yom Rosh ha-Cho-desh ha-zeh.

Zach-reinu Adonoy Elo-heinu bo l'to-vah, u-fa-k'deinu vo li-v'ra-chah, v'ho-shi-einu vo l'cha-yim, u-vi-d'var y'shu-ah v'ra-cha-mim, chus v'cha-neinu v'ra-cheim alei-nu v'ho-shi-einu, ki ei-lecha ei-neinu, ki Eil Melech cha-nun v'ra-chum Atah.

אֱלֹהֵינוּ וֵאלֹהֵי אֲבוֹתֵינוּ, יַעֲלֶה, וְיָבוֹא, וְיַגִּיעַ, וְיֵרָאֶה, וְיֵרָצֶה, וְיִשָּׁמַע, וְיִפָּקֵד, וְיִזָּכֵר זִכְרוֹנֵנוּ וּפִקְדוֹנֵנוּ, וְזִכְרוֹן אֲבוֹתֵינוּ, וְזִכְרוֹן מָשִׁיחַ בֶּן דָּוִד עַבְדֶּךָ, וְזִכְרוֹן יְרוּשָׁלַיִם עִיר קָדְשֶׁךָ, וְזִכְרוֹן כָּל עַמְּךָ בֵּית יִשְׂרָאֵל לְפָנֶיךָ, לִפְלֵיטָה לְטוֹבָה, לְחֵן וּלְחֶסֶד וּלְרַחֲמִים, לְחַיִּים וּלְשָׁלוֹם בְּיוֹם רֹאשׁ הַחֹדֶשׁ הַזֶּה.

זָכְרֵנוּ יְיָ אֱלֹהֵינוּ בּוֹ לְטוֹבָה, וּפָקְדֵנוּ בוֹ לִבְרָכָה, וְהוֹשִׁיעֵנוּ בוֹ לְחַיִּים, וּבִדְבַר יְשׁוּעָה וְרַחֲמִים, חוּס וְחָנֵּנוּ וְרַחֵם עָלֵינוּ וְהוֹשִׁיעֵנוּ, כִּי אֵלֶיךָ עֵינֵינוּ, כִּי אֵל מֶלֶךְ חַנּוּן וְרַחוּם אָתָּה.

Second Closing Blessing: Thank You, Hashem

 Take a minute or two to review the following list and focus on the things for which you feel especially thankful today. Say, "Thank you, Hashem, for…."

- Life
- Health
- Intellect
- Sight
- Hearing
- Speech
- Parents
- Teachers
- Friends
- Grandparents
- Spouse
- Children

- Movement
- Memories
- Freedom of Choice
- Making Me a Jew
- My Jewish Soul
- Mitzvot
- Torah (which provides me with direction in life)
- The Ability to Talk to You
- Watching Over Me
- Making Me Your Partner in Creation
- A Place in the Next World (*Olam HaBa*)
- Wonders of Nature
- Material Possessions (home, car, clothes, furniture, dishes, books, etc.)
- Grandchildren
- Family
- Israel
- Peace
- Forgiveness
- Respect and Honor
- Personal Growth
- Meaning and Purpose
- The Desire to Be Good
- The Power to Change Things
- My Favorite Things
- A Way to Pay Expenses
- Pleasure (physical, intellectual, emotional, spiritual, etc.)
- Add in your own personal thoughts…

> **Kavanah:** *I have so much to be thankful for, every second of the day. I can't even begin to enumerate all the things that I have to be thankful for. And I know that Hashem gives it all to me.*

Bow on *Modim* and stand upright on *lach*.

We thank You, Hashem, our eternal G-d and the G-d of our ancestors. You are the One we depend on in our lives, who shields us from one generation to the next. We thank You for our lives, which are in Your hands, for our souls, which are watched by You, for the miracles that You do for us every day, and for the wonders and good things that you do for us all the time — every evening, morning, and afternoon. You are the Source of goodness and compassion whose kindness never ends. We always put our hope in You.

Mo-dim a-nach-nu lach sha-atah hu Adonoy Elo-heinu vei-lo-hei avo-teinu l'olam va-ed. Tsur cha-yeinu, ma-gein yish-einu atah hu l'dor va-dor. No-deh l'cha u-n'sa-peir t'hi-la-techa al cha-yeinu ha-m'su-rim b'ya-decha, v'al nish-mo-teinu ha-p'ku-dot lach, v'al ni-secha she-b'chol yom ima-nu, v'al nif-l'o-techa v'tovo-techa she-b'chol eit, erev va-vo-ker v'tsa-ha-ra-yim. Ha-tov ki lo cha-lu ra-cha-mecha, v'ha-m'ra-cheim ki lo ta-mu cha-sa-decha, mei-olam ki-vi-nu lach.

מוֹדִים אֲנַחְנוּ לָךְ שָׁאַתָּה הוּא יְיָ אֱלֹהֵינוּ וֵאלֹהֵי אֲבוֹתֵינוּ לְעוֹלָם וָעֶד. צוּר חַיֵּינוּ, מָגֵן יִשְׁעֵנוּ אַתָּה הוּא לְדוֹר וָדוֹר. נוֹדֶה לְּךָ וּנְסַפֵּר תְּהִלָּתֶךָ עַל חַיֵּינוּ הַמְּסוּרִים בְּיָדֶךָ, וְעַל נִשְׁמוֹתֵינוּ הַפְּקוּדוֹת לָךְ, וְעַל נִסֶּיךָ שֶׁבְּכָל יוֹם עִמָּנוּ, וְעַל נִפְלְאוֹתֶיךָ וְטוֹבוֹתֶיךָ שֶׁבְּכָל עֵת, עֶרֶב וָבֹקֶר וְצָהֳרָיִם. הַטּוֹב כִּי לֹא כָלוּ רַחֲמֶיךָ, וְהַמְרַחֵם כִּי לֹא תַמּוּ חֲסָדֶיךָ, מֵעוֹלָם קִוִּינוּ לָךְ.

For all of this, Master of the World, may Your name be acknowledged, blessed continually, and forever.

V'al ku-lam yit-ba-rach v'yit-ro-mam shim-cha Mal-keinu ta-mid l'olam va-ed.

וְעַל כֻּלָּם יִתְבָּרַךְ וְיִתְרוֹמַם שִׁמְךָ מַלְכֵּנוּ תָּמִיד לְעוֹלָם וָעֶד.

NOTE: From Rosh Hashanah to Yom Kippur we add in the following line:

Inscribe all of the Jewish People for good life.

U-ch'tov l'cha-yim to-vim kol b'nei v'ri-techa.

וּכְתוֹב לְחַיִּים טוֹבִים כָּל בְּנֵי בְרִיתֶךָ.

Bend knees on *Baruch*, bow on *atah*, and stand upright on *Adonoy*.

And all that lives will acknowledge You and will thank, praise, and bless You forever, for that is a good thing to do. Hashem, You are our help and salvation, the G-d of goodness. Adonoy, Source of all blessings, it is proper to give thanks to you.

V'chol ha-cha-yim yo-du-cha selah, vi-ha-l'lu et shim-cha be-emet. Ha-El y'shu-a-teinu v'ez-ra-teinu selah. Baruch atah Adonoy, *ha-tov shim-cha u-l'cha na-eh l'ho-dot.*

וְכֹל הַחַיִּים יוֹדוּךָ סֶּלָה, וִיהַלְלוּ אֶת שִׁמְךָ בֶּאֱמֶת, הָאֵל יְשׁוּעָתֵנוּ וְעֶזְרָתֵנוּ סֶּלָה. בָּרוּךְ אַתָּה יְיָ, הַטּוֹב שִׁמְךָ וּלְךָ נָאֶה לְהוֹדוֹת.

Third Closing Blessing: For Inner Peace and a Life of Goodness

> **Kavanah:** *Inner turmoil and strife within our Jewish family are the greatest blocks to a life of happiness and fulfillment. Help me to use the Torah and Torah's values to achieve a life of inner and external peace. I want to be a peaceful, kind person who brings goodness and peace to my people and to my world.*

Hashem, give us and all of Israel, Your people, peace, goodness, blessing, life, good favor, kindness, and compassion. Our Father, bless us all as one with Your special light. For with Your special light, You have given us the Torah, our instructions for living, and a love of kindness, righteousness, blessing, compassion, life, and peace. May You find it good to bless us and all of Israel, Your People, at all times with Your peace.

Sim shalom, to-vah, u-v'ra-chah, chein, va-che-sed, v'ra-cha-mim alei-nu v'al kol Yisrael a-mecha. Bar-cheinu avi-nu, ku-la-nu k'echad b'or pa-ne-cha, ki v'or pa-necha na-ta-ta la-nu, Adonoy Elo-heinu, Torat cha-yim v'a-ha-vat che-sed, u-ts'da-kah, u-v'ra-chah, v'ra-cha-mim, v'cha-yim, v'shalom. V'tov b'ei-necha l'va-reich et kol am-cha Yisrael, b'chol eit u-v'chol sha-ah bi-sh'lo-mecha.

שִׂים שָׁלוֹם, טוֹבָה, וּבְרָכָה, חֵן, וָחֶסֶד, וְרַחֲמִים עָלֵינוּ וְעַל כָּל יִשְׂרָאֵל עַמֶּךָ. בָּרְכֵנוּ אָבִינוּ, כֻּלָּנוּ כְּאֶחָד בְּאוֹר פָּנֶיךָ, כִּי בְאוֹר פָּנֶיךָ נָתַתָּ לָּנוּ, יְיָ אֱלֹהֵינוּ, תּוֹרַת חַיִּים וְאַהֲבַת חֶסֶד, וּצְדָקָה, וּבְרָכָה, וְרַחֲמִים, וְחַיִּים, וְשָׁלוֹם. וְטוֹב בְּעֵינֶיךָ לְבָרֵךְ אֶת כָּל עַמְּךָ יִשְׂרָאֵל, בְּכָל עֵת וּבְכָל שָׁעָה בִּשְׁלוֹמֶךָ.

NOTE: From Rosh Hashanah to Yom Kippur we conclude this blessing with the following paragraph, instead of the usual concluding blessing:

In the Book of Life, Blessing, Peace, and Good Livelihood, may we and all of the People of Israel be remembered and inscribed for good life and peace. You, Adonoy, the Source of all Blessing, make peace.

B'sei-fer cha-yim b'rachah v'shalom, u-far-na-sah to-vah, ni-za-cheir v'ni-ka-teiv l'fa-necha, a-nach-nu v'chol am-cha Beit Yisrael, l'cha-yim to-vim u-l'shalom. Baruch atah Adonoy, oseh ha-sha-lom.

בְּסֵפֶר חַיִּים בְּרָכָה וְשָׁלוֹם, וּפַרְנָסָה טוֹבָה, נִזָּכֵר וְנִכָּתֵב לְפָנֶיךָ, אֲנַחְנוּ וְכָל עַמְּךָ בֵּית יִשְׂרָאֵל, לְחַיִּים טוֹבִים וּלְשָׁלוֹם. בָּרוּךְ אַתָּה יְיָ, עֹשֵׂה הַשָּׁלוֹם.

On a regular day, continue with the conclusion of the blessing, as follows:

You, Adonoy, Source of all blessings, bless Israel, His People, with peace.

Baruch atah Adonoy, ha-m'va-reich et amo Yisrael ba-shalom.

בָּרוּךְ אַתָּה יְיָ, הַמְבָרֵךְ אֶת עַמּוֹ יִשְׂרָאֵל בַּשָּׁלוֹם.

A Request for Hashem's Help to Control Speech, Jealousy, and Anger

Kavanah: I have just used the power of speech that Hashem has given me to speak to Him… to request His help, to pray for me and my people, to remember who I am, and to bring me closer to Hashem. But that same power, if used improperly, can be so damaging. Help me to channel the awesome power of speech only for good and not for slander, gossip, lying, or other words that are unbefitting for me. Help me to be humble, and not to be jealous or angry. And help me to be open to Hashem's Torah and mitzvot.

My G-d, please guard my tongue from improper speech and my lips from lying. To those who curse me, let me keep silent and let me be as humble as dust to everyone. Open my heart to Your Torah so that my soul will perform Your mitzvot. And as for those who wish to harm me, quickly erase their advice and destroy their ideas.

Hashem, my G-d and the G-d of my ancestors, may it be Your will that none should be jealous of me, nor I of them; that I should not get angry today, nor should I do something to make You angry with me. Save me from the Evil Inclination and put in my heart the desire for humility and submission.

Hashem, our King and G-d, cause the entire world to recognize Your name, rebuild Your city (Jerusalem), build Your home (the Temple), gather your exiled nation, and fill them with joy. Do this for Your sake, for Your Torah's sake, and for the sake of Your holiness. As the verse in Psalms says, "So that your beloved ones may rest, let Your hand of kindness save us and respond to me."

Elo-hai, n'tsor l'sho-ni mei-ra, u-s'fa-tai mi-da-beir mir-mah, v'lim-ka-l'lai naf-shi ti-dom, v'naf-shi ke-afar la-kol ti-h'yeh. P'tach li-bi b'Tora-techa, u-v'mits-vo-techa tir-dof naf-shi. V'chol ha-chosh-vim a-lai ra-ah, m'hei-rah ha-feir atsa-tam v'kal-keil ma-cha-shav-tam. Asei l'ma-an sh'mecha, asei l'ma-an y'mi-necha, asei l'ma-an k'du-sha-techa, asei l'ma-an Tora-techa. L'ma-an yei-chal-tsun y'di-decha, ho-shi-ah y'min-cha va-a-nei-ni.

אֱלֹהַי, נְצוֹר לְשׁוֹנִי מֵרָע, וּשְׂפָתַי מִדַּבֵּר מִרְמָה, וְלִמְקַלְלַי נַפְשִׁי תִדֹּם, וְנַפְשִׁי כֶּעָפָר לַכֹּל תִּהְיֶה. פְּתַח לִבִּי בְּתוֹרָתֶךָ, וּבְמִצְוֹתֶיךָ תִּרְדֹּף נַפְשִׁי. וְכָל הַחוֹשְׁבִים עָלַי רָעָה, מְהֵרָה הָפֵר עֲצָתָם וְקַלְקֵל מַחֲשַׁבְתָּם. עֲשֵׂה לְמַעַן שְׁמֶךָ, עֲשֵׂה לְמַעַן יְמִינֶךָ, עֲשֵׂה לְמַעַן קְדֻשָּׁתֶךָ, עֲשֵׂה לְמַעַן תּוֹרָתֶךָ. לְמַעַן יֵחָלְצוּן יְדִידֶיךָ, הוֹשִׁיעָה יְמִינְךָ וַעֲנֵנִי.

Let my words and the thoughts in my heart be acceptable to You, G-d, my Redeemer, upon whom I rely. May He, who makes peace in the heavens, make peace upon us and upon all of Israel; and let us say, Amein (that is, I believe this to be the truth).

Yi-h'yu l'ra-tson im-rei fi v'he-g'yon li-bi l'fa-necha. Adonoy tsu-ri v'go-a-li.

יִהְיוּ לְרָצוֹן אִמְרֵי פִי וְהֶגְיוֹן לִבִּי לְפָנֶיךָ, יְיָ צוּרִי וְגוֹאֲלִי.

*Oseh shalom bi-m'ro-mav,
hu ya-aseh shalom alei-nu,
v'al kol Yisrael. V'im-ru, Amein.*

עֹשֶׂה שָׁלוֹם בִּמְרוֹמָיו, הוּא יַעֲשֶׂה שָׁלוֹם עָלֵינוּ, וְעַל כָּל יִשְׂרָאֵל. וְאִמְרוּ: אָמֵן.

Take three steps back and bow slightly to the left, right, and center as if taking leave from the king.

The Final Stanza: Rebuild the Temple

> *Kavanah: The prayer that I have just finished takes the place of the Temple service. But it is merely a temporary replacement. We ask Hashem to rebuild the Temple where we will achieve clarity of purpose and of Truth and where we will achieve a real and everlasting closeness to Him. Help us to learn Torah and fulfill the mitzvot.*

Hashem, our G-d and the G-d of our ancestors, may it be Your will that You rebuild the Temple speedily in our days and make the Torah the center of our lives. Then we will serve You with reverence as we did in previous times. And the offerings of Judah and Jerusalem will be pleasing to You as they were in the days of old.

Y'hi ra-tson mil-fa-necha Adonoy Elo-heinu vei-lo-hei avo-teinu, she-yi-ba-neh Beit ha-Mik-dash bim-hei-rah v'ya-meinu, v'tein chel-keinu b'Tora-techa. V'sham na-ava-d'cha b'yir-ah, ki-mei olam u-ch'sha-nim kad-mo-ni-yot. V'ar-vah la-donoy min-chat Y'hudah vi-ru-sha-la-yim, ki-mei olam u-ch'sha-nim kad-mo-ni-yot.

יְהִי רָצוֹן מִלְפָנֶיךָ יי אֱלֹהֵינוּ וֵאלֹהֵי אֲבוֹתֵינוּ, שֶׁיִבָּנֶה בֵּית הַמִּקְדָשׁ בִּמְהֵרָה בְיָמֵינוּ, וְתֵן חֶלְקֵנוּ בְּתוֹרָתֶךָ.
וְשָׁם נַעֲבָדְךָ בְּיִרְאָה, כִּימֵי עוֹלָם וּכְשָׁנִים קַדְמוֹנִיוֹת.
וְעָרְבָה לַיי מִנְחַת יְהוּדָה וִירוּשָׁלַיִם, כִּימֵי עוֹלָם וּכְשָׁנִים קַדְמוֹנִיוֹת.

Concluding Friday Night Shabbat Prayers

1. *Aleinu*: See page 146-147.

2. Mourner's Kaddish: If there is a mourner and a *minyan* of ten Jewish men is present, the mourners recite the Mourner's Kaddish slowly and together. See page 124-125.

3. *Adon Olam*: Some have the tradition to conclude with this prayer. See page 150-151.

ADDITIONAL PRAYERS FOR VARIOUS TIMES AND EVENTS IN LIFE

Prayer for the Soldiers of the Israel Defense Forces

The holy soldiers of Israel not only guard and watch over more than six million of our Jewish brothers and sisters and all of the other people who live in and who visit Israel, they guard the Land and all of its holy places. This allows us to go to Israel whenever we want to, and to be inspired by the beauty, the energy, and the spirituality of the Holy Land. The soldiers risk life and limb for us without receiving any thanks or recognition. At the very least, we can, and should, pray on their behalf.

May He who blessed our forefathers Avraham, Yitzchak, and Yaakov, bless the soldiers of the Israel Defense Forces, who stand on guard over our Land and the Cities of G-d. From the Lebanese border to the Egyptian desert, and from the Great Sea (i.e., the Mediterranean) to the approach of the Arava, on land, in the air, and upon the sea.

May Hashem cause the enemies who rise up against us to be struck down. May the Holy One, blessed is He, watch over and save our soldiers from all troubles and distress and from every plague and illness. May He send blessing and success in their every endeavor. May He put our enemies under our soldiers' power and may He crown our soldiers with the crowns of salvation and victory.

And may it be fulfilled for them the verse, "For it is Hashem, your G-d, who goes to battle with you, to battle your enemies for you, in order to save you."

And let us all say, Amein (i.e., I am in complete agreement!).

Mi she-bei-rach Avo-teinu Avra-ham Yitz-chak v'Ya-akov, Hu yi-va-reich et cha-ya-lei ts'va ha-haga-nah l'Yisrael, ha-om-dim al mish-mar ar-tzeinu v'arei Elo-heinu, mig-vul ha-L'va-non v'ad Mid-bar Mits-ra-yim, u-min ha-Yam ha-Ga-dol ad l'vo ha-Ara-vah, ba-ya-ba-shah ba-avir u-va-yam.

מִי שֶׁבֵּרַךְ אֲבוֹתֵינוּ אַבְרָהָם יִצְחָק וְיַעֲקֹב, הוּא יְבָרֵךְ אֶת חַיָּלֵי צְבָא הַהֲגָנָה לְיִשְׂרָאֵל, הָעוֹמְדִים עַל מִשְׁמַר אַרְצֵנוּ וְעָרֵי אֱלֹהֵינוּ, מִגְּבוּל הַלְּבָנוֹן וְעַד מִדְבַּר מִצְרַיִם, וּמִן הַיָּם הַגָּדוֹל עַד לְבוֹא הָעֲרָבָה, בַּיַּבָּשָׁה בָּאֲוִיר וּבַיָּם.

Yi-tein Adonoy et oi-veinu ha-ka-mim alei-nu ni-ga-fim lif-nei-hem.

יִתֵּן יי אֶת אוֹיְבֵינוּ הַקָּמִים עָלֵינוּ נִגָּפִים לִפְנֵיהֶם.

Ha-Kadosh Baruch Hu yish-mor v'ya-tzil et cha-ya-leinu mi-kol tsa-rah v'tsu-kah, u-mi-kol ne-ga u-ma-cha-lah, v'yish-lach b'ra-chah v'hats-la-chah b'chol ma-asei y'dei-hem.

הַקָּדוֹשׁ בָּרוּךְ הוּא יִשְׁמוֹר וְיַצִּיל אֶת חַיָּלֵינוּ מִכָּל צָרָה וְצוּקָה, וּמִכָּל נֶגַע וּמַחֲלָה, וְיִשְׁלַח בְּרָכָה וְהַצְלָחָה בְּכָל מַעֲשֵׂה יְדֵיהֶם.

Yad-beir son-einu tach-tei-hem, vi-at-reim b'che-ter y'shu-a u-v'a-teret ni-tsa-chon.

יַדְבֵּר שׂוֹנְאֵינוּ תַּחְתֵּיהֶם, וִיעַטְּרֵם בְּכֶתֶר יְשׁוּעָה וּבַעֲטֶרֶת נִצָּחוֹן.

Vi-ku-yam ba-hem ha-ka-tuv: Ki Adonoy Elo-heichem ha-ho-lech i-ma-chem, l'hi-la-cheim la-chem im oi-veichem l'ho-shi-a et-chem. V'no-mar: Amein.

וִיקֻיַּם בָּהֶם הַכָּתוּב: כִּי יְיָ אֱלֹהֵיכֶם הַהֹלֵךְ עִמָּכֶם, לְהִלָּחֵם לָכֶם עִם אֹיְבֵיכֶם לְהוֹשִׁיעַ אֶתְכֶם. וְנֹאמַר: אָמֵן.

Prayers Before Going to Sleep at Night

This day of life is now coming to an end. I am about to return my soul to Hashem and go into the state of sleep, from which I hope to awaken refreshed and with renewed strength and vigor.

This day of life will never recur again. I look back and evaluate what I accomplished today and will set out what I wish to accomplish tomorrow. I want to end this day on a strong note and with a smile.

 Take a minute to review the events of the past day. Identify all the positive things you did and the areas in which you wish to improve tomorrow and beyond.

Declaration of Forgiveness

*Kavanah: Now this is hard to do.
But if I can, I will forgive those who hurt me in any way,
whether purposefully or inadvertently, and release them from any severe
punishment they may have deserved for hurting me.
If I cannot forgive them at this time, maybe I will be able to forgive
them at some time in the future, especially if we have discussed the matter
openly and if they have made a serious effort to apologize and correct their error.
In return, may Hashem forgive me for my transgressions.*

Master of the World, I forgive anyone who angered me, belittled me, or sinned against me, whether it was against me physically or monetarily, against my honor, or against anything of mine. And may no one be punished because of what they did to me.

Ri-bo-no shel Olam, ha-rei-ni mo-chel v'so-lei-ach l'chol mi she-hich-is v'hik-nit o-ti, o she-cha-ta k'neg-di bein b'gu-fi, bein b'ma-mo-ni, bein bi-ch'vo-di, bein b'chol asher li, bein bo-nes bein b'ra-tson, bein b'sho-geig bein b'mei-zid, bein b'di-bur bein b'ma-aseh, bein b'gil-gul zeh bein b'gil-gul a-cheir, v'lo yei-a-neish shum adam b'si-ba-ti.	רִבּוֹנוֹ שֶׁל עוֹלָם, הֲרֵינִי מוֹחֵל וְסוֹלֵחַ לְכָל מִי שֶׁהִכְעִיס וְהִקְנִיט אוֹתִי, אוֹ שֶׁחָטָא כְּנֶגְדִּי בֵּין בְּגוּפִי, בֵּין בְּמָמוֹנִי, בֵּין בִּכְבוֹדִי, בֵּין בְּכָל אֲשֶׁר לִי, בֵּין בְּאֹנֶס בֵּין בְּרָצוֹן, בֵּין בְּשׁוֹגֵג בֵּין בְּמֵזִיד, בֵּין בְּדִבּוּר בֵּין בְּמַעֲשֶׂה, בֵּין בְּגִלְגּוּל זֶה בֵּין בְּגִלְגּוּל אַחֵר, וְלֹא יֵעָנֵשׁ שׁוּם אָדָם בְּסִבָּתִי.

Prayer for a Restful Sleep

> **Kavanah:** *I ask Hashem to provide me with pure, peaceful, refreshing, and rejuvenating sleep so that I wake up ready to do mitzvot and make a positive difference tomorrow!*

You, Adonoy our G-d, Source of all blessing, King of the World, are the One who makes my eyes close when I am tired and provides sleep to rejuvenate me, and You are the One who rejuvenates me with shining eyes when I wake up in the morning. May it be Your will, Adonoy, my G-d and the G-d of my ancestors, to provide me with peaceful rest and wake me up in peace. When I sleep, protect me from strange ideas, bad dreams, and impure thoughts. May my sleep be proper, and may I awake with shining eyes and not experience the sleep of death tonight.

You, Adonoy, Source of all blessing, enlighten the entire world with Your glory.

Baruch atah Adonoy Elo-heinu Melech ha-olam, ha-ma-pil chev-lei shai-nah al ei-nai, u-t'nu-mah al af-a-pai. V'y'hi ra-tson mil-fa-necha Adonoy Elo-hai vei-lo-hei avo-tai, she-tash-ki-veini l'shalom v'ta-ami-deini l'shalom. V'al y'va-ha-lu-ni ra-a-yo-nai, va-cha-lo-mot ra-im, v'har-ho-rim ra-im. U-t'hei mi-ta-ti sh'lei-mah l'fa-necha. V'ha-er ei-nai pen i-shan ha-ma-vet. Ki atah ha-mei-ir l'ishon bat ayin. Baruch atah Adonoy ha-mei-ir la-olam ku-lo bich-vo-do.	בָּרוּךְ אַתָּה יְיָ אֱלֹהֵינוּ מֶלֶךְ הָעוֹלָם, הַמַּפִּיל חֶבְלֵי שֵׁנָה עַל עֵינָי, וּתְנוּמָה עַל עַפְעַפָּי. וִיהִי רָצוֹן מִלְּפָנֶיךָ יְיָ אֱלֹהַי וֵאלֹהֵי אֲבוֹתַי, שֶׁתַּשְׁכִּיבֵנִי לְשָׁלוֹם וְתַעֲמִידֵנִי לְשָׁלוֹם. וְאַל יְבַהֲלוּנִי רַעְיוֹנַי, וַחֲלוֹמוֹת רָעִים, וְהִרְהוּרִים רָעִים. וּתְהֵא מִטָּתִי שְׁלֵמָה לְפָנֶיךָ. וְהָאֵר עֵינַי פֶּן אִישַׁן הַמָּוֶת. כִּי אַתָּה הַמֵּאִיר לְאִישׁוֹן בַּת עָיִן. בָּרוּךְ אַתָּה יְיָ הַמֵּאִיר לָעוֹלָם כֻּלּוֹ בִּכְבוֹדוֹ.

Shema Yisrael

[See Page 59 for a full explanation of this prayer and of this mitzvah.]

Part I. *Shema* Meditation: The Oneness of Hashem

> **Kavanah:** *Hashem is the one life force behind all things.*
> *Everything that Hashem does is for the good.*
> *Part of Hashem is within me.*
> *I am one with Hashem and He is one with me.*
> *I will try to follow Hashem's directions and connect with Him*
> *by using the forces of love and awe that Hashem has put in my soul.*

 Cover your eyes with your right hand while saying the opening line of the *Shema*.

שְׁמַע יִשְׂרָאֵל, יי אֱלֹהֵינוּ, יי אֶחָד:
(whisper)
בָּרוּךְ שֵׁם כְּבוֹד מַלְכוּתוֹ לְעוֹלָם וָעֶד

Shema Yisrael, Adonoy Elo-heinu, Adonoy Echad.
(whisper)
Baruch sheim k'vod mal-chu-to l'olam va-ed.

Listen Israel, Adonoy is our G-d, Adonoy is One.
(whisper)
May Hashem be acknowledged as the Source of blessing forever.

(from *Devarim* (Deuteronomy), Chapter 6, verses 5 to 9)

V'a-hav-ta eit Adonoy Elo-hecha, b'chol l'va-v'cha, u-v'chol naf-sh'cha, u-v'chol m'o-decha. V'ha-yu ha-d'va-rim ha-eileh, asher ano-chi m'tsa-v'cha ha-yom, al l'va-vecha. V'shi-nan-tam l'va-necha, v'di-bar-ta bam, b'shiv-t'cha b'vei-techa, u-v'lech-t'cha va-derech, u-v'shach-b'cha u-v'ku-mecha. U-k'shar-tam l'ot al ya-decha, v'ha-yu l'to-ta-fot bein ei-necha. U-ch'tav-tam al m'zu-zot bei-techa u-vish-a-recha.

וְאָהַבְתָּ אֵת יי אֱלֹהֶיךָ, בְּכָל לְבָבְךָ, וּבְכָל נַפְשְׁךָ, וּבְכָל מְאֹדֶךָ. וְהָיוּ הַדְּבָרִים הָאֵלֶּה, אֲשֶׁר אָנֹכִי מְצַוְּךָ הַיּוֹם, עַל לְבָבֶךָ. וְשִׁנַּנְתָּם לְבָנֶיךָ, וְדִבַּרְתָּ בָּם, בְּשִׁבְתְּךָ בְּבֵיתֶךָ, וּבְלֶכְתְּךָ בַדֶּרֶךְ, וּבְשָׁכְבְּךָ וּבְקוּמֶךָ. וּקְשַׁרְתָּם לְאוֹת עַל יָדֶךָ, וְהָיוּ לְטֹטָפֹת בֵּין עֵינֶיךָ. וּכְתַבְתָּם עַל מְזֻזוֹת בֵּיתֶךָ, וּבִשְׁעָרֶיךָ.

And you shall love Hashem, your G-d, with all your heart, with all your soul, and with all that is dear to you. These words which I command you today shall always be in your heart. Teach them to your children. Speak about them when you are at home, when you travel, when you lay down, and when you arise. Bind them as a sign on your arm (i.e., *tefillin* on the arm) and as *tefillin* upon the center of your head and write them as *mezuzot* for the doorposts of your house and your gates.

Part II. *V'hayah Im Shamo'a*
Cause and Effect: The Results of the Jewish People's Choices and Behavior

> **Kavanah:** *What I do matters to me and to the Jewish People. All of my actions will be recorded and evaluated. Each action has an effect upon me and on the Jewish Nation. There is cause and effect and consequence to my actions, words, thoughts, and decisions.*

(from *Devarim* (Deuteronomy), Chapter 11, Verses 13 to 21)

וְהָיָה, אִם שָׁמֹעַ תִּשְׁמְעוּ אֶל מִצְוֹתַי, אֲשֶׁר אָנֹכִי מְצַוֶּה אֶתְכֶם הַיּוֹם, לְאַהֲבָה אֶת יְיָ אֱלֹהֵיכֶם וּלְעָבְדוֹ, בְּכָל לְבַבְכֶם וּבְכָל נַפְשְׁכֶם. וְנָתַתִּי מְטַר אַרְצְכֶם בְּעִתּוֹ, יוֹרֶה וּמַלְקוֹשׁ, וְאָסַפְתָּ דְגָנֶךָ וְתִירֹשְׁךָ וְיִצְהָרֶךָ. וְנָתַתִּי עֵשֶׂב בְּשָׂדְךָ לִבְהֶמְתֶּךָ, וְאָכַלְתָּ וְשָׂבָעְתָּ. הִשָּׁמְרוּ לָכֶם, פֶּן יִפְתֶּה לְבַבְכֶם, וְסַרְתֶּם וַעֲבַדְתֶּם אֱלֹהִים אֲחֵרִים, וְהִשְׁתַּחֲוִיתֶם לָהֶם. וְחָרָה אַף יְיָ בָּכֶם, וְעָצַר אֶת הַשָּׁמַיִם, וְלֹא יִהְיֶה מָטָר, וְהָאֲדָמָה לֹא תִתֵּן אֶת יְבוּלָהּ, וַאֲבַדְתֶּם מְהֵרָה מֵעַל הָאָרֶץ הַטֹּבָה אֲשֶׁר יְיָ נֹתֵן לָכֶם. וְשַׂמְתֶּם אֶת דְּבָרַי אֵלֶּה, עַל לְבַבְכֶם וְעַל נַפְשְׁכֶם, וּקְשַׁרְתֶּם אֹתָם לְאוֹת עַל יֶדְכֶם, וְהָיוּ לְטוֹטָפֹת בֵּין עֵינֵיכֶם. וְלִמַּדְתֶּם אֹתָם אֶת בְּנֵיכֶם, לְדַבֵּר בָּם בְּשִׁבְתְּךָ בְּבֵיתֶךָ, וּבְלֶכְתְּךָ בַדֶּרֶךְ, וּבְשָׁכְבְּךָ וּבְקוּמֶךָ. וּכְתַבְתָּם עַל מְזוּזוֹת בֵּיתֶךָ, וּבִשְׁעָרֶיךָ. לְמַעַן יִרְבּוּ יְמֵיכֶם וִימֵי בְנֵיכֶם, עַל הָאֲדָמָה אֲשֶׁר נִשְׁבַּע יְיָ לַאֲבֹתֵיכֶם לָתֵת לָהֶם, כִּימֵי הַשָּׁמַיִם עַל הָאָרֶץ.

V'ha-yah, im sha-mo-a tish-m'u el mits-votai, asher a-no-chi m'tsa-veh et-chem ha-yom, l'a-ha-vah et Adonoy Elo-heichem u-l'av-do, b'chol l'vav-chem u-v'chol naf-sh'chem, v'na-ta-ti m'tar ar-ts'chem b'i-to, yo-reh u-mal-kosh, va-saf-ta d'ga-necha, v'ti-ro-sh'cha v'yits-ha-recha. V'na-ta-ti ei-sev b'sa-d'cha liv-hem-techa, v'a-chal-ta v'sa-va-ta. Hi-sham-ru la-chem, pen yif-teh l'vav-chem, v'sar-tem va-ava-d'tem Elo-him achei-rim, v'hish-ta-cha-vitem la-hem. V'cha-rah af Adonoy ba-chem, v'a-tsar et ha-sha-ma-yim, v'lo yi-h'yeh ma-tar, v'ha-ada-mah lo ti-tein et y'vu-lah, va-ava-d'tem m'hei-rah mei-al ha-arets ha-tovah asher Adonoy no-tein la-chem. V'sam-tem et d'va-rai ei-leh, al l'vav-chem v'al naf-sh'chem, u-k'shar-tem o-tam l'ot al yed-chem, v'ha-yu l'to-ta-fot bein ei-nei-chem. V'li-ma-d'tem o-tam et b'nei-chem, l'da-beir bam b'shiv-t'cha b'vei-techa, u-v'lech-t'cha va-derech, u-v'shach-b'cha u-v'ku-mecha. U-ch'tav-tam al m'zu-zot bei-techa, u-vish-a-recha. L'ma-an yir-bu y'mei-chem vi-mei v'nei-chem, al ha-ada-mah asher nish-ba Adonoy la-avo-tei-chem la-teit la-hem, ki-mei ha-sha-ma-yim al ha-arets.

And if you are careful to listen to My commandments, which I am commanding you today, and if you love Hashem, your G-d, and serve Him with all your heart and all your soul, then I, Hashem, have made this promise: I (Hashem) will provide rain to your land in its proper times so that you can harvest grain, wine, and olive oil. I will provide grass in your fields for your cattle and you will have sufficient food to eat and be satiated. Be careful not to be led astray by your heart's temptations to worship other gods or to bow to them. If you do follow other gods, Hashem will be angry with you and will restrain the heavens and there will be no rain and the earth will not yield produce. And you will vanish quickly from the good land which Hashem is giving you. Place these words of Mine upon your heart and soul. Bind them (for *tefillin*) as a sign on your arm and let them be *tefillin* in the center of your head. Teach these words to your children. Discuss them at home, when you travel, when you lay down, and when you get up. And write them on *mezuzot* for the doorposts of your homes and gates. If you do this, you and your children will endure for a long time upon the land that Hashem swore to your ancestors, that He would to give them, for as long as the heavens remain above the earth (i.e., forever).

Part III. *Vayomeir*
Remember the Exodus from Egypt and Be Careful to Do the Right Thing

> **Kavanah:** *I will strive to be constantly aware that I am part of the Jewish People and its mission in the world. Hashem helps us to break through our perceived barriers and limitations to achieve personal growth.*

Identify those issues that are holding you back from growing, achieving, and being the best you can be today. Ask yourself, "Am I sad, angry, lazy, self-focused?" Ask Hashem to help you break out of your personal "Egypt," i.e., your personal barriers and limitations.

(from *Bamidbar* (Numbers), Chapter 15, verses 37 to 41)

Va-yo-meir Adonoy el Mosheh lei-mor: Da-beir el b'nei Yisrael, v'a-mar-ta alei-hem, v'a-su la-hem tsi-tsit, al kan-fei vig-dei-hem l'doro-tam, v'nat-nu al tsi-tsit ha-kanaf, p'til t'chei-let. V'ha-yah la-chem l'tsi-tsit, u-r'item oto, u-z'char-tem et kol mits-vot Adonoy, va-asi-tem o-tam, v'lo ta-tu-ru acha-rei l'vav-chem v'a-cha-rei einei-chem, asher a-tem zo-nim acha-rei-hem. L'ma-an tiz-k'ru, va-asi-tem et kol mits-votai vi-h'yi-tem k'do-shim lei-lo-hei-chem.

וַיֹּאמֶר יי אֶל מֹשֶׁה לֵּאמֹר: דַּבֵּר אֶל בְּנֵי יִשְׂרָאֵל, וְאָמַרְתָּ אֲלֵהֶם, וְעָשׂוּ לָהֶם צִיצִת, עַל כַּנְפֵי בִגְדֵיהֶם לְדֹרֹתָם, וְנָתְנוּ עַל צִיצִת הַכָּנָף, פְּתִיל תְּכֵלֶת. וְהָיָה לָכֶם לְצִיצִת, וּרְאִיתֶם אֹתוֹ, וּזְכַרְתֶּם אֶת כָּל מִצְוֹת יי, וַעֲשִׂיתֶם אֹתָם, וְלֹא תָתוּרוּ אַחֲרֵי לְבַבְכֶם וְאַחֲרֵי עֵינֵיכֶם, אֲשֶׁר אַתֶּם זֹנִים אַחֲרֵיהֶם. לְמַעַן תִּזְכְּרוּ, וַעֲשִׂיתֶם אֶת כָּל מִצְוֹתָי, וִהְיִיתֶם קְדֹשִׁים לֵאלֹהֵיכֶם.

Ani Adonoy Elo-heichem, asher ho-tsei-ti et-chem mei-erets Mits-ra-yim, li-h'yot la-chem lei-lo-him; Ani Adonoy Elo-heichem. Emet.

אֲנִי יְיָ אֱלֹהֵיכֶם, אֲשֶׁר הוֹצֵאתִי אֶתְכֶם מֵאֶרֶץ מִצְרַיִם, לִהְיוֹת לָכֶם לֵאלֹהִים, אֲנִי יְיָ אֱלֹהֵיכֶם. אֱמֶת.

And Hashem spoke to Moshe and instructed him to speak to the Jewish People and have them make *tzitzit* (special tassels) on the corners of four-cornered garments for all generations. These should include a thread of sky-blue wool (dyed from a source that is no longer available today). These shall be your *tzitzit*. When you see them, you will remember all of Hashem's commandments and keep and follow them. Thus, you will not be led astray by the desires of your heart and eyes, which have a tendency to lead you astray. You will remember and keep all of My commandments and will be holy to your G-d. I am Hashem, your G-d, who brought you out of Egypt to be your G-d. I am Hashem, your G-d. This is truth.

1. *Y'va-re-ch'cha Adonoy v'yish-m'recha. Ya-eir Adonoy pa-nav ei-lecha vi-chu-nekah. Yi-sa Adonoy pa-nav ei-lechah v'ya-seim l'cha shalom.*

יְבָרֶכְךָ יְיָ וְיִשְׁמְרֶךָ.
יָאֵר יְיָ פָּנָיו אֵלֶיךָ וִיחֻנֶּךָּ.
יִשָּׂא יְיָ פָּנָיו אֵלֶיךָ וְיָשֵׂם לְךָ שָׁלוֹם.

2. *Hi-nei lo ya-num v'lo yi-shan sho-meir Yisrael.*

הִנֵּה לֹא יָנוּם וְלֹא יִישָׁן שׁוֹמֵר יִשְׂרָאֵל.

3. *B'sheim Adonoy Elo-hei Yisrael, mi-mi-ni Mi-cha-el, u-mis-mo-li Ga-vri-el, u-mil-fa-nai U-ri-el, u-mei-acho-rai R'fa-eil, v'al ro-shi Sh'chi-nat El.*

בְּשֵׁם יְיָ אֱלֹהֵי יִשְׂרָאֵל, מִימִינִי מִיכָאֵל, וּמִשְּׂמֹאלִי גַּבְרִיאֵל, וּמִלְּפָנַי אוּרִיאֵל, וּמֵאֲחוֹרַי רְפָאֵל, וְעַל רֹאשִׁי שְׁכִינַת אֵל.

1. May Adonoy bless you and guard you. May Adonoy shine His light upon you and be gracious to you. May Adonoy turn toward you and give you peace and fulfillment.

2. (Hashem,) the Guardian of Israel does not slumber or sleep.

3. May Adonoy, the G-d of Israel, instruct the angels Michael to be at my right, Gavriel at my left, Uriel before me, and Refael behind me, and above my head, the Presence of Hashem will watch over me.

Adon Olam

> **Kavanah:** *There are many things that I can't understand and will never understand about Hashem. But I do know that Hashem is with me in every step that I take. So I will go to sleep without fear, confident that Hashem will watch over me.*

Master of the World, who reigned before all creation,
At the time when His Will created all form,
He was then proclaimed as the Ruler.

And after all may cease to be,
He, the awesome One, will rule alone.

He was, He is, and He will be forever, in Splendor.

He is One; there is no other who can compare to Hashem.

He is without beginning and without end.

He holds all the power.

And He is my G-d, my living redeemer, the one I rely upon in my time of trouble.

Hashem is my banner, a place of refuge for me, my cup's fill when I call to Him.

I will trust my spirit in His hand when I go to sleep and when I awake.

Hashem is with me. I shall not fear.

Adon olam asher ma-lach, *b'te-rem kol y'tsir niv-ra.*	אֲדוֹן עוֹלָם אֲשֶׁר מָלַךְ, בְּטֶרֶם כָּל יְצִיר נִבְרָא.
L'eit na-asah v'chef-tso kol, *a-zai me-lech sh'mo nik'ra.*	לְעֵת נַעֲשָׂה בְחֶפְצוֹ כֹּל, אֲזַי מֶלֶךְ שְׁמוֹ נִקְרָא.
V'a-cha-rei ki-ch'lot ha-kol, *l'va-do yim-loch no-ra.*	וְאַחֲרֵי כִּכְלוֹת הַכֹּל, לְבַדּוֹ יִמְלוֹךְ נוֹרָא.
V'hu ha-yah v'hu ho-veh, *v'hu yi-h'yeh b'tif-a-rah.*	וְהוּא הָיָה וְהוּא הֹוֶה, וְהוּא יִהְיֶה בְּתִפְאָרָה.

V'hu echad v'ein shei-ni, l'ham-shil lo l'hach-bi-rah.	וְהוּא אֶחָד וְאֵין שֵׁנִי, לְהַמְשִׁיל לוֹ לְהַחְבִּירָה.
B'li rei-sheet b'li tach-lit, v'lo ha-oz v'ha-mis-rah.	בְּלִי רֵאשִׁית בְּלִי תַכְלִית, וְלוֹ הָעֹז וְהַמִּשְׂרָה.
V'hu ei-li v'chai go-ali, v'tsur chev-li b'eit tsa-rah.	וְהוּא אֵלִי וְחַי גּוֹאֲלִי, וְצוּר חֶבְלִי בְּעֵת צָרָה.
V'hu ni-si u-ma-nos li, m'nat ko-si b'yom ek-ra.	וְהוּא נִסִּי וּמָנוֹס לִי, מְנָת כּוֹסִי בְּיוֹם אֶקְרָא.
B'ya-do af-kid ru-chi, b'eit ishan v'a-irah.	בְּיָדוֹ אַפְקִיד רוּחִי, בְּעֵת אִישָׁן וְאָעִירָה.
V'im ru-chi g'vi-ya-ti, Adonoy li v'lo i-ra.	וְעִם רוּחִי גְוִיָּתִי, יְיָ לִי וְלֹא אִירָא.

 Smile and sleep peacefully...

PRAYERS THROUGHOUT THE DAY

There is an appropriate prayer or blessing for every occurrence in life (remember that scene in *Fiddler on the Roof* where the students ask the Rabbi to teach them a blessing for the cruel Czar?). There is a prayer when one hears good news or bad news; when one sees a natural wonder, a rainbow, or a genius; when one experiences a new child or a new fruit for the first time that year; and for virtually every circumstance in life.

King David taught the concept of saying one hundred blessings in a day. These short moments of awareness, and often of thanks, can assist a person in becoming acutely "G-d-conscious" and thereby lead to living an aware, meaningful, thankful, and purposeful life.

Listed below are some of the more frequently-used blessings. (See the NCSY *Bencher* for the complete blessing after eating and for the meals for Shabbat and Jewish Holidays. See the Artscroll Siddur for a more extensive list of blessings in Hebrew and English).

Prayer After Using the Washroom

After using the washroom, wash your hands and say *Asher Yatsar*, the Blessing for Our Bodies.

> **Kavanah:** *I thank you, Hashem, that all of the complicated functions of my body work. Without Your life force, I could not survive for even one moment.*

You, Adonoy our G-d, Source of all blessings, Master of the World, created people with wisdom and made our bodies so complex, with many cavities and many openings. It is obvious to You that if even one of them were to rupture or become blocked, it would be impossible to survive and stand before You for even one moment. You, Adonoy, Source of all blessings, Master of the World, heal our bodies and make wondrous creations.

Baruch atah Adonoy Elo-heinu Me-lech ha-olam asher ya-tsar et ha-adam b'choch-mah u-va-ra vo n'ka-vim n'ka-vim, cha-lu-lim cha-lu-lim. Ga-lu-i v'ya-du-a lif-nei chi-sei ch'vo-decha she-im yi-pa-tei-ach echad mei-hem o yi-sa-tem echad mei-hem

בָּרוּךְ אַתָּה יי אֱלֹהֵינוּ מֶלֶךְ הָעוֹלָם אֲשֶׁר יָצַר אֶת הָאָדָם בְּחָכְמָה וּבָרָא בוֹ נְקָבִים נְקָבִים חֲלוּלִים חֲלוּלִים. גָּלוּי וְיָדוּעַ לִפְנֵי כִסֵּא כְבוֹדֶךָ שֶׁאִם יִפָּתֵחַ אֶחָד מֵהֶם

i ef-shar l'hit-ka-yeim v'la-a-mod l'fa-necha a-fi-lu sha-ah echat.

Baruch atah Adonoy, ro-fei chol ba-sar u-maf-li la-asot.

אוֹ יִסָּתֵם אֶחָד מֵהֶם אִי אֶפְשָׁר לְהִתְקַיֵּם וְלַעֲמוֹד לְפָנֶיךָ אֲפִילוּ שָׁעָה אֶחָת.

בָּרוּךְ אַתָּה יי רוֹפֵא כָל בָּשָׂר וּמַפְלִיא לַעֲשׂוֹת.

As You Leave on an Out-of-Town Journey

> **Kavanah:** *Hashem, please keep my family and me safe on our journey. The guardian angels that reside in our home will stay behind, so please send Your forces to protect us from any occurrence that could turn the trip into a dangerous one.*

May it be Your will, Adonoy, our G-d and the G-d of our ancestors, that You lead and guide us toward peace and help us reach our destination for life, happiness, and peace. Please rescue us from all enemies, ambushes, robbers, dangerous animals, or winds along the way and from any form of punishment that could come to the world.

Send blessings to our efforts and grant us grace, kindness, and compassion in the eyes of all those who meet us. Please hear the sound of our prayers, as You are the G-d who hears prayers and listens to our requests. You, Adonoy, Source of all blessing, listen to our prayers.

Y'hi ra-tson mil-fa-necha Adonoy Elo-heinu vei-lo-hei avo-teinu she-toli-chenu l'shalom, v'tats-i-deinu l'shalom, v'ta-d'ri-cheinu l'shalom. V'ta-gi-einu lim-choz chef-tseinu l'cha-yim u-l'sim-chah u-l'shalom, v'ta-tsi-leinu mi-kaf kol o-yeiv v'o-reiv v'lis-tim v'cha-yot ra-ot ba-de-rech, u-mi-kol mi-nei fur-ani-yot ha-mit-rag-shot u-va-ot la-olam, v'tish-lach b'ra-chah b'ma-asei ya-deinu, v'ti-t'nei-nu l'chein u-l'che-sed u-l'ra-cha-mim b'ei-necha u-v'ei-nei chol ro-einu, v'tish-ma kol tacha-nu-neinu. Ki El sho-mei-a t'fi-lah v'ta-cha-nun atah. Baruch atah Adonoy, sho-mei-a t'fi-lah.

יְהִי רָצוֹן מִלְּפָנֶיךָ יי אֱלֹהֵינוּ וֵאלֹהֵי אֲבוֹתֵינוּ שֶׁתּוֹלִיכֵנוּ לְשָׁלוֹם, וְתַצְעִידֵנוּ לְשָׁלוֹם, וְתַדְרִיכֵנוּ לְשָׁלוֹם. וְתַגִּיעֵנוּ לִמְחוֹז חֶפְצֵנוּ לְחַיִּים וּלְשִׂמְחָה וּלְשָׁלוֹם, וְתַצִּילֵנוּ מִכַּף כָּל אוֹיֵב וְאוֹרֵב וְלִסְטִים וְחַיּוֹת רָעוֹת בַּדֶּרֶךְ, וּמִכָּל מִינֵי פֻּרְעָנִיּוֹת הַמִּתְרַגְּשׁוֹת וּבָאוֹת לָעוֹלָם. וְתִשְׁלַח בְּרָכָה בְּמַעֲשֵׂי יָדֵינוּ, וְתִתְּנֵנוּ לְחֵן וּלְחֶסֶד וּלְרַחֲמִים בְּעֵינֶיךָ וּבְעֵינֵי כָל רוֹאֵינוּ, וְתִשְׁמַע קוֹל תַּחֲנוּנֵינוּ. כִּי אֵל שׁוֹמֵעַ תְּפִלָּה וְתַחֲנוּן אָתָּה. בָּרוּךְ אַתָּה יי שׁוֹמֵעַ תְּפִלָּה.

Blessings Before Eating

Kavanah: Hashem could have created us in such a way that we would not have to eat. He could have made us able to survive through the process of photosynthesis as plants do. Even if we were meant to survive by eating food and drinking, Hashem could have provided us with food only once a day or He could have fed us with only oatmeal or bland foods.

Instead, Hashem provides us with nourishment through multiple foods, in multiple colors, flavors, textures, and combinations, many times each day. So, before we eat, we ought to take out a moment to recognize the wonder of the food Hashem has provided to us. It is one of the ways in which Hashem tells us repeatedly that we are His children and that He loves and cares for us. Bon appétit!

It is a beautiful thing to share this sentiment by saying the blessing out loud and allowing others to respond, "Amein!"

(Please note that there are many nuances to the blessings on food, such as food combinations, categorizations (e.g., a blueberry is considered a fruit, while a banana is considered a vegetable), and many other issues. The best thing is to start getting into the habit of saying the blessings before eating and then ask a knowledgeable Rabbi when a particular question arises.)

On fruit:

Adonoy, You who are the Source of all blessing, Master of the World, creates the fruits of the trees.

Baruch atah Adonoy Elo-heinu Melech ha-olam, bo-rei p'ri ha-eits.   בָּרוּךְ אַתָּה יי אֱלֹהֵינוּ מֶלֶךְ הָעוֹלָם, בּוֹרֵא פְּרִי הָעֵץ.

On vegetables:

Adonoy, You who are the Source of all blessing, Master of the World, creates the produce of the earth.

Baruch atah Adonoy Elo-heinu Melech ha-olam, bo-rei p'ri ha-ada-mah.   בָּרוּךְ אַתָּה יי אֱלֹהֵינוּ מֶלֶךְ הָעוֹלָם, בּוֹרֵא פְּרִי הָאֲדָמָה.

On cakes, crackers, and cookies:

Adonoy, You who are the Source of all blessing, Master of the World, creates various forms of nourishment.

Baruch atah Adonoy Elo-heinu Melech ha-olam, bo-rei mi-nei m'zo-not.

בָּרוּךְ אַתָּה יי אֱלֹהֵינוּ מֶלֶךְ הָעוֹלָם, בּוֹרֵא מִינֵי מְזוֹנוֹת.

On wine and grape juice:

Adonoy, You who are the Source of all blessing, Master of the World, creates the fruit of the vine.

Baruch atah Adonoy Elo-heinu Melech ha-olam, bo-rei p'ri ha-ga-fen.

בָּרוּךְ אַתָּה יי אֱלֹהֵינוּ מֶלֶךְ הָעוֹלָם, בּוֹרֵא פְּרִי הַגָּפֶן.

On drinks, candies, ice cream, meat:
(NOTE: This is also the default blessing when you aren't sure which blessing to say before eating)

Adonoy, You who are the Source of all blessing, Master of the World, makes everything exist through Your word.

Baruch atah Adonoy Elo-heinu Melech ha-olam, she-ha-kol ni-h'yeh bi-d'va-ro.

בָּרוּךְ אַתָּה יי אֱלֹהֵינוּ מֶלֶךְ הָעוֹלָם, שֶׁהַכֹּל נִהְיֶה בִּדְבָרוֹ.

On washing your hands before eating bread:

Before we eat bread, we must wash our hands in a special way. We fill up a cup with water and pour the water over our right hand twice and then fill the cup again and pour it over our left hand twice. (NOTE: Jews from the Sephardic tradition wash each hand three times rather than twice). Before we dry our hands, we say the following blessing:

Adonoy, You who are the Source of all blessing, Master of the World, commanded us regarding washing the hands.

Baruch atah Adonoy Elo-heinu Melech ha-olam, asher ki-d'sha-nu b'mits-vo-tav, v'tsi-vanu al n'ti-lat ya-da-yim.

בָּרוּךְ אַתָּה יי אֱלֹהֵינוּ מֶלֶךְ הָעוֹלָם, אֲשֶׁר קִדְּשָׁנוּ בְּמִצְוֹתָיו, וְצִוָּנוּ עַל נְטִילַת יָדָיִם.

On bread, matzah, bagels:

Adonoy, You who are the Source of all blessing, Master of the World, who takes bread out of the earth.

Baruch atah Adonoy Elo-heinu Melech ha-olam, ha-mo-tsi le-chem min ha-arets.

בָּרוּךְ אַתָּה יי אֱלֹהֵינוּ מֶלֶךְ הָעוֹלָם, הַמּוֹצִיא לֶחֶם מִן הָאָרֶץ.

Blessings After Eating

 **After Concluding a Meal with Bread**

NOTE: This is only the first of four blessings that make up the *bentching* (the commonly used Yiddish term to refer to the prayers after a meal that includes bread). However, reciting the first blessing, the only blessing mandated by the Torah, is a good way to begin. For the full version, purchase the NCSY Bencher (Orthodox Union) or see one of the English translations of the traditional siddur (see the For Further Reading section).

> **Kavanah:** *Thank you, Hashem, for providing me with food as you have done every day since my birth. You provide food for all of the creatures in the world. Please continue to provide sustenance and nourishment for us for our entire lives.*

**You, Adonoy, Source of all Blessings, our G-d and Master of the World, provide food with His goodness for the whole world, with grace, kindness, and mercy. He supplies sustenance for all living creatures, for His kindness is everlasting. Because of His great goodness, we have never lacked for food nor will we. Because of His great name, He is the G-d who feeds, provides for all and is good to all. He prepares food for all of His creations.
You, Adonoy, the Source of all Blessings, provide food for all.**

Baruch atah Adonoy Elo-heinu Melech ha-olam, ha-zan et ha-olam ku-lo, b'tu-vo, b'chein b'che-sed u-v'ra-cha-mim, hu no-tein le-chem l'chol ba-sar, ki l'olam chas-do. U-v'tu-vo ha-ga-dol ta-mid lo cha-sar la-nu v'al yech-sar la-nu ma-zon l'olam va-ed, ba-avur sh'mo ha-ga-dol, ki hu El zan u-m'far-neis la-kol, u-mei-tiv la-kol, u-mei-chin ma-zon l'chol b'ri-yo-tav asher ba-ra.

בָּרוּךְ אַתָּה יי אֱלֹהֵינוּ מֶלֶךְ הָעוֹלָם, הַזָּן אֶת הָעוֹלָם כֻּלּוֹ, בְּטוּבוֹ, בְּחֵן בְּחֶסֶד וּבְרַחֲמִים, הוּא נוֹתֵן לֶחֶם לְכָל בָּשָׂר, כִּי לְעוֹלָם חַסְדּוֹ. וּבְטוּבוֹ הַגָּדוֹל תָּמִיד לֹא חָסַר לָנוּ וְאַל יֶחְסַר לָנוּ מָזוֹן לְעוֹלָם וָעֶד, בַּעֲבוּר שְׁמוֹ הַגָּדוֹל, כִּי הוּא אֵל זָן וּמְפַרְנֵס לַכֹּל, וּמֵטִיב לַכֹּל, וּמֵכִין מָזוֹן לְכָל בְּרִיּוֹתָיו אֲשֶׁר בָּרָא.

Baruch atah Adonoy, ha-zan et ha-kol.

בָּרוּךְ אַתָּה יי, הַזָּן אֶת הַכֹּל.

After Eating Cake, Cookies, or Crackers:

(NOTE: A variation of this "After Blessing" is said after drinking wine or eating olives, dates, grapes, figs, or pomegranates — the fruits of Israel, which are designated in the Torah as being extra-special.)

You, Adonoy, Source of all Blessings, Master of the World, provide sustenance and nourishment for the trees and their fruits, for the vine and its fruits, for the produce, and for the beautiful, good, and spacious Land, which you gave as an inheritance to our ancestors to eat from its fruit and to be satisfied with its goodness.

Please, Adonoy our G-d, have compassion on Israel, Your nation, on Jerusalem, Your city, on Zion, the home of Your honor, on Your altar, and on Your dwelling place. Build Jerusalem, the Holy City, quickly, in our time.

Bring us up to that place so that we can rejoice in its rebuilding and eat of its fruits and be satisfied with its goodness.

And there we will acknowledge, in holiness and purity, that You are the Source of our blessings. For You, Adonoy, are good and You do good for all. We thank You for the land and its produce.

You, Adonoy, are the Source of blessing for the the land and its produce.

Baruch atah Adonoy Elo-heinu Melech ha-olam, al ha-mich-yah v'al ha-kal-ka-lah, v'al t'nu-vat ha-sa-deh, v'al erets chem-dah to-vah u-r'cha-vah, she-ra-tsi-ta v'hin-chal-ta la-avo-teinu, le-echol mi-pir-yah v'lis-bo-a mi-tu-vah.
Ra-cheim na Adonoy Elo-heinu al Yisrael a-mecha, v'al Y'ru-sha-la-yim i-recha, v'al Tsi-yon mish-kan k'vo-decha, v'al miz-b'che-cha, v'al hei-cha-lecha. U-v'nei Y'ru-sha-la-yim ir ha-ko-desh bim-hei-rah v'ya-meinu, v'ha-alei-nu l'to-chah, v'sam-cheinu b'vin-ya-nah, v'no-chal mi-pir-yah, v'nis-ba mi-tu-vah u-n'va-re-ch'cha ale-ha bi-k'du-shah u-v'ta-ha-rah.
Ki atah Adonoy tov u-mei-tiv la-kol, v'no-deh l'cha al ha-arets v'al ha-mich-yah. Baruch atah Adonoy, al ha-arets v'al ha-mich-yah.

בָּרוּךְ אַתָּה יי אֱלֹהֵינוּ מֶלֶךְ הָעוֹלָם, עַל הַמִּחְיָה וְעַל הַכַּלְכָּלָה, וְעַל תְּנוּבַת הַשָּׂדֶה, וְעַל אֶרֶץ חֶמְדָּה טוֹבָה וּרְחָבָה, שֶׁרָצִיתָ וְהִנְחַלְתָּ לַאֲבוֹתֵינוּ, לֶאֱכוֹל מִפִּרְיָהּ וְלִשְׂבּוֹעַ מִטּוּבָהּ.
רַחֵם נָא יי אֱלֹהֵינוּ עַל יִשְׂרָאֵל עַמֶּךָ, וְעַל יְרוּשָׁלַיִם עִירֶךָ, וְעַל צִיּוֹן מִשְׁכַּן כְּבוֹדֶךָ, וְעַל מִזְבְּחֶךָ, וְעַל הֵיכָלֶךָ.
וּבְנֵה יְרוּשָׁלַיִם עִיר הַקֹּדֶשׁ בִּמְהֵרָה בְיָמֵינוּ, וְהַעֲלֵנוּ לְתוֹכָהּ, וְשַׂמְּחֵנוּ בְּבִנְיָנָהּ, וְנֹאכַל מִפִּרְיָהּ, וְנִשְׂבַּע מִטּוּבָהּ וּנְבָרֶכְךָ עָלֶיהָ בִּקְדֻשָּׁה וּבְטָהֳרָה.
כִּי אַתָּה יי טוֹב וּמֵטִיב לַכֹּל, וְנוֹדֶה לְּךָ עַל הָאָרֶץ וְעַל הַמִּחְיָה.
בָּרוּךְ אַתָּה יי, עַל הָאָרֶץ וְעַל הַמִּחְיָה.

After Eating or Drinking Foods that Don't Require the Other "After Blessings":

You, Adonoy, Source of all blessing, our G-d and Master of the World, Creator of many living things, each with its particular needs — for everything You created in order to sustain all life; we recognize that You, the Eternal One, are the Source of all blessings.

Baruch atah Adonoy Elo-heinu Melech ha-olam bo-rei n'fa-shot ra-bot v'ches-ro-nan al kol mah she-ba-ra-ta l'ha-cha-yot ba-hem ne-fesh kol chai. Baruch chei ha-ola-mim.

בָּרוּךְ אַתָּה יי אֱלֹהֵינוּ מֶלֶךְ הָעוֹלָם בּוֹרֵא נְפָשׁוֹת רַבּוֹת וְחֶסְרוֹנָן עַל כָּל מַה שֶּׁבָּרָאתָ לְהַחֲיוֹת בָּהֶם נֶפֶשׁ כָּל חָי. בָּרוּךְ חֵי הָעוֹלָמִים.

BIKUR CHOLIM: VISITING THE SICK

Introduction

Illness is one of the great equalizers in life. All people experience illness during their lifetime in one way or another. Either they will become ill at some time in their lives or their parents, children, relatives, or friends will. Illness touches the wealthy and the modest, the wise and the simple, people of all religions, statures, professions, walks of life, race, and levels of influence.

But what can we do when someone we care about is ill? Judaism teaches that there is always something you can do to help better a situation. In the case of illness it begins with sensitivity and the mitzvah of visiting the ill person. A visitor, teaches the Talmud, can even take away a measure of illness from the patient.

The first time that we learn about the mitzvah of *bikur cholim,* visiting the sick, is when Hashem visited our forefather Avraham on the third day following his circumcision at age 100. Avraham was feeling hot, lonely, and in pain when Hashem appeared to him. As we are to pattern ourselves after the qualities of G-d, we learn from this biblical account that we, too, are to visit the sick.

The Talmud teaches that those who take care to perform this mitzvah are saved from strict justice in the Next World. Rabbi Akiva teaches that visiting the sick gives life to the ill person, both physically and emotionally. On the other hand, failure to visit those who are seriously ill can be akin to ending their lives prematurely.

Guidelines for Performing *Bikur Cholim*:

When a patient is quite ill or has just had surgery, only immediate family and close friends should visit for the first three days. If you are a close friend and feel that your visit will help, then it is best to check first with the family to make sure that it is all right for you to visit. After the third day, anyone can visit.

There are no age restrictions on this mitzvah; the young can visit the old and the old can visit the young.

Depending on the circumstances, when someone is ill, it may be an opportune time to settle past differences. If this is the case, you must first ask permission from a family member to make sure your visit is welcome by the patient.

It is best not to visit too early in the morning or too late in the evening. Generally, the afternoon is the preferred time. Friday or the day of the eve of a major Jewish holiday is also a very good time to visit, as the patient is usually feeling quite lonely and depressed knowing that they will be in the hospital over the special days and away from family, friends, and their community.

An essential part of fulfilling the mitzvah of *bikur cholim* is to recite a prayer in front of the sick person, as the *Shechinah* (the "mothering" presence of G-d) is present in the room of an ill person. You can recite the prayers in any language. Before saying a prayer, it is best to ask patients for permission to say a prayer for them in their presence. If they are not comfortable with this, then say the prayer outside the room. (See appropriate prayers listed below.)

It is a tremendous *Kiddush Hashem* (a G-dly act) to visit all kinds of Jews and non-Jews alike, especially if the Jewish person you are visiting is sharing a room with a Gentile person.

It is best *not* to focus on the illness when visiting. Discuss the patient's regular daily activities and share an uplifting thought if the person is up to listening.

Be sensitive not to trouble or bother the ill person in any way.

Be careful not to shame the person if he or she is not dressed properly (e.g., after surgery) or is dealing with an embarrassing physical challenge. Sometimes it is best to stay outside of the curtain in the hospital room and address the patient from there.

Don't stay too long (sometimes five to ten minutes might be just enough). Watch for signs of fatigue and take them as a sign to say goodbye, with a smile.

The Goals of This Mitzvah:

To visit and pray for the ill person.

See if you can get the patient to *smile*. This will leave both the patient and you feeling better.

Visiting the sick has "a mitzvah behind a mitzvah." People can focus exclusively on the patient, while forgetting about the spouse, children, and parents of the patient. You can help out with shopping, providing meals, babysitting, and other chores, *and by giving the family members words of encouragement and hope.*

Remember that it has been proven scientifically that an ill person with a positive attitude and an optimistic outlook has a far better chance of survival and recuperation.

Sometimes, when it seems there is nothing else to do, those present with the ill person can sing the patient's favorite songs or sweet traditional songs of the Shabbat and Jewish holiday prayers (e.g., "Shalom Aleichem"). Singing changes the environment in the room and provides a spirit of calm and sweetness.

WHERE THERE IS LIFE, THERE IS HOPE. The visitor must exude a positive attitude, projecting *optimism* and *hope*.

When one is seriously ill, it is a good time to do examine one's lifestyle, add in the performance of mitzvot, and give *tzedakah*. It is most appropriate for the visitor to perform a mitzvah and give charity in the merit of the patient's recovery.

REMEMBER: There is *always* something you can do.

Visit, smile, sing, say a prayer, perform a mitzvah, give *tzedakah* on behalf of the ill person, and provide companionship, encouragement, hope, and perhaps some welcome assistance to the patient's family members.

Prayers to Recite on Behalf of Someone Who Is Seriously Ill

The Prayer for the Sick (known as the *Mi Shebeirach* prayer)

May He (G-d) who blessed our ancestors, Abraham, Isaac, and Jacob, Moshe, Aaron, King David, and King Solomon, bless and heal (first name, ideally the patient's Jewish name) **the son/daughter of** (their mother's name, ideally the patient's mother's Jewish name), **because I am praying on their behalf and I will try to give charity in his/her merit.**

As a reward for these efforts, may the Holy One, Blessed is He, be filled with compassion for the patient and provide him/her with restored health, healing, strength, and reinvigorated life and send from the Heavens a speedy and complete recovery to all of his/her organs and limbs, among the other sick people of our Nation, including both a healing of body and of spirit, (On Shabbat we add the line: **and although on Shabbat it is inappropriate to cry out**) **may the recovery come very soon. And let us respond,** *Amein*.

Prayer for a male who is seriously ill:

Mi she-bei-rach avo-teinu Avra-ham Yitz-chak v'Ya-akov, Mo-sheh Aharon Da-vid u-Shlo-mo, Hu y'va-rech vira-pei et (patient's first name, ideally his Jewish name) ben (his mother's name, ideally her Jewish name), ba-avur she-ani mit-pa-leil ba-avu-ro u-ba-avur she-ani notein bli neder tse-dakah ba-avu-ro.

B's'char zeh, Ha-kadosh Baruch Hu yi-ma-lei ra-cha-mim alav, l'hach-li-mo u'l'ra-po-to u'l'ha-cha-zi-ko u'l'ha-cha-yo-to, v'yish-lach lo m'hei-rah r'fu-ah sh'lei-mah min ha-sha-ma-yim, lir-mach ei-va-rav, u-sh'sah gi-dav, b'toch sh'ar cho-lei Yisrael, r'fu-at ha-neh-fesh u-r'fu-at ga-guf, (On Shabbat insert the line: Shabat hi mi-liz-ok, u-r'fu-ah k'ro-va la-vo) hash-ta, ba-aga-la u-viz-man ka-riv.
V'no-mar, Amein.

מִי שֶׁבֵּרַךְ אֲבוֹתֵינוּ אַבְרָהָם יִצְחָק וְיַעֲקֹב, מֹשֶׁה אַהֲרֹן דָּוִד וּשְׁלֹמֹה, הוּא יְבָרֵךְ וִירַפֵּא אֶת, patient's first name, ideally his Jewish name בֶּן his mother's name, ideally her Jewish name בַּעֲבוּר שֶׁאֲנִי מִתְפַּלֵּל בַּעֲבוּרוֹ וּבַעֲבוּר שֶׁאֲנִי נוֹתֵן בְּלִי נֶדֶר צְדָקָה בַּעֲבוּרוֹ.

בִּשְׂכַר זֶה, הַקָּדוֹשׁ בָּרוּךְ הוּא יִמָּלֵא רַחֲמִים עָלָיו, לְהַחְלִימוֹ וּלְרַפֹּאתוֹ וּלְהַחֲזִיקוֹ וּלְהַחֲיוֹתוֹ, וְיִשְׁלַח לוֹ מְהֵרָה רְפוּאָה שְׁלֵמָה מִן הַשָּׁמַיִם, לְרַמַ"ח אֵבָרָיו, וּשְׁסָ"ה גִידָיו, בְּתוֹךְ שְׁאָר חוֹלֵי יִשְׂרָאֵל, רְפוּאַת הַנֶּפֶשׁ וּרְפוּאַת הַגּוּף, (בשבת יאמר: שַׁבָּת הִיא מִלִּזְעֹק, וּרְפוּאָה קְרוֹבָה לָבֹא), הַשְׁתָּא, בַּעֲגָלָא וּבִזְמַן קָרִיב. וְנֹאמַר: אָמֵן.

Prayer for a female who is seriously ill:

Mi-she-bei-rach avo-teinu Avraham, Yitz-chak v'Ya-akov, Mo-sheh Aharon Da-vid u-Shlo-mo, Hu y'va-rech vira-pei et (patient's first name, ideally her Jewish name) bat (her mother's name, ideally her Jewish name), ba-avur she-ani mit-pa-leil ba-avu-rah u-ba-avur she-ani notein bli neder tse-dakah ba-avu-rah.

B's'char zeh, Ha-kadosh Baruch Hu yi-ma-lei ra-cha-mim aleha, l'hach-li-mah u'l'ra-po-tah u'l'ha-cha-zi-kah u'l'ha-cha-yo-tah, v'yish-lach lah m'hei-rah r'fu-ah sh'lei-mah min ha-sha-ma-yim, l'chol eiva-reha, u-l'chol gi-deha, b'toch sh'ar cho-lei Yisrael, r'fu-at ha-ne-fesh u-r'fu-at ha-guf, (On Shabbat insert the line: Shabat hi mi-liz-ok, u-r'fu-ah k'ro-vah la-vo) hash-ta, ba-aga-la u-viz-man ka-riv.
V'no-mar, Amein.

מִי שֶׁבֵּרַךְ אֲבוֹתֵינוּ אַבְרָהָם יִצְחָק וְיַעֲקֹב, מֹשֶׁה אַהֲרֹן דָּוִד וּשְׁלֹמֹה, הוּא יְבָרֵךְ וִירַפֵּא אֶת, בַּת patient's first name, ideally her Jewish name her mother's name, ideally her mother's Jewish name בַּעֲבוּר שֶׁאֲנִי מִתְפַּלֵּל בַּעֲבוּרָהּ וּבַעֲבוּר שֶׁאֲנִי נוֹתֵן בְּלִי נֶדֶר צְדָקָה בַּעֲבוּרָהּ.

בִּשְׂכַר זֶה, הַקָּדוֹשׁ בָּרוּךְ הוּא יִמָּלֵא רַחֲמִים עָלֶיהָ, לְהַחְלִימָהּ וּלְרַפֹּאתָהּ וּלְהַחֲזִיקָהּ וּלְהַחֲיוֹתָהּ, וְיִשְׁלַח לָהּ מְהֵרָה רְפוּאָה שְׁלֵמָה מִן הַשָּׁמַיִם, לְכָל אֵבָרֶיהָ, וּלְכָל גִּידֶיהָ, בְּתוֹךְ שְׁאָר חוֹלֵי יִשְׂרָאֵל, רְפוּאַת הַנֶּפֶשׁ וּרְפוּאַת הַגּוּף, (בשבת יאמר: שַׁבָּת הִיא מִלִּזְעֹק, וּרְפוּאָה קְרוֹבָה לָבֹא), הַשְׁתָּא, בַּעֲגָלָא וּבִזְמַן קָרִיב. וְנֹאמַר: אָמֵן.

Additional Prayers for the Sick

The book of Psalms (*Tehillim*) contains 150 poems and prayers written by ten different authors (including Adam, Moses, and King Solomon). The compiler of the book and the writer of most of the Psalms was King David. There is an appropriate Psalm to recite at literally every occurrence and for every request in life. Rebbe Nachman of Breslov taught that the Psalms are "the keys to heaven."

There are various views as to which Psalms are the ideal ones to say on behalf of someone who is seriously ill. Some say thirty-seven different Psalms on behalf of an ill person. Others have different traditions. As this can be quite arduous for those who are unfamiliar with the Psalms, we have chosen three of the most familiar Psalms.

Psalm 20: Answer Me in My Time of Distress

A hymn by (King) **David for the musicians** (in the Temple);

May Adonoy answer you on the day of your distress.
May the Name of the "G-d of Jacob" (our forefather) protect you.

May He send you help from the Holy Place and provide you with support from Zion.

May He remember all of your prayers and pleas, as if they were offerings in the Holy Temple.

May He grant your heart's desire and fulfill your plans.

We will sing when G-d provides your deliverance and in the Name of G-d we will raise our banners.

May Adonoy fulfill all of your requests.

We will sing, "Now I know that Adonoy has delivered his chosen one. He has answered him from His holy heavens with the strength of His right hand."

Some place their trust in chariots and horsepower, but we call out in the name of Adonoy, our G-d.

They were brought to their knees and fell, but we rose up and stood tall. Adonoy, save us. Master of the World, answer us on the day we call to You.

Lam-na-tsei-ach miz-mor l'Da-vid.
Ya-an-cha Adonoy b'yom tsa-rah,
y'sa-ge-v'cha sheim Elo-hei Ya-akov.
Yish-lach ez-r'cha mi-ko-desh,
u-mi-Tsi-yon yis-a-decha.
Yiz-kor kol min-cho-techa,
v'o-la-t'cha y'dash-neh selah.
Yi-tein l'cha chil-va-vecha,
v'chol atsa-t'cha y'ma-lei.
N'ra-n'nah bi-shu-a-techa,
u-v'sheim Elo-heinu nid-gol,
y'ma-lei Adonoy kol mish-alo-techa.
Atah ya-da-ti ki ho-shi-a Adonoy m'shi-cho,
ya-a-nei-hu mish-mei kad-sho,
bi-g'vu-rot yei-sha y'mi-no.
Ei-le va-rechev v'ei-le va-su-sim,
va-a-nach-nu b'sheim Adonoy Elo-heinu
naz-kir.
Hei-mah kar-u v'na-fa-lu,
va-a-nach-nu kam-nu va-nit-o-dad.
Adonoy ho-shi-ah,
ha-Melech ya-a-neinu v'yom kar-einu.

לַמְנַצֵּחַ מִזְמוֹר לְדָוִד.
יַעַנְךָ יי בְּיוֹם צָרָה,
יְשַׂגֶּבְךָ שֵׁם אֱלֹהֵי יַעֲקֹב.
יִשְׁלַח עֶזְרְךָ מִקֹּדֶשׁ,
וּמִצִּיּוֹן יִסְעָדֶךָּ.
יִזְכֹּר כָּל מִנְחֹתֶךָ,
וְעוֹלָתְךָ יְדַשְּׁנֶה סֶלָה.
יִתֶּן לְךָ כִלְבָבֶךָ,
וְכָל עֲצָתְךָ יְמַלֵּא.
נְרַנְּנָה בִּישׁוּעָתֶךָ,
וּבְשֵׁם אֱלֹהֵינוּ נִדְגֹּל,
יְמַלֵּא יי כָּל מִשְׁאֲלוֹתֶיךָ.
עַתָּה יָדַעְתִּי כִּי הוֹשִׁיעַ יי מְשִׁיחוֹ,
יַעֲנֵהוּ מִשְּׁמֵי קָדְשׁוֹ, בִּגְבֻרוֹת יֵשַׁע יְמִינוֹ.
אֵלֶּה בָרֶכֶב וְאֵלֶּה בַסּוּסִים,
וַאֲנַחְנוּ בְּשֵׁם יי אֱלֹהֵינוּ נַזְכִּיר.
הֵמָּה כָּרְעוּ וְנָפָלוּ,
וַאֲנַחְנוּ קַּמְנוּ וַנִּתְעוֹדָד.
יי הוֹשִׁיעָה,
הַמֶּלֶךְ יַעֲנֵנוּ בְיוֹם קָרְאֵנוּ.

Psalm 23: Hashem is my Shepherd

A hymn by (King) **David. Adonoy is my shepherd, I will not be lacking.**

He lays me down in green meadows.
He leads me to calm waters.

He restores my soul.
He guides me along the path of righteousness, for His Name's sake.

Though I walk in the valley under the shadow of death,
I fear no evil, for You are with me.
Your rod (of affliction) and Your staff (of kindness) comfort me.

You set a table before me, against my enemies.
You anointed my head with oil (to indicate that I am special to You); my cup overflows.

May only goodness and kindness pursue me all the days of my life, and may I live in Adonoy's house for all of my days.

Miz-mor l'Da-vid; Adonoy ro-i, lo ech-sar.
Bin-ot de-she yar-bi-tsei-ni,
al mei m'nu-chot y'na-ha-lei-ni.

מִזְמוֹר לְדָוִד; יְיָ רֹעִי, לֹא אֶחְסָר.
בִּנְאוֹת דֶּשֶׁא יַרְבִּיצֵנִי,
עַל מֵי מְנֻחוֹת יְנַהֲלֵנִי.

Naf-shi y'sho-veiv,
yun-chei-ni v'mag-lei tse-dek l'ma-an sh'mo.

נַפְשִׁי יְשׁוֹבֵב,
יַנְחֵנִי בְמַעְגְּלֵי צֶדֶק לְמַעַן שְׁמוֹ.

Gam ki ei-leich b'gei tsal-ma-vet,
lo i-ra ra ki Atah i-ma-di shiv-t'cha u-mish-
an-techa hei-mah y'na-cha-mu-ni.

גַּם כִּי אֵלֵךְ בְּגֵיא צַלְמָוֶת,
לֹא אִירָא רָע כִּי אַתָּה עִמָּדִי שִׁבְטְךָ
וּמִשְׁעַנְתֶּךָ הֵמָּה יְנַחֲמֻנִי.

Ta-a-roch l'fa-nai shul-chan ne-ged tso-r'rai,
di-shan-ta va-she-men ro-shi, ko-si r'va-yah.

תַּעֲרֹךְ לְפָנַי שֻׁלְחָן נֶגֶד צֹרְרָי,
דִּשַּׁנְתָּ בַשֶּׁמֶן רֹאשִׁי, כּוֹסִי רְוָיָה.

Ach tov va-che-sed yir-d'fu-ni kol y'mei cha-
yai, v'shav-ti b'veit Adonoy l'o-rech ya-mim.

אַךְ טוֹב וָחֶסֶד יִרְדְּפוּנִי כָּל יְמֵי חַיָּי,
וְשַׁבְתִּי בְּבֵית יְיָ לְאֹרֶךְ יָמִים.

Psalm 130: From the Depths I Call to You

A song written to be sung on the Temple steps.
From the depths I called to you, Adonoy.
Adonoy, hear my voice, let Your ears hear the sound of my pleas.

If You preserve misdeeds, Adonoy, who could survive?

For with You is forgiveness, so that You will be feared.

I have yearned for You, Adonoy, my soul has yearned, and for His word
I have waited. My soul longs for Adonoy, more than those (in the deepest
darkness) who continually long for the dawn.

Let the People of Israel place their hope in Adonoy, for with Adonoy is
kindness and with Him is abundant redemption.

And He will redeem the People of Israel from all of its misdeeds.

Say your own personal prayer, in your own words.

Shir ha-ma-a-lot,
mi-ma-ama-kim k'ra-ti-cha Adonoy.

שִׁיר הַמַּעֲלוֹת,
מִמַּעֲמַקִּים קְרָאתִיךָ יְיָ.

Adonoy shim-a v'ko-li,
ti-ye-nah az-ne-cha ka-shu-vot,
l'kol ta-cha-nu-nai.

אֲדֹנָי שִׁמְעָה בְקוֹלִי,
תִּהְיֶינָה אָזְנֶיךָ קַשֻּׁבוֹת,
לְקוֹל תַּחֲנוּנָי.

Im avo-not tish-mar Yah,
Adonoy mi ya-a-mod?

אִם עֲוֹנוֹת תִּשְׁמָר יָהּ,
אֲדֹנָי מִי יַעֲמֹד.

Ki imcha ha-s'li-chah,
l'ma-an ti-va-rei.

כִּי עִמְּךָ הַסְּלִיחָה,
לְמַעַן תִּוָּרֵא.

Ki-vi-ti Adonoy kiv-tah naf-shi,
v'li-d'va-ro ho-chal-ti.

קִוִּיתִי יי קִוְּתָה נַפְשִׁי,
וְלִדְבָרוֹ הוֹחָלְתִּי.

Naf-shi La-Donoy, mi-shom-rim la-bo-ker,
shom-rim la-bo-ker.

נַפְשִׁי לַאדֹנָי, מִשֹּׁמְרִים לַבֹּקֶר,
שֹׁמְרִים לַבֹּקֶר.

Ya-chel Yisrael el Adonoy, ki im Adonoy
ha-che-sed, v'har-bei i-mo f'dut.

יַחֵל יִשְׂרָאֵל אֶל יי, כִּי עִם יי הַחֶסֶד,
וְהַרְבֵּה עִמּוֹ פְדוּת.

V'Hu yif-deh et Yisrael, mi-kol avo-no-tav.

וְהוּא יִפְדֶּה אֶת יִשְׂרָאֵל, מִכֹּל עֲוֹנֹתָיו.

What to Pray for When There is Little Chance of the Patient's Recovery

You can pray and ask G-d to provide some or all of the following:

- For excellent medical care

- For a caring, kind nursing team

- For a pain-free palliative experience

- For meaning and purpose in the final period of the patient's life

- For moments of laughter and good memories

- For good relationships with family members and close friends

- For openness to reconciliation and forgiveness with those with whom the patient may have been at odds

- For the opportunity to say the Final Prayers with a knowledgeable person or rabbi

- For awareness that G-d is very close to them at this time

- For anticipation of a sweet and fulfilling life in the hereafter, the World of Truth and Reward

- For the opportunity and desire to perform additional mitzvot (such as charity, kind words, etc.)

- For the patient to be an inspiration to those he/she leaves behind

- For a peaceful end to his/her life in this world

- and for the family to make the right decisions regarding the patient's life and passing

NOTE: As there can be very challenging issues to deal with in today's hospital and medical environment, it is crucial for a family dealing with end-of-life issues to seek the guidance of a knowledgeable Orthodox Rabbi. He can contact the world's leading Rabbinic medical authorities for insight, advice, and guidance. Each case has its own unique circumstances. The Torah provides clear guidance in each case.

PRAYER STORIES

The Tattered Siddur

The Holy Ba'al Shem Tov (Master of the Good Name) was one of the greatest Jews ever to have lived. He had the custom of travelling throughout Russia to meet both the simplest and the most holy of Jews.

One day he entered a *shtibl* (a small synagogue) in a small shtetl and, as was his custom, the Ba'al Shem Tov went to the back of the shul to pray with the simple but pure Jews. After the service ended, one of the simple Jews approached the Ba'al Shem Tov.

The simple Jew owned only one tattered siddur, which he could barely read. The binding of the siddur had long since disintegrated and the pages had fallen out many times. The simple Jew had picked up the pages and kissed them lovingly each time they had fallen to the floor. He placed the pages back inside the tattered covers of the book as best he could, but they were no longer in the proper order as the word "siddur" (i.e., order) implied.

The simple Jew asked the Ba'al Shem Tov to assemble the pages in the proper order. The Ba'al Shem Tov readily agreed to help a simple Jew in need, and he took each page from the tattered siddur and put it in its proper place. When he finished, the Ba'al Shem Tov blessed the simple Jew and left the *shtibl* to journey to the next shtetl.

As he left, a wind rushed in through the doorway and blew the pages of the tattered siddur onto the floor. The simple Jew looked at the pages in horror as he saw them scattered over the floor, and he bent to pick them up. He kissed each one and put it back between the covers of his tattered siddur. Though replaced, once again the pages were out of their proper order.

The simple Jew was determined to pursue the Ba'al Shem Tov and beseech the holy Rabbi to again put the siddur in the prescribed order. By this time, though, the Ba'al Shem Tov, who had the custom of travelling at a very quick pace, was far ahead of the simple Jew.

But the simple Jew was determined. He ran after the Ba'al Shem Tov with all his strength. He ran down the dirt road that led out of the shtetl. He ran through a path in the forest and through the fields that lay beyond the forest. Slowly he began to gain ground on the Ba'al Shem Tov, and he could see the holy man off in the distance.

The Ba'al Shem Tov came to a river and, as was his custom (you see, true holy people are accustomed to miracles), he took out a handkerchief and placed it on the ground at the bank of the river. He stood on the handkerchief and it carried him across the river as if it were a raft. Once he reached the other side, he simply put the handkerchief in his pocket and continued his journey.

The simple Jew knew no better and, having witnessed what the Ba'al Shem Tov had done, when he came to the river he too took out his handkerchief and placed it upon the riverbank. The simple Jew stood on the handkerchief just as the Ba'al Shem Tov had done, and it carried him across to the other side, where he continued to pursue the Ba'al Shem Tov.

The Ba'al Shem Tov reached the next shtetl and went to the *shtibl*. He sat down at a wooden table and prepared to greet the Jews of that town, when suddenly the door of the *shtibl* burst open. "Rebbe," the simple Jew cried out, between gasps of much-needed air. "I am so happy that I caught up to you." And he related to the Ba'al Shem Tov what had happened since their last encounter.

The Ba'al Shem Tov invited the simple Jew to sit at the table next to him and poured the exhausted man a drink. After reciting the appropriate blessing, the simple Jew quenched his thirst and asked the Ba'al Shem Tov if his tattered siddur could once again be placed back in the proper order that was ordained by the prophets and scholars of the Great Assembly some 2,200 years earlier.

The Ba'al Shem Tov took the siddur and stared at the simple Jew with a look of bewilderment. "Your efforts to follow me all this way are most praiseworthy, my dear friend and fellow Yid. But tell me, please, how did you get across the river?" asked the holy man.

"Well," said the simple Jew. "I saw that the Rebbe took out his handkerchief, laid it at the bank of the river, stood upon it, and it took the Rebbe across to the other side. So I did the same thing. I took out my handkerchief, stood on it, and it too took me to the other side of the river."

The Ba'al Shem Tov stared deeply into the eyes of the simple Jew (you see, according to Jewish mysticism, the eyes are the windows of the soul). "If that is the case, my dear friend, then it is best to leave the pages of your siddur in the exact order that you have them. Keep praying just as you have been praying. There is nothing at all wrong with the order of *your* siddur."

The Dove

(Jewish tradition teaches a number of vitally important lessons in the story of The Dove.)

At the time of creation, Hashem created all of the animals, birds, and fishes of the sea, and He looked and saw that all had potential for good. But one was extra special. It was the dove. The dove was small, but it was pure and snow white. Hashem sent all the creatures to the earth to live happily ever after. The mission of the dove was to inspire purity, gentleness, and song among the other creatures of the world.

But the animals were jealous of the dove because it sang so sweetly and looked so beautiful. However, it was also small, vulnerable, and defenceless. Time after time, various animals attempted to harm the dove: first the bear, then the snake, the tiger, the jackal, and the lion.

Each time, although wounded, the dove managed to run and escape the evil plans of its tormentors. But each subsequent attack took its toll upon the dove. So it turned to Hashem and cried out for redemption from its plight. It was proud of its pristine whiteness, its purity, and its talent for song. But it could no longer stand to be under constant threat of attack. It longed for the day when it could just rest quietly and sing its harmonious tunes.

Hashem heard the anguished cries of the dove and, as it was the most beloved of all the creatures, Hashem promised it redemption from its torment in a most special way. Hashem would provide the dove with the most awesome of all creations. Hashem would give it wings! No other creation would have anything similar. Only the dove would carry this precious gift of Hashem's.

The dove stood proudly as Hashem affixed the wings to its shoulders. It returned to the forest and marched proudly through the main thoroughfare, showing its new wings to one and all.

But now the other animals became furious. They flew into a jealous rage for none of them had wings. They gathered together and conspired to put an end to the dove once and for all. They would lay in wait and, when the dove approached, they would pounce upon it and violently end its life.

The next day, the dove strolled happily through the forest singing a joyful tune. When it reached a clearing in the trees, the animals attacked from every direction. The dove attempted to run away as it had done so many times before. But this time it found itself unable to gather enough speed as the wings weighed it down. Though it attempted to outrun its attackers, it was woefully unsuccessful. The animals swiped and swatted and stomped upon the little dove and left it there to die.

As it lay upon the ground, mortally wounded, the dove turned to Hashem and cried out, "Hashem, you were so unfair to me. Before I had wings, I was at least able to outrun my attackers. This time I had no chance to escape, and the wings will cost me my life. I will be able to sing no more, and the world will have no one to look up to as a model of purity and gentleness. How could you do this to me?"

Hashem turned to the dove, picked it up lovingly, and restored it to health. Then Hashem told the dove, "If you do not use your wings, indeed they will be burdensome. They will weigh you down and will lead to your demise. But if you use your wings for flying, you will soar high above all the other creatures. You will reach heights you never imagined were possible. You will become so close to Me, you will exceed your dreams and all will look up to you. Now go back to the earth and listen to what I have told you."

The dove returned to the earth. When the animals spotted the dove, they were astonished. They had assumed that they had long ago rid themselves of the beacon of purity that lived in their midst. So now they convened a conference and devised a plan to obliterate the dove with absolute certainty.

As the dove once again strode proudly through the forest, the animals ferociously attacked it. But this time, instead of attempting to run from the onslaught, the dove began to flap its wings and slowly it lifted from the ground. The more it flapped its wings, the higher it soared. It flew over the heads of all the attacking beasts. It rose above the trees and above the mountains. And the dove caught a great wind and flew towards the heavens. All the creatures were astonished, even the dove itself. It was just as Hashem had promised.

From that day on, all the animals looked towards the dove with awe and with great respect. The dove would fly each and every day, soaring ever higher and returning to the earth to share its sweet song with everyone.

(Note: This story served as the inspiration for the song, "Higher and Higher," which was written by the author of this work and performed as the title song of the album, "Higher and Higher," by the Jewish-music singing star, Yehuda. The song concludes with the following words: "Our story has concluded, but my friends there's one more thing. The little dove, that's you and me, and the Torah, that's our wings…").

The Holy Whistler

Prior to reciting *Kol Nidrei* one Yom Kippur night, a famous Rebbi (I can't recall which one) addressed the congregation in his *shtibl*. He told them that there was a heavenly decree against the inhabitants of that particular shtetl as they had been lax in some particularly important observances. More was expected of them. He begged them to pray to Hashem with all their hearts. He urged them to reach new heights of sincerity, to search their hearts for true repentance, and to beseech Hashem with all their strength to change the decree.

An air of extreme trepidation filled the *shtibl*. The Rebbi had never spoken such words before. They lived an already perilous existence with poverty and roaming Cossack bands as the norms of their daily life. They tried to lead a pious and holy existence. But obviously they had fallen short. There was no choice but to pour out their hearts in pure, uninhibited prayer.

And so the *Chazzan* began the *Kol Nidrei* and the people prayed as never before. Late that night, when they had no more strength to continue, the Rebbi sent them home with instructions to return at dawn for the Yom Kippur morning prayers. He would stay behind and spend the night begging the Heavenly Court to reverse its decree.

At dawn, the *shtibl* was filled as each participant wondered if their prayers and those of their Rebbi had convinced the Heavenly Court to rescind its decree. The Rebbi, who, as a genuine holy man, had access to the discussions of the Heavenly Court, declared that, sadly, the people of the shtetl had not been successful. But with a full day of prayer ahead and the extra measure of compassion that Hashem shows to all on Yom Kippur, he was certain that they would achieve success. And so the morning service began.

Everyone put forth their best efforts. Tears flowed. With eyes focused only on the letters of their High Holiday prayer books, their lips uttered one prayer after another. But, after some time, the Rebbi sensed that they had not yet broken through the gates of Heaven. So the Rebbi instructed that the one who led the prayers should be replaced with another *chazzan* and perhaps that would effect the necessary change. One person after another went to the bimah (the *chazzan*'s pedestal) to lead the congregation in prayer. In each case, the Rebbi could sense no difference in the effect of their collective prayers upon the heavens.

All of the scholars took their turn leading the congregation, then the community leaders, the members of the burial society, the teachers, and the overseers of kosher food. Each one attempted to lead the congregation to the level at which their prayers would find full acceptance by the heavenly court. Each of the recognized and important members of the *shtibl* took his turn. None were successful.

Finally, as the time for *Neilah*, the final prayer service of Yom Kippur approached, the Rebbi himself went to the bimah. The entire congregation joined in tearful prayer, as they attempted one last time to achieve the seemingly impossible. But after an hour of heartfelt prayer, the Rebbi sensed that the congregation had still not been successful. And with the final moments of Yom Kippur approaching, the distraught Rebbi turned to the congregation and asked if there was anyone present who thought that he could accomplish what no one had been able to accomplish over the past twenty-five hours of Yom Kippur.

No one moved. No one would dare to assume that they could achieve what the holy Rebbi could not. But one illiterate man in the back of the *shtibl*, a shepherd by trade and apparently the simplest of Jews, strode to the bimah. He placed his *tallit* over his head and began to whistle a tune. Everyone was appalled (for it is inappropriate to whistle on a holy day and especially on the holiest of all days), and they rushed to remove him from the bimah. "Stop!" cried the Rebbi. "Let him continue." So the simple shepherd continued to whistle his plaintive tune. Louder and louder he whistled.

The *shtibl* was filled with the aura of holiness. There was a sense that the whistling had pierced the previously impenetrable walls of Heaven. The shepherd continued, until the Rebbi signalled for him to stop. The Rebbi then turned to the congregation and informed them that, indeed, the whistling had reached the highest level of heaven, carrying with it the prayers of the whole shtetl that Yom Kippur. The heavenly decree had indeed been overturned.

All of those present burst into great smiles of relief, coupled with joy. The congregation joined in a robust recitation of *Shema Yisrael* and the closing verses of Yom Kippur. Then the congregation burst into the traditional closing song of hope, "L'shanah Haba'ah Birushalayim" (Next Yom Kippur in Rebuilt Jerusalem).

But when the song concluded, no one left the *shtibl*. What had transpired? Who was this shepherd? How had his whistling accomplished what no one's prayers had been able to? They turned to the Rebbi for an explanation and he turned to the simple shepherd. Not a sound was heard in the *shtibl* as all waited for the shepherd's explanation.

"My name is Moishele, and I am just a simple shepherd. Each day I take the sheep out to graze. As they graze among the grass and clover, I sit on the verdant hills and contemplate the greatness of Hashem. I want so much to speak to Hashem. I want to tell Him all of my feelings, all that I need, to thank Him for all that He has done for me and for my people. But I don't know how to read Hebrew, and I don't know how to pray. Still, I do know how to whistle. I spend most of the day whistling.

"When I am happy, I whistle, and when I am sad, I whistle. I can express my deepest feelings, my longing, my appreciation by whistling. Tonight I just did what I do every day. I turned to Hashem and whistled a plea from my heart. Hashem, I whistled, these are good people. They are Your people. They are trying so hard and if, in the eyes of the Heavenly Court, they have come up short of Your expectations, please forgive them and overlook their shortcomings. If not for their merit, then please do it for the merit of their forefathers and mothers who stayed loyal to You, no matter what befell them. That is what I thought of as I whistled my prayer."

The Rebbi turned to the people and said, "Hashem listens to prayers in any language, so long as they are prayers from the heart."

And that year was the most peaceful and prosperous year that the Jews of the shtetl had ever experienced.

The Price of a Prayerbook

When the Second World War ended, Rabbi Eliezer Silver received permission from the American Army to accompany American troops into the former concentration camps and labor camps. His goal was to meet Jews who had survived the unspeakable horrors of the Holocaust and help them in any way that he could. Rabbi Silver received an American army uniform, a senior army rank, and an escort to take him wherever he wished to travel.

At each site, he would ask to meet each of the surviving Jews individually so that they could pour out their hearts to him. He would provide words of solace and encouragement. In one such camp, he sat at a desk and, as was his custom, Rabbi Silver asked to meet every Jew individually. One by one they came. They had not seen nor had they spoken to a rabbi in many years. At the time, they had thought that the promise of the Jews as the Eternal Nation had been abandoned. Tears flowed and the souls of the surviving Jews connected with that of the great Rabbi.

One elderly survivor came to the Rabbi for his private audience and informed him that there was a young teenager who refused to see the Rabbi. Under no circumstances would the young man meet with the Rabbi. Messengers were sent to ask the young man to come to the Rabbi, but each request was answered with a terse refusal.

When the Rabbi had finished meeting with all the survivors, he searched out the young man. He wished to talk to him and find out why the young man refused to meet with him even for a few moments. If he was angry with Hashem, then why not express that anger? If he was deeply depressed and saddened by the loss of his family members, perhaps the Rabbi could help search for any surviving blood relatives and long-lost childhood friends.

The Rabbi found the young man. He asked the teenager why he had refused to meet with him. The young man responded that he had been disgusted with the behavior of a religious Jew in the camp. This Jew had managed to smuggle in a siddur. He was the only one who possessed a Jewish prayer book. In the nightmare that was life in the labor/death camp, a siddur could provide guidance, hope, optimism, and faith. But this man refused to allow anyone to use the siddur unless the one who wished to borrow it gave up his daily ration of bread in return.

And thus it happened, day after day. Someone would give up his meager daily ration of bread in order to pray from the lone siddur in the camp. The young man was repulsed at how a seemingly religious man could demand that his fellow Jew, his fellow prisoner, starving from the minute daily rations that were provided, give up his food ration to pray to Hashem. Therefore, he refused to meet with any other religious Jew.

The wise Rabbi Silver thought for a few moments. He empathized with the emotions of the young man for he, too, while not judging another under circumstances that he thankfully had not experienced, was dismayed at the actions of the seemingly religious Jew.

But then Rabbi Silver put his arm around the shoulder of the young man and said to him, "Why is it that you choose to focus on the behavior of one wayward Jew? Why not focus instead on the hundreds of Jews who gave up their only daily food ration in order to pray from an authentic siddur for just a few moments?"

The truth of the Rabbi's words struck deep into the heart of the young man. His anger dissipated and his spirit was revived. He left the camp to rebuild his life and to inspire the world. The young man's name was Elie Wiesel, noted author, lecturer, and Nobel Peace Prize Winner.

(NOTE: This story was told by the legendary Nazi hunter, Simon Wiesenthal z"l.)

Reb Feivel and the Cossack

The great Rabbi Tzvi Elimelech told the following story about his sainted father, Reb Feivel. In the eighteenth and nineteenth centuries, the Jewish educational system in Europe was very different from the school system today. Most of the schooling was done at home by the parents or by *melamdim*, Jewish teachers who were hired by a small group of parents. The wealthy could afford to hire great Torah scholars, who were themselves very poor, to teach their children. The scholars would leave their shtetls and move into the homes of the wealthy from Sukkot until Pesach (Passover) in order to teach the children of the wealthy. During this time, the scholars would usually be required to leave their homes and families, but their financial situation was so desperate that there was often no other viable option of providing for their families. Reb Feivel was one such Torah scholar.

Reb Feivel was a renowned scholar who was terribly impoverished. He was contacted by a wealthy man in a town far away from his shtetl and offered the position of private tutor for the wealthy man's son. For this, the wealthy man would provide room, board, and the handsome sum of five hundred rubles to be paid before Reb Feivel returned home for Pesach.

Reb Feivel had no choice. His large family required a substantial sum of money to pay for food, clothing, education, weddings, and dowries. There were no teaching opportunities closer to home that would provide anywhere near the sum of five hundred rubles. So Reb Feivel discussed the matter with his wife and reluctantly he accepted the position as tutor to the rich man's son.

Reb Feivel packed his few personal items and walked a few kilometers to the nearest wagon station. There he caught a wagon ride to the nearest train station and from there he took a train to the town of the wealthy man. The wealthy man sent one of his servants to greet Reb Feivel and to escort him to his handsome home. Reb Feivel was shown to his quarters and was introduced to the wealthy man's son. The two of them began their daily curriculum of Torah study.

When the first Shabbat arrived, Reb Feivel prepared and put on his special Shabbat clothing. He went downstairs to wish the entire family a *gut Shabbes*, and he inquired of his host how many guests would be joining them for Shabbat. Reb Feivel expected that such a wealthy home would surely host many poor people, itinerant travelers, some elderly, some lonely, and some wayward Jews. He looked forward with great anticipation all week to greeting the guests and sharing some uplifting Torah thoughts with them.

He was most surprised, and frankly quite shocked, when the wealthy man informed him that there would be no guests at all. "I am not about to spend my hard-earned money on people I hardly know or, worse, on those I have never met," he said gruffly. Reb Feivel pleaded with him to invite some guests home from shul. Surely there would be those waiting to be invited to their only decent meal of the week. If the wealthy man did not invite them, who would?

The rich man refused to change his mind. But he did tell Reb Feivel that if inviting guests was so important to him, then guests would be invited, but the cost of their meals would be deducted from Reb Feivel's salary. Reb Feivel readily agreed. And so a number of poor people were invited to be guests of the wealthy man that Shabbat. The same thing occurred week after week. Poor people, travelers, the lonely, the distraught, and the confused would all share the magnificence of Shabbat at the wealthy man's table. They would be satiated by the princely meal and uplifted by Reb Feivel's words of Torah.

In the meantime, back in his hometown, Reb Feivel's wife had no money to feed and clothe the family. But she knew that her husband would return home before Pesach with five hundred rubles. This sum was more than enough to pay their bills for many months. So she went to the grocer, the fish store, the butcher, and the other merchants whose fare she required and begged them for credit. She promised to repay them promptly when her husband returned before Pesach.

But as the months passed, the storekeepers and merchants felt that they had extended far too much credit to Reb Feivel's wife and they refused to sell to her on credit any longer. For many weeks before Pesach, the family had to subsist on bread and potatoes as she had few staples left in her home. She longed for the day when Reb Feivel would return.

As the Pesach holiday neared, Reb Feivel prepared for his journey home. He arranged for a train ticket. He finished teaching the curriculum that he had planned for the wealthy man's son. He bade farewell to all the poor guests from the town in which he had lived over these past six months. Finally the day had come to receive his remuneration and to head back home to his beloved wife and family.

Reb Feivel approached the wealthy man and asked for his five hundred rubles.

"You want me to pay you five hundred rubles?" asked the rich man. "You owe me five hundred rubles!"

"How is that possible? I did everything you asked and more," queried Reb Feivel. The rich man replied, "Yes, but remember that you told me that the costs of all the guests who were invited for the Shabbat meals were to be paid from your salary. I have been keeping an accurate accounting and the cost was a thousand rubles. As such, I will keep the five hundred rubles that I was to have paid you and you owe me another five hundred rubles. You can pay me when you return next Sukkot."

Reb Feivel was shocked. Not only would he be going home penniless, but he owed an additional sum of five hundred rubles. He could see no way of ever repaying such a large sum. How could he face his wife? He could surmise what creditors and outstanding debts waited for him at home. The rich man's carriage dropped Reb Feivel at the train station and he began the long journey home.

Reb Feivel got off the train, caught the wagon ride, and walked the last few kilometers to his shtetl in a state of bewilderment. He had no idea what to do or what to say to his wife. He arrived in the middle of the night. Rather than confronting his wife, he went to the *shtibl*, which was always open, and began to recite the Psalms.

When morning came, the men of the shtetl came to the *shtibl* to study and to pray the morning prayers. Among the group was Reb Feivel's eldest son. When he saw his father, he ran towards him and shouted, "Father, when did you arrive? I will immediately run home and tell mother that you are here!"

Reb Feivel pleaded with his son to stay for the morning prayers and promised him that they would walk home together immediately following the concluding prayer. The son prayed excitedly next to his father. But he could hardly concentrate on the words. The family had not had a decent meal in more than a month. He knew that his father had returned with a large sum of money. That night there would be a great feast at home. A real meal! With fresh bread, vegetables, fruit, and meat! The family's debts would be paid. All of the children would receive new clothes for the holiday, and there would be gifts for every member of the family! He could hardly wait.

Reb Feivel prayed for Hashem to send him some idea of what he was to do. When the prayers ended, Reb Feivel slowly put away his *tefillin* and folded his *tallit*. He put them in his old leather suitcase and called his son to escort him home. His son grabbed his father's hand and pulled him home. But rather than walking along the quick route, which followed the main road of the shtetl, Reb Feivel insisted that they take the much longer route along the road that separated the shtetl from the non-Jewish area outside the shtetl.

"But isn't this way dangerous?" asked Reb Feivel's son.

"No, it's morning so there is really nothing to be afraid of. No Cossack would dare attack us in broad daylight. I need the walk in order to clear my mind and gather my thoughts."

"Okay, Father. As you wish. But please let me carry your suitcase. You have come from a long journey and, as I am almost a man now, I can carry your suitcase."

"What a nice mitzvah, Tzvi Elimelech," said Reb Feivel, as they slowly walked along the route home.

Suddenly a Cossack jumped onto the road and shouted, "Stop, Jew!"

Reb Feivel jumped in front of his son and said, "What is it you want?"

"I am looking for a Jew named Reb Feivel," said the Cossack. "Do you know where he is?"

"I am Reb Feivel. What is it you want of me?"

"Here," said the Cossack. "This is for you." He tossed a small purse towards Reb Feivel, then turned and ran away. Reb Feivel opened the purse and found it filled with gold coins. These would be worth many thousands of rubles. He would have to teach for many, many years to earn such a large sum of money.

Reb Feivel took his son by the hand and they quickly went home. Reb Feivel greeted his wife with much joy. The family was reunited. There was now more than enough money to pay all of the creditors, including the wealthy man whose son Reb Feivel had taught. There would indeed be a great reunion feast for the family that night and there would be new clothes and the finest food available for the Pesach Seders.

Great joy permeated the walls of their small home as Reb Feivel's family prepared for the Pesach holiday. Hashem had performed an open miracle for Reb Feivel. But who was that Cossack who tossed the gold coins to Reb Feivel and then turned and ran without saying so much as a word? No one knew.

At the first Seder, all of the grand Pesach traditions were carried out in meticulous detail. Profound Torah thoughts were exchanged. The children asked the Four Questions and received the 3,000-year-old answer from Reb Feivel with new insights. The joyous songs shook the walls of the modest home.

When it came time, near the end of the Seder, to open the door for Elijah the prophet (known in Hebrew as Eliyahu Hanavi), Reb Feivel gave the honor to his eldest son, Tzvi Elimelech. Tzvi Elimelech opened the door to let in Elijah (who only appears in physical form for righteous people at the time of their greatest need) and suddenly slammed the door shut! He turned pale. All of those at the Seder wondered what had happened.

"What is it, Tzvi Elimelech?" asked Reb Feivel.

"Nothing, father. I must have imagined what I saw or maybe it was all the wine that I drank."

Tzvi Elimelech opened the door again. The traditional prayer was said in unison and, at its conclusion, Tzvi Elimelech closed the door and returned to the Seder table.

"Father," he said, bending close to Reb Feivel's ear, "I could swear that when I opened the door for Eliyahu, there was a Cossack standing there and waving to me. Does Hashem sometimes send Eliyahu dressed as a Cossack?"

Reb Feivel just smiled. Hashem answers prayers with messengers disguised in many different ways.

ONE MORE STORY

Cyril "Reb Yisrael" Newman *a"h*

As we were going to press with this book, I was awakened by an early morning call informing me that my dear father and best friend had passed away unexpectedly, but sweetly, during his pre-Shabbat rest in Jerusalem. He was just shy of ninety-three years of age.

I had the privilege of delivering one of the eulogies to the overwhelmingly large audience in attendance at his late night funeral on Har HaMenuchos (Mountain of Those at Rest) in western Jerusalem. My remarks were based on one section of the daily morning prayers (see pages 81-82). I related just a few of the many stories about my father's exemplary life, based on the themes itemized in this section of the siddur. The following are just a few of them.

It's Always Sunny Above the Clouds

The Jerusalem Talmud teaches: "These are the obligations for which a person benefits in this world, but the ultimate reward is reserved for the World to Come."

Our father loved doing these things so he most definitely received the fruits of his efforts in this world. It will take all of eternity to reward him for the everlasting impact of his immeasurable good deeds and kind words.

"Honoring one's father and mother"

When our parents married in 1947, our paternal grandfather (my namesake) was too sick to work. All of his other sons had left to make their fortunes in America but our father remained with his parents in Toronto. He worked diligently each day, as did our mother, who worked as a bookkeeper for a meager salary.

Each week our father presented his entire paycheck to his elderly parents while our parents lived very modestly on our mother's very small salary. They rented a room in a rooming house with three families per floor and one shared bathroom, so that they could properly support our father's elderly parents.

"Acts of kindness"

Our father was involved with acts of kindness his entire life. For example:

• Two people related to me that when it came time for them to open businesses in order to support their families in a more substantive way, they decided to go into the insurance business, our father's chosen profession.

Each told the same story. Our father had approached them privately and offered to assist them in any and every way so that they could achieve success in their newly chosen careers. When they commented that this would mean that he would in effect be training his competitors, who would market to the Toronto Jewish community in which he was active, our father replied that he was confident that there was more than enough business to go around and that he relished the idea that he could help someone else achieve success in their career – considered to be the highest level of charity.

• When our mom *a"h* died in the year 2000, our father experienced a deep sense of loneliness for the first time in his life. Rather than retreat into his own grief-stricken world, he decided to see who else was faced with this great life challenge and what he could do to help alleviate their pain.

He felt that widowers, especially those within his circle, had a built-in support system due to their attendance at shul twice a day, as well as at many daily and weekly Torah study classes. But in his neighborhood there were few similar opportunities for widows. And thus began a new project, which took up much of our father's time each week for the next 700 (!!) weeks. He gathered a long list of widows in his community, including some who had moved to Israel from Toronto and "referrals" from one widow to another.

If they lived outside of his Jerusalem neighborhood, he would call them every Thursday or Friday to inquire as to their well-being, offer his assistance in any way, relate stories, and make them smile and laugh. If they lived within his neighborhood, he had a driver take him every Friday to buy the Shabbat flowers that each one preferred and the magazines they each preferred to read on Shabbat. Then he would himself deliver the personalized package to each one, inquiring as to her wellbeing while standing outside the door of her Jerusalem home. One widow related to me that when our father was not in town, her weekly pre-Shabbat gift would arrive by taxi.

"Attending at the place of Torah study in the morning and evening"

Aside from his office in a large office complex, our father had a home office downstairs. He would arise at 5:00 a.m. every morning, go down to his office and review the difficult Aramaic words of the Talmud, which he had written in a myriad of steno pads, over and over again before leaving for shul for the daily morning prayers.

On the kitchen table there was always a Chumash, a copy of the Torah with commentary, so that he could study the weekly section before going to bed.

"Providing hospitality to guests"

When we grew up in the 1960s, our parents' home was among the very best host homes in the city for Shabbat, Jewish holidays, and whenever a visitor from another city or country needed to be housed or hosted for a meal in a warm and friendly environment.

Each weekend brought a new round of faces whom our father had greeted and invited in shul or who had been referred by a previous guest. At times we would have up to twenty-five guests join us for a laughter-filled, meaningful feast of delicacies for the holiday dinner or luncheon, always accompanied by songs and relevant Torah thoughts.

"Visiting the sick"

Our father carried two pads of colored paper in his car. When the white one was on the dashboard it meant that he needed to fill up the car with gas. When the yellow pad was on the dash, it meant that my father needed to visit someone who was seriously ill. More often than not, he drove around town with a yellow pad on the dashboard.

"Providing for a bride"

Our father loved to attend weddings and make the bride and groom and their parents happy by dancing enthusiastically and getting others to join in the traditional Jewish wedding dances as well. Our mother made sure that he was very well dressed and he wore the finest custom-tailored suits. Our father would come home from these weddings and his suits would be drenched with sweat after dancing for hours.

Three days before our father's passing, he had been convalescing in Jerusalem's Herzog Hospital after cracking his hip bone in a fall in his home. That day the nurses had made some medical errors that caused internal bleeding. So they sent our father by ambulance to the emergency ward at Shaare Zedek Medical Center. After being admitted and hooked up to intravenous, our father calmly left the emergency ward, put on his best wedding suit and left for a family wedding (still hooked to the IV), where he danced in the center of the circle on both the groom's and the bride's side of the mechitzah (the separation screen that allows for modesty at traditional Jewish weddings). He loved every minute of it, even though he returned to the hospital late that night, completely exhausted, as one might expect.

"Escorting the deceased"

Sometimes our father would come home for the daily family dinner with his bespoke suits covered in mud. Not only was he a member of our synagogue's burial society ("The Holy Friends") for more than twenty-five years, he was the only person I have ever met who carried tall rubber boots and an army shovel in the trunk of his car.

While in very traditional Jewish funerals, the graves are always filled with earth by the friends and relatives of the deceased, in less traditional funerals the custodians will either fill in just a small part of the grave or they will cover the top of the grave with a piece of artificial grass, dismiss those in attendance, and let the cemetery workers complete the task of filling the grave.

Our father could not bear to attend the funeral of a fellow Jew and not see to it that the final act of kindness that one can do for another was performed. So literally hundreds of times, he stayed behind after all the attendees had left, put on his rubber boots, grabbed his trusty shovel, and filled the grave until there was a mound of earth on top of the grave to mark the site, in accordance with Jewish tradition. It mattered not to our father if the funerals took place in the harsh Toronto winters, the scorching summer heat, or the torrential spring rains.

"Praying intensely"

Our father loved going to shul. He was a shul builder, a one-man welcoming committee, and in Israel he also served in the lofty role of the "candyman," giving out candies during the services to both children and adults alike. He was a founding member of Shaarei Tefillah in Toronto in 1951. He was active in two shuls in the Talpiot Mizrach district of Jerusalem, as well as in two other Jerusalem synagogues. He hosted weekly Friday night and Saturday night services in his Jerusalem home.

And it is most fitting that for his eighty-fifth birthday, his closest friends and family members dedicated, in his honor, a new shul and a Yeshiva (advanced Torah academy) in the community of Netzer Ariel for Jews who were expelled from the Gaza Strip in 2005. Our father felt such deep anguish for these fine people who had everything taken from them and were then shunted to an empty university dormitory until the fall semester was about to begin.

The shul and yeshiva, which also serves as the focal point of the community, breathed new life into the hundreds of people who felt forsaken by their own government and were left to fend for themselves with little assistance or hope for a better future.

Today they have a thriving, energetic, and dedicated community, which provides many services to the people of Ariel and of Israel, all centered around Beit Yisrael ("The House of Israel," our father's Jewish name), the name of our father's most recent shul project.

"Bringing peace between one person and another and between husband and wife"

Our father was known colloquially as "The Preacher" as he would work diligently to bring peace between people who were having severe disagreements. He would explain to them how in the scale of a lifetime, the matter over which they were fighting was likely much smaller than it appeared to be and that making peace was better than being right almost all of the time.

He asked forgiveness, compromised, and walked away from monetary disputes many times in order to achieve the higher goal of peace in the family and among members of the community.

"And know that Torah study is equivalent to all of these"

As a young boy growing up in Toronto in the 1920s and '30s, our father attended the small synagogue (*shtibl*) of the saintly Rebbi of Strettin. The synagogue was so small that when the tables were set for the weekly Third Shabbat Meal, the children were sent outside to play while the men sat in the room to hear their Rebbi's deep Torah thoughts and soulful songs.

The Rebbi knew that one small boy wished to stay in the room so he had that boy — our father — sit under the table at his feet. He fed him by passing food under the tablecloth. And from his position on the floor sitting at the

Rebbi's feet, our father would stare intently at the Rebbi's eyes as he reached lofty spiritual levels during the songs and his deep Torah thoughts.

This image influenced our father throughout his entire life. He attended classes in his shuls and in two Jerusalem seniors' kollels, and for his entire adult life he both gave and raised funds for the spread of Torah education for both children and adults.

He loved his Torah teachers and gave them great respect, honor, and support. Perhaps this is the main reason why he and our mother can boast of having twenty-five well-educated, deeply connected and highly dedicated Jewish children, grandchildren, and great-grandchildren (thus far).

In summary, our father had great trust in G-d. This manifested itself in him being a man of joy, perpetual song, smiles, gratitude, and relentless optimism. He loved the G-d, the People, and the Land of Israel. And while we will miss him deeply, we will bear in mind, as he was wont to say (the words which serve as the title of his autobiography), "It's always sunny above the clouds." Indeed.

FOR FURTHER READING

Put aside at least eighteen minutes a day for Torah study.

Torah:

The Jewish Bible, which contains G-d's instructions for living a successful and meaningful life. Hey, you gotta read this book!

Aryeh Kaplan, *The Living Torah* (Moznaim Publishing Corporation Inc.).
A great translation of the Torah. A must-read for every Jew.

The Artscroll Series/Stone Edition of the Chumash (Mesorah Publications, Ltd.).
A popular traditional translation of the Torah, with some commentaries.

Gutnick Edition *Chumash* (Kol Menachem).
A single volume edition of the Torah with commentary by the Lubavitcher Rebbe.

Prayer:

More insights and deeper explanations of Jewish prayers and their meanings

Artscroll Transliterated Linear Siddur (Mesorah Publications, Ltd.).

Avraham Davis, *The Complete Metsudah Siddur: A New Linear Prayer Book with English Translation and Anthology of the Classic Commentaries* (Metsudah Publications).

Interlinear Tehillim (Artscroll Mesorah Publications, Ltd.).

Yaakov Yosef Iskowitz, (Psalms) *Tehillim Eit Ratzon, Harkham Edition* (Feldheim Publishers).

Aryeh Kaplan, *Jewish Meditation: A Practical Guide* (Schocken Books).

Heshy Kleinman, *Praying with Fire*, 2 volumes (Artscroll/Mesorah Publications, Ltd.).

Nissan Mindel, *My Prayer*, 2 volumes (Kehot Publication Society).

David Olivestone, *NCSY Bencher: A Book of Prayer and Song* (OU/NCSY Publications).

Shimshon Dovid Pinkus, *Gates of Prayer* (Feldheim Publishers).

Jonathan Sacks, *The Koren Sacks Siddur* (Koren Publishers Jerusalem).

Jacob Immanuel Schochet, *Deep Calling unto Deep* (Kehot Publication Society).

Tehillim Ohel Yoseph Yitzchok (Kehot Publications Society).

Jewish Life:

Shabbat and Holidays

Shimon Apisdorf, *Rosh Hashanah Yom Kippur Survival Kit* (Leviathan Press).

Shimon Apisdorf, *Passover Survival Kit* (Leviathan Press).

The Breslov Haggadah (Breslov Research Institute).

Aryeh Kaplan, *Sabbath: Day of Eternity* (OU/NCSY Publications).

Eliyahu Kitov, *The Book of Our Heritage: The Jewish Year and Its Days of Significance* (Feldheim Publishers).

Lori Palatnik, *Friday Night and Beyond: The Shabbat Experience Step-by-Step* (Jason Aronson).

Mitzvot and Milestones

Chafetz Chaim, *Ahavas Chesed* (published in English by Feldheim Publishers).

Aryeh Kaplan, *Waters of Eden: The Mystery of the Mikveh* (OU/NCSY Publications).

Maurice Lamm, *The Jewish Way in Love and Marriage* (Jonathan David Publishers).

Maurice Lamm, *The Jewish Way in Death and Mourning* (Jonathan David Publishers).

Lori Palatnik, *Remember My Soul* (Leviathan Press).

Zalman Posner, Eliezer Danzinger, Nissan Mangel, *Kuntres Ahavat Yisrael* (published in English by Kehot Publication Society, about the mitzvah of loving our fellow Jews).

Rivkah Slonim, *Total Immersion: A Mikvah Anthology* (Jason Aronson Publishers).

Adin Steinsaltz, *Teshuvah: A Guide for the Newly Observant Jew* (Jason Aronson Publishers).

The Traditional Jewish Perspective

David Aaron, *Endless Light: The Ancient Path of the Kabbalah to Love, Spiritual Growth, and Personal Power* (Simon & Schuster).

David Aaron, *Seeing G-d: Ten Life-Changing Lessons of the Kabbalah* (Jeremy P. Tarcher/Putnam).

Shalom Arush (translated by Lazer Brody), *The Garden of Emuna: A Practical Guide to Life* (Chut Shel Chessed Institutions).

Irving M. Bunim, *Ethics from Sinai* (Feldheim Publishers).

Hayim Halevi Donin, *To Be a Jew: A Guide to Jewish Observance in Contemporary Life* (Basic Books).

Avraham Greenbaum, *Under the Table and How to Get Up: Jewish Pathways of Spiritual Growth* (Tsohar Publishing).

Simon Jacobson, *Toward a Meaningful Life* (HarperCollins Publishers).

Esther Jungreis, *The Committed Life: Principles for Good Living from Our Timeless Past* (HarperCollins Publishers).

Esther Jungreis, *Life is a Test: How to Meet Life's Challenges Successfully* (The Shaar Press).

Additional books by Aryeh Kaplan, published by OU/NCSY Publications:

The Aryeh Kaplan Anthology (2 volumes)
Jerusalem: The Eye of the Universe
Tzitzith: A Thread of Light
Tefillin

Moshe Chaim Luzzato (translated by Aryeh Kaplan), *Derech HaShem: The Way of G-d* (Feldheim Publishers).

Moshe Chaim Luzzato, *Mesilat Yesharim: Path of the Just* (Feldheim Publishers).

Zelig Pliskin, *Guard Your Tongue* (Bnay Yakov Publications).

M. Rothschild and S. Finkelman, *Chofetz Chaim: A Daily Companion* (Artscroll/Mesorah Publications, Ltd.).

Jonathan Sacks, *A Letter in the Scroll* (The Free Press).

Adin Steinsaltz, *The Thirteen-Petalled Rose* (Basic Books).

Abraham J. Twerski, *Visions of the Fathers* (Shaar Press).

Additional books by Abraham J. Twerski (there are 77 in total), published by Artscroll/Mesorah Publications and others:
Growing Each Day
Living Each Day
Smiling Each Day
Wisdom Each Day

And other books written by Rabbis David Aaron, Zvi Freeman, Avraham Greenbaum, Simon Jacobson, Aryeh Kaplan, Jonathan Sacks, Adin Steinsaltz, Abraham J. Twerski, Rebbetzin Esther Jungreis, or by the Leviathan Press.

Websites:

Aish.com (website of Aish HaTorah; provides excellent introduction to all aspects of Jewish teachings and life)

Azamra.org (website of Rabbi Avraham Greenbaum, translator of teachings of Rebbe Nachman of Breslov)

Breslov.org (website of the Breslov Research Institute)

Chabad.org (website of the Chabad Lubavitch Organization)

Dailyhalacha.com (online learning about Jewish law for daily life with Rabbi Eli Mansour)

Israelight.org (website of Rabbi David Aaron)

OU.org (Orthodox Union site with many Torah classes)

Rabbiwein.com (website of Rabbi Berel Wein, founder of the Destiny Foundation, which creates programming on Jewish history and life)

Torah.org (Torah learning)

yutorah.org (Yeshiva University online learning about the Jewish holidays, Torah, Halacha, and Talmud)

APPROBATIONS

BAIS MEDRASH N'SIV OLAM
TORAH INSTITUTE
155 Palm Drive / Toronto, ON M3H 2C6 / 416.782.8816
Harav Reuven Silver, Dean

בס"ד
ט"ו בכסלו, תשע"ה

Rabbi Zale Newman has attended my Torah classes for the past thirty-six years. Even with his very busy schedule, including frequent trips out of town, he rarely misses a class. This has created a very close bond between us and, as such, I feel I am in a qualified position to speak about him and his valuable accomplishments.

Zale has been involved in Kiruv work for many years, both independently, as well as in conjunction with some of the major Kiruv organizations, such as NCSY, Ohr Somayach and Aish HaTorah. He can truly be called a pioneer in the Kiruv movement!

Zale has now produced a Siddur to be used as an introductory guide to the full Hebrew Siddur. I know that he has spent many years in the writing of this Siddur, and has had it reviewed by two Torah scholars. I have no doubt that it will be very well received and useful for those to whom it is intended. As usual, Zale has used his multiple talents to bring out the beauty and sweetness of our Sages' holy words.

I wish him many years of continued success in his work on behalf of Klal Yisroel.

ראובן סילבר

יחיאל מיכל טווערסקי
באאמו"ר הרה"צ כמוהר"ר יעקב ישראל זצללה"ה מהאָרנאָסטײַפּאָל

Rabbi Michel Twerski

בס"ד

The last half century witnessed an unparalleled resurgence to Torah and its practices, from sectors believed to be hopelessly estranged and lost from Judaic identification. By the hundreds and thousands, Jews of every ilk, gender and culture, young & old, singles and marrieds, intellectuals, artists and entertainers, found their way back to the faith of their ancestors. Their journey was heroic, their spiritual contribution electric, their aspirations, humbling, their pure, sincere faith, inspiring. Yet, the "frum", in-bred community, was ill-prepared for the magnitude of this phenomenon, and ill-equipped to meet its needs and demands. To be sure, new educational institutions appeared on the scene, brilliant and charismatic teachers stepped up to the plate , all determined to arm the newcomers with the requisite skills to sustain their growth, and achieve parity with their "frume-from-birth" counterparts. These efforts notwithstanding, significant gaps remained, impeding the neophytes in their ascent to the summits of Torah and Avodah.

One of the more conspicuous and painful voids centered on the area of Tefillah, a major pillar in the day-to-day expression of Divine service and connection. Our Siddurim, regardless of the outpouring of literate and scholarly translations and commentaries, failed to provide an adequate bridge to an experience of prayer which would slake the thirst of the Ba'al Teshuvah in his deep yearning for religious adequacy.

Rabbi Zale Newman, a highly regarded veteran and veritable star on the stage of Kiruv, seems to have successfully addressed this void, and authored an insightful and engaging manual, appropriately named **Stairway to Heaven**, to allow religious novices the tools for full immersion in the heart-Avodah of Klal Yisroel. Frankly, I am convinced that many long-standing native "shomrei Torah" will benefit equally from this remarkably crafted work. That being said, I confess that because of severe time constraints I was unable to scrutinize every page of this manuscript meticulously. However, my personal knowledge of Rabbi Newman's religious credentials, and my even cursory perusal of **Stairway to Heaven,** satisfies me that Rabbi Newman is to be much congratulated for offering all of us, beginners and old-timers alike, a thoughtful, instructive, and accessible guidebook to escort us through the world of Tefillah. It offers us the possibility of approaching the Divine throne, with heart and mind, passion and humility, and perhaps, most importantly, the powerful sense that our prayers are actually being heard.

I trust that **Stairway to Heaven** will be warmly received, and offer my warmest brochois for success and ne'sius chain.

With every good wish, I am
Respectfully yours,

Rabbi Michel Twerski
Rosh Chodesh Teves 5775

Congregation Beth Jehudah • 3100 N. 52nd Street • Milwaukee, WI 53216 • ph. 414 442-5730 • Fax 414 442-6171
Home Study • 3259 N. 51st Boulevard • Milwaukee, WI 53216 • ph. 414 442-6983 • Fax 414 447-6995

Rabbi Y. Fuhrer
Cong. Chasidei Bobov
Toronto ON M6A 2EB
Tel. 416-787-7251

הרב יהושע פיהרער
ראש הכולל
דחסידי באבוב
טאראנטא, קאנאדע

יום ט' לחודש חשון, שנת תשע"ה לפ"ק

הנה מע"כ ידידנו היקר והנכבד, איש החסד ורב פעלים לתורה ולתעודה למען הכלל והפרט, ובפרט בענין קירוב לבבות לעבודתו ית"ש ה"ה מו"ה בצלאל נוימאן הי"ו, חתן הרב הגאון הגדול המפורסם ר' פנחס הירשפרונג זצ"ל אב"ד מונטריאל, אשר הנה זה יותר משלשים שנים, כולם שוים לטובה, אשר יושב וקובע עתים לתורה ערב ובוקר לא ישבותו בין כותלי בית מדרשנו.

ועכשיו הראני את הסידור שמתכונן להו"ל בעז"ה למתחילים בעבודת ד', מטובל בפירושים נעים לעורר נפש היהודי לטעום מתיקות התפלה, ולהתקשר על ידה להשי"ת באהבה, ולהיכלל בשם כל ישראל, בדרך המסורה לנו מדור דור ששמו דגוש עזה בעבודה שבלב זו תפלה.

והננו לברכו שיצליח ד' דרכו בקודש, ויתאהב שם שמים על ידו, וחפץ ד' בידו יצליח מתוך בריות גופא ונהורא מעליא, בהרחבת הדעת ומנוחת הנפש, ומתוך רב נחת ושמחה, עדי נזכה שישמע ד' לקול תפלתנו, בביאת גואל צדק במהרה בימנו אמן.

החותם בברכה.

יהושע פיהרער

ישיבת ראשית חכמה
Yeshivas Reishis Chochma

Rabbi Elazar Robinson,
Rosh Yeshiva
Yeshivas Reishis Chochma
Toronto Canada

בס"ד

The author of this work, Zale Newman, has been my talmid/chaver for the past 31 years. He felt there was a need for a beginner's siddur and through many years of careful thought, he produced a masterpiece.

This siddur will inspire the readers to understand that through their davening they are developing a relationship with the Creator. In truth it would be ideal if ALL of us would come to pray as beginners for then we would not fall into the pitfall of "mitzvos anashim milumada" - praying by rote.

Once the Bobover Rebbe *t"zl* was told by his ophthalmologist that the Rebbe need not worry about his upcoming eye operation because the doctor had performed this operation so many times, he could do it blindfolded. The Rebbe responded that although he had been putting on tefillin since his Bar Mitzvah, he still put them on each day as if it was his first time.

This siddur is to show the beginner the basics of prayer and to help the reader eventually progress to the regular siddur. However even when the reader has "graduated" to the new level, he should not lose sight of the fact that each day he is a beginner once again.

In the merit of all of the tefilos (prayers) that will emanate from this siddur, Hashem should grant Zale and his family much shefa brochos and siyata dishmaya in all of their endeavors and may we all be davening very soon in the Beis HaMikdash HaShlisi.

Elazar Robinson
Menachem Av 5774

בס"ד

חסד לאורחים
Chesed L'Orchim

Mordechai Machlis, Director

ברוך השומע תפילת עמו ישראל ברחמים - ט לחודש התשיעי תשע'ה

Dearest Rav Zale א שליט"

שלום וברכה ! Thank you so much for allowing me the privilege of reading and studying your most outstanding singular and original format of the סידור. I was especially appreciative of your exciting and eye-opening informative notes and commentaries. Unquestionably, your monumental work will revolutionize many aspects of Tefillah and will successfully open the gateways of prayer even to those who are not yet closely connected to our cherished liturgical texts.

Rav Zale – in my opinion, Hashem has blessed you to be one of the most outstanding מחנכים and משפיעים in כלל ישראל. Your many years of experience in קירוב קרובים and קירוב רחוקים coupled with your keen insights into properly studying and teaching all aspects of תורה של שלימותה are evident to any serious user of your precious סידור. During the many years that ה' has blessed me with the זכות of learning from you, I have always sensed your special drive to bring all facets of our precious תורה and מסורה to the millions of our brothers and sisters who were not granted the gift of a living Torah tradition in their families. Your סידור here in ירושלים עיר הקודש will spiritually uplift prayer in the very city of prayer!

"יודע היה בצלאל לצרף אותיות שנבראו בהן שמים וארץ". Your Torah namesake knew the secret of combining and joining the letters of heaven with the letters of earth. Your *Stairway to Heaven* brings all of us ever so close to that sublime synthesis. With the special blessings of Hashem, your סידור will be found in בתי כנסת and בית מדרש throughout the world as well as in the hearts and homes of all those seeking to improve their pathways of prayer. I wholeheartedly and enthusiastically endorse and recommend your סידור and סדר תפילה, and I am anxiously awaiting your many future תורה works as well.

יהי רצון ששומע תפילת כל פה ימלא את כל משאלות לבכם לטובה ולברכה בבריאות איתנה ובשמחה עצומה יחד עם תפילותיהם ובקשותיהם של כל אחינו ואחיותינו בכל מקום שהם

באהבה רבה ובברכה נפשית,

מרדכי מכליס
ירושלים עיר הקודש

בס"ד
26 Av, 5774

The author of this wonderful work, Reb Zale Newman, epitomizes the time honoured title of "askan", a full time volunteer for Klal Yisrael. His personal acts of chesed, whether fundraising for individuals in dire need, or giving of his time in weekly visits to hospitals, are lessons for all of us to behold. His Ahavas Yisroel was and is the motivation for his pioneering efforts in Kiruv Rechokim over the past four decades. NCSY, Aish HaTorah and Chabad Lubavich, among scores of others, have benefited from his many talents.

We have tremendous hakaras hatov to Reb Zale as The Village Shul and Aish HaTorah Learning Centre have been the recipients of his gifts and been a major priority of his efforts since its founding 25 years ago. Together with his Aishes Chayil Rochel, countless individuals at The Village Shul have been impacted and inspired by their love, focus and attention.

A major priority of The Village Shul is to create a community that is outwardly focused and where its impact is felt around the world. Our work here has been an inspiration, as other communities around the world have learned from and replicated our model. It therefore gives me tremendous pleasure that Reb Zale's Torah will now be spread beyond these four walls, teaching and inspiring so many Jews to have a meaningful connection with their Creator through Tefillah. May HaKadosh Baruch Hu bless Reb Zale with continued strength to continue helping, inspiring and educating in his own inimitable way.

Rabbi Ahron Hoch

Dear Reader,

I was elated to learn that my esteemed friend and mentor Rabbi Zale Newman has written a book on the most essential element of the of our relationship with the Almighty- prayer. Prayer is of prominent importance in our tradition and Stairway to Heaven is more than just another aid to prayer, it's a step by step handbook to successfully connect to Hashem and the Tefillah experience.

Any work committed to uplifting Jewish life is most crucial, but coupled with the knowledge that this work was written by a Talmid Chacham who also deeply understands and has dedicated his life to inspire both young and old is very exciting.

I highly recommend this wonderful book and commend Rabbi Newman on this monumental effort. The words on each page will surely inspire the reader to a greater awareness and appreciation of the power of prayer as it is rich in both content and style.

Rabbi Glenn Black,
Chief Executive Officer, NCSY

ABOUT THE AUTHOR

"Reb Zale" Newman was born and raised in Toronto, Ontario, Canada. His parents were passionate about the Jewish People, Torah study, the Land of Israel, and acts of outreach and kindness. They imbued these values in their children and sacrificed greatly to provide advanced Jewish education to all of their children.

As a result, Reb Zale attended Eitz Chaim Day School, Ner Israel Yeshiva High School of Toronto, Bais Medrash l'Torah (BMT) and Kerem B'Yavneh (KBY) yeshivas in Israel, and Yeshiva University in New York, where he studied Talmud and completed a BA in economics.

After completing his MBA studies at McGill University in Montreal and York University in Toronto, he spent the bulk of his professional life in the field of Canadian financial services. He is the founder and President of Bond Street Mercantile, where the concentration is on various opportunities to invest in Israel. The flagship product is the Holy Land Investment Fund, the only fund of its kind available to Canadians who wish to invest in Israel.

Reb Zale's passion is partaking in daily Torah study that encompasses many different areas, from Talmud and Halachah to Chassidic thought. He has studied for the past thirty-six years with Rabbi Reuven Silver of Bais Medrash N'siv Olam from whom he received Rabbinic ordination, and for thirty-two years with Rabbi Elazar Robinson, Rosh Yeshiva of Reishis Chochma at the Bobov Kollel in Toronto. He studied Chassidic thought with Rabbi Immanuel Schochet *a"h* and Rabbi Elisha Schochet. He considers Rabbi Mordechai Machlis of Jerusalem his teacher in the area of G'milut Chessed (acts of kindness) and has many additional Torah teachers in North America and Israel. He developed a close, personal relationship with the Lubavitcher Rebbe and corresponded with the Rebbe on a regular basis.

Reb Zale's first love and "real" work is in the area of outreach to Jews who are unaffiliated or marginally affiliated with their Jewish heritage. To this end, he has served in every level of NCSY over the past forty years, including a stint as the International Director. He continues his high-school outreach activities with daily involvement in NCSY Canada and the Torah High program for Jewish public school teens. He has been involved with Aish HaTorah for more than twenty-five years. Toronto's Village Shul, of which he is a founding member, is Reb Zale's primary base for adult outreach. He runs the "Stairway to Heaven" weekly Shabbat service for the novice, where this particular work has been "beta-tested" over the past many years, as well as teaching the weekly Soul Spa program for women and various educational series. He has assisted with outreach activities of Chabad Lubavitch in locales across North America and serves as an advisor, teacher, consultant, and speaker for a number of outreach organizations around the world.

Reb Zale works with numerous charitable projects for needy people in Israel and continues his efforts on behalf of widows, orphans, handicapped children, the sick, and the needy in Toronto and beyond. He is a member of Toronto's Bikur Cholim, the Jewish Volunteer Services, where he serves Jewish patients at Sunnybrook Hospital and North York General Hospital.

Reb Zale's musical talents have allowed him to contribute to the field of Jewish music as a musician, songwriter, and record and concert producer. He served as the music producer of the legendary Shlomo Carlebach *a"h* and as the producer/songwriter for Yehuda, the popular Chassidic pop singer, among many others. Perhaps his best known work is the Uncle Moishy and the Mitzvah Men project for Jewish children, which has spawned eighteen albums, fifteen DVDs, and multiple world tours over the past thirty-five years.

Reb Zale is married to Rochel, a family therapist, who is a daughter of Rabbi Pinchas Hirschprung *zt"l*, the late Chief Rabbi of Montreal and world-renowned Torah scholar, and Rebbetzin Hirschprung *a"h*. Together they have been blessed with three children, Chayim, Batsheva, and Dovid Tzvi ("DZ"); their son-in-law, Amram; their four grandchildren, Yaakov Shlomo, Pinchas Yadin, Keira Biba, and Yehuda; and thousands of students and Shabbat guests.

Reb Zale can be reached via email at at zale@stairwaytoheaven.ca and at the StairwaytoHeaven website.

(written by F. Silver)

www.ingramcontent.com/pod-product-compliance
Lightning Source LLC
Chambersburg PA
CBHW051940290426
44110CB00015B/2047